MW00884062

Contents

10,000 Better Days

Promise of the Appalachian Trail

David J. Knobbe

For my father.

Backstory

It was August 2016. I was making the Laugavegur Trek in Iceland from Landmannalaugar to Thórsmörk. The trail wound through black lava fields, steaming hot springs, colorful mountains, and spectacular falls. Snow and ice was everywhere even though it was the end of summer.

I wasn't feeling great. Still, I was doing okay considering most of my hiking partners were less than half my age. That's when my heart started doing things it shouldn't have – beating too fast and failing to recover like it used to. As I slogged up a particularly steep slope, my heart skipped to one-hundred-eighty beats per minute. I stumbled, caught myself, hit the ground softly and lay still at the top of the slope panting. A young woman took my hand. She was my co-leader. Her eyes were full of concern that bordered on panic. "I'm okay," I assured her, but she knew differently. I was pale and sweating profusely despite the chill in the air. I tried to keep cool, but that's next to impossible when your heart's screaming like a bullet train. "So, this is what it's like to die," I thought. I was pretty sure I'd need to be helicoptered out -- if I lasted long enough.

An hour or so later, my heart calmed. I didn't need a helicopter, but I knew I wasn't the same. I hid my fear behind a smile and tried to be upbeat. I knew if I wasn't convinced that I was alright, nobody else would be either. I struggled to my feet, threw on my pack, and made my way up the trail ever so slowly and with uncertainty. I was less sturdy and as unsteady as I'd ever been before. Crap. I knew something was wrong – dreadfully wrong. I just wasn't sure what it was. My discomfort eased as the day wore on but I never fully recovered. Deep, full breathes seemed a thing of the past as did feelings that I could walk a good long way without getting tired. I caught up to the group carrying a backpack that no longer felt like the friend it had been when I'd carried it in places like Scotland, Croatia, and China. It was ten times heavier than it had been earlier that morning. I gave the group of ten college students a sheepish smile, dropped my head and pushed on down the trail right past them without stopping. Something, I knew, was wrong – seriously so – but I didn't tell anyone.

For the next few days, whether slogging up a slope or sitting absolutely still, filling my lungs with that pristine Iceland air – something that should have been nothing but joy -- was pure labor. My heart skipped around like a child hyped up on sugar and sleep was anything but easy or rejuvenating. My dreams were wild and fractured and frightening.

I pushed on dutifully, more stumbling than walking with purpose. I remember being driven more by the fear of having to explain why me -- the expedition leader -- had to be helicoptered out. I imagined news headlines describing my untimely and inconvenient demise and how I'd left my group alone and against the elements in the wilds of Iceland.

That's hardly how any of us want to be remembered.

I pushed on and completed the trip on my own power but barely.

In Atlanta, a few days later, the doctor's news was as welcome as a hammer to the head. "Good and bad," she said. "Your heart's in remarkable shape -- not a single blockage. Your mitral valve is shot, though. You'll need an open heart procedure to fix it."

"Open heart surgery?" That was a hard one to wrap my head around. "But I don't have problems like that", I told myself. I turned to the doctor and asked, "And if I don't have the surgery?"

"You'll continue to decline. Quality will diminish. Life will be shortened." She pulled no punches as she held my stare. "You'll survive a year or two -- Maybe."

That's hard news to swallow – I was slowly dying.

Just two weeks home from hiking in Iceland, and I was sliding downhill fast. A flight of stairs was suddenly more than I could handle without stopping to rest, and it seemed like a decade since I'd last filled my lungs fully with fresh air. There weren't many choices – none really. I guessed my days hiking and adventuring and maybe even working in the yard were now over. It was a heavy burden to manage.

I'd never felt further from memories of the Appalachian Trail as I did then. And though it had been twenty-nine years since I completed a southbound thru-hike on Springer Mountain, as I would discover, the lessons learned then were closer and more critical than I could have realized. "Still paying tremendous dividends," I'd eventually understand about my thru-hike when I viewed it through the lens of surviving the unexpected.

A few doctor visits and a couple weeks later, I had open-heart surgery. Fourteen days after that, I sat uncomfortably in my office at the University trying to re-establish balance. I should have taken more time off, I suspected, but ego and middle-age make for a dangerous combination. I was upright and above ground, though, and breathing deeply for the first time in what seemed several decades. All of that felt pretty good. In reality, though, it had only been eight weeks since the onset of significant symptoms on that hillside in Iceland, and the real challenges were just beginning.

Fortunately, age and health qualified me for a relatively new and less invasive surgical procedure. The five-hour surgery still required stopping my heart and hooking me to a heart-lung machine, but it didn't involve cracking my chest. Instead of sawing through my breastbone and opening me to the world, the surgeon turned me on my side, lowered tiny lights into my chest cavity through holes he'd drilled between my ribs, made an incision, stretched me wide enough so he could get his hands inside, and re-built the damaged structures inside my heart. He used a titanium ring and Gortex thread. The results were impressive. I woke feeling as if someone had danced all over my chest and shoulders. Though it hurt like hell for the next week, I at least felt like I was on my way to a better place -- And that place was neither heaven nor hell.

Pain, though, is a short-termed monster, beatable if you learn to live with it rather than fight it and you don't let it stoke self-destructing anger or fuel misery that makes you want to quit.

DePriest Mountain is in Virginia. I hadn't been there for twenty-nine years. People simply know it as "the Priest". Southbound AT hikers don't like to talk about it. Climbing that slope lacks the spiritual nature of climbing Katahdin or any of the mountains in the Presidential Range. There's no glamor in hiking up it. Hell, it's not even one of the fifty highest mountains in Virginia. The mountain rises, though, from the valley below for three and a half miles at a near-consistent slope that's not exactly steep, but it' unrelenting. There are few places to catch a breather that aren't sloping upward. I don't remember a single gorgeous view on the way up. I hated that climb.

Most hikers are spent when they get to the top, exhausted more by the false summits that have lured them into believing they were almost to the top only to reveal that there was still a good long way to go. Walking up that mountain proved, thirty years later, to be an invaluable metaphor for dealing with the pain and struggle of heart surgery recovery. Neither was a pleasant struggle. Neither was glamorous. Both felt like they'd go on forever. And, yes, both experiences sucked. But I knew that if I kept moving, I'd eventually make it to the top. There were no choices in either case but to push through the pain, the frustration, the boredom, and the feelings of smallness. After surgery, I reminded myself, over and over, "You can do this. You've proved that before. Just keep pushing on, and you'll get there. Eventually."

Post-surgery, the surgeon explained that everything went as expected. He'd been able to fix things without stitching a pig or cow valve into my heart-- which was a relief since such things don't last as long as fixing the original equipment. It concerned me, too, irrationally, I know, that having a pig valve stitched into me might leave me snorting like a pig now and then and resisting the temptation to root around in the dirt nose-first or to roll in the mud. I told my children goofy things like that often enough that I almost started believing if they dropped an animal valve into me, I might wake up mooing or worse. The impact of a lack of blood to the brain during the pre-surgery month or two made me little crazy.

So, heart surgery resulted in the best possible physical outcomes. I could breathe again; I would soon be able to run and play and hike and climb again; I didn't have a horrendous scar down the center of my chest; and I'd soon be back to my old self – for better or for worse. I was on the road to rapid recovery. Or so it seemed.

What does any of this have to do with the Appalachian Trail? Well, recovering from heart surgery got harder before it got easier. Pushing through the tough parts called for the same skills required to complete a thru-hike: consistency, determination, focus, vision, a rock-solid spirit, pain-tolerance, and luck.

The physical recovery wasn't hard. I was walking miles in a few weeks and pounding on a punching bag a few weeks after that. From the moment I awoke in the recovery room, it became easier and easier to take big, deep, satisfying breaths.

As I was ready to proclaim the whole affair a complete success and even volunteer to be the poster child for successful and rapid recovery from heart surgery, I encountered an unwanted truth. Heart surgery impacts more than the heart. Most notably, it messes with the brain. Thinking and remembering suddenly felt different – like I was using somebody else's brain instead of my own. I wrestled with a growing sense that I wasn't the same person anymore. My brain didn't work like it had, and as a result, I struggled every minute of every day to feel like myself. As days and months went by, I wondered if full recovery was even possible.

It had only been a few months since Iceland, and I could recall little more than shadowy images from that trip. That's a scary thing – to think back on something you know happened and not be able to recall much detail at all. It was as if it had taken place forty years before instead of four months prior. There had been twenty of us organized into two groups. I could remember five by name and face. That's all. Even today, I likely wouldn't recognize the others if I ran into them on the street. All of that shook me to the core.

Besides not remembering details of that trip, things like dates, phone numbers, and names no longer stuck in my head like they once had.

Memories became more important than ever. I started thinking about my time on the Appalachian Trail more and more, especially when I got frustrated with my recovery and sought sources of peace and strength. "I didn't quit when I was hiking," I'd remind myself and that would provide some comfort. "I stayed focused," I told myself and recalled how lonely it was hiking solo from Massachusetts down to Harpers Ferry after my partners quit. "I didn't give up then," I told myself, and I knew I wasn't likely to give up post-surgery either. It was the lessons learned along a successful thru-hike thirty years before that bolstered me in those tough times.

I remembered how much I wanted to give up at the hardest moments along the AT, but I never did. Why not? Because, I came to understand, quitting is not something I tend to do. It wasn't in me then – along the AT -- and I was pretty sure it still wasn't me thirty years later.

I encouraged myself with the thru-hiker's mantra, "No regrets," and remembered how I resisted temptations to skip challenges like the climb over the Priest in Virginia. For twenty-one hundred miles and five million steps, I didn't skip a single section of trail, I reminded myself. There was, I knew, no room for shortcuts or to bypass any of the doctor's prescriptions for recovery.

"You can't wish yourself to the end," I reminded myself. "If you put the required miles in every day, even if you take a few zero-mile days now and then, eventually you'll get where you want to go." Those thoughts – rooted in memories and real experiences -- kept me going even when I wanted so badly to quit post-surgery and give into just being less than I'd been for the whole of my previous life.

Through it all, though, because of the knowledge about myself that resulted from my experiences as a thru-hiker, I was pretty sure that I could and would push through the hardships. After all, I'd been doing just that ever since I took those first steps on the Appalachian Trail in 1987. I knew deep down – because I'd been tested by uphills and downs and long days and tough moments -- that the pain and struggle would eventually yield to satisfaction and new understanding. All I needed to do was to stay focused. Knowing that I'd pushed through such tribulations in 1987, I was pretty certain I would do the same in 2016.

Supported by lessons learned hiking the AT, I adopted a routine intended to "exercise" my gray matter -- writing for 30 minutes each morning.

When I started my thru-hike in Maine, I could push through about ten tough miles. That's it. By North Carolina, I could click off twenty or even thirty with relative ease. How had I gotten to that point? By simply doing what needed to be done, a little each day, until I eventually found myself where I needed to be.   Writing as "exercise" became more important than walking or riding an exercise bike. Eventually, I woke up to realize I'd written nearly two thousand pages. It was akin to the experience of waking up and realizing I'd hiked two-thousand miles of the Appalachian Trail and had less than one hundred miles to Springer Mountain...

10,000 Better Days: Promise of the Appalachian Trail is an outcome of my "exercise" routine. I wrote this book in pursuit of health and normalcy in much the same spirit I hiked the Appalachian Trail – a few miles at a time. I'm fairly certain I wouldn't have completed either journey had I not been able to break each one into the five or so million steps required. Two-thousand miles in one bite is too much to wrap your head around.   Putting ten miles in a day or crossing the next stream or climbing the next hill is easier to imagine.

I'm not sure which was more difficult -- writing a book or hiking the Appalachian Trail. One was definitely more enjoyable and gave me a chance to eat in some remarkable out-of-the-way diners and to connect with some amazing human beings. One challenge included one-hundred-fifty-nine nights beneath a billion stars, gorgeous vistas, and a million opportunities to learn.

The strengths and habits required to finish a thru-hike weren't so different from those required to complete a book or to recover from heart surgery – which I'm still doing. You can't wish your way to the end of any of them – the Appalachian Trail or a book when you're writing or reading it or any other great challenge. Some might be able to write a 200-page text in a single night, but most of us can't. It takes a little focused effort every day for a lot of days to get where you want to go. That's an enduring lesson of the Appalachian Trail.

The Appalachian Trail shaped my life and made a lot of things possible.

Thirty years after I finished a thru-hike at the top of Springer Mountain, my AT experience is still an invaluable part of a healthy life. That's the moment I started thinking critically about the value of epic adventures like thru-hikes and mountain climbs and traveling through unknown lands. Such experiences are of critical and enduring importance in our lives. The value of such experiences does not diminish.

Filling our heads with adventures when we're young is no different than socking away a few dollars to ensure a comfortable future. When we do so, we're not likely to reap huge rewards the day after our adventure ends. The pay-off comes over the next 10,000 days or so, mostly a little at a time, and sometimes as unexpectedly as a substantial raise, a refund check, or winning the lottery.

I hope anyone reading this book will embrace this idea: adventuring's not just for the young; you're never too old to start; and you're always too young to stop.

Happy trails.

10,000 Better Days

10,000 better days -- That's the promise of an Appalachian Trail thru-hike or any adventure that's big enough and doesn't guarantee success or even survival. 10,000 days, each better than they might otherwise have been --- that's the likely return when you invest more than you can afford to lose in an adventure that pushes you beyond what you know, taxes you thoroughly in all manners, and stretches your understanding of how the world works and where you fit in.

Survive such an adventure, one that's bigger than you, and you'll likely go on to thrive each day after that. That's the promise of the Appalachian Trail or any life-sized adventure. Is it worth it? Absolutely, if done well.

Humans are engineered for adventure – thanks to my friend Matt Marcus for that brilliant term – "engineered for adventure". It captures, I think, the nature of who we are and how we best grow and learn. Without experiences that stretch boundaries and feed our soul, we stagnate and miss opportunities to become the people we want to be. If we avoid stretching our boundaries and increasing self-understanding – something achieved nearly predictably when we meet adventures head-on – then we're likely to go nowhere, at least not anywhere we intended to go. Without such experiences to stand upon, we lack a foundation from which we can manage future challenges.

When I think of the importance of adventure in our lives, I am drawn to this quote:

Everyone therefore who hears these words of mine, and does them, I will liken him to a wise man, who built his house on a rock. The rain came down, the floods came, and the winds blew, and beat on that house; and it didn't fall, for it was founded on the rock. Everyone who hears these words of mine, and doesn't do them will be like a foolish man, who built his house on the sand. The rain came down, the floods came, and the winds blew, and beat on that house; and it fell—and great was its fall.

— *Matthew 7:24–27*

Better days aren't guaranteed just because you set out to do something big and then endured discomfort long enough to finish what you started. Finishing's not enough. Adventures can be pursued in ways that increase the likelihood that thirty years on you might look back and say, "Because of that experience, every step since – for the whole of my life -- was somewhat better, and I lived more completely as a result."

A life-sized adventure done well can define life and re-shape all its possibilities for a long, long time to come.

There are wrong ways to approach adventures. If you charge in blindly and without purpose, for example, then the likelihood of getting what you want from your adventure isn't so predictable. A thru-hike – or any adventure of similar scale – marred by shortcuts and half-assed efforts is not the same as one marked by absolute bests. The benefits of coasting through such an experience half-heartedly and without intent are likely somewhat less than one seeks and maybe will prove even the opposite of anything positive.

"No regrets" has been the mantra of many thru-hikers. It should be the line drawn in the sand by anyone setting off on an adventure of impressive proportions. "No regrets" means no shortcuts, nothing half-assed, and no surrender.

This book is about getting the most from epic experiences whether it's hiking the Appalachian Trail, serving in the Peace Corps or the armed forces, studying abroad for a year, finishing an engineering degree, or paddling the Mississippi River from Lake Itasca all the way to the Gulf of Mexico. This is the story of a single thru-hike that took place thirty years ago. It was relatively unremarkable in comparison with most others. Nonetheless, it is one that's continued to pay significant dividends for this particular hiker.

The message I hope to convey is this: done right, an epic adventure can be a game-changer. If, however, in the face of a grand adventure, you leave too much to chance and only follow a trail someone else has set or if you give only half your best, then you'll likely walk away in the end with less -- and maybe much less – than you sought. If instead, you embrace a vision, stick to it in good times and bad, forge your own path, and push through moments when you want to lay down and quit, then you're likely to reap far more benefits than you expected.

In 1987, I lived half-a-year along the Appalachian Trail. I started on Mount Katahdin in Maine with three partners and finished one-hundred-sixty days later on Springer Mountain. I was with three different partners then. I made it a point to take every step of the 2,139.5 mile trail – approximately five million of them. I went through two pairs of boots, carried less-than-state-of-the-art equipment, and spent twelve-hundred dollars in 1987 monies not including the cost to mail food to post offices along the trail. Airfare from Missouri to Maine and back to Missouri from Georgia five months later was extra, too. It cost a few hundred dollars each way.

For two-thousand miles, I never had a blister or diarrhea. I got bit by bugs, burned by the sun, and ate more oatmeal, pop tarts, and mac and cheese than could possibly be healthy. My pack weighed too much, and I didn't carry a gun or a machete or anything more than a two-inch long pocket knife. I didn't have a cell phone or a laptop. Neither had been invented yet.

Most of the close calls and near misses were the result of my own choices and none stemmed from getting drunk in places I shouldn't have been. I drank just one beer along the way. I found it floating in an ice cold spring in the middle of nowhere somewhere in Maine. It still ranks as one of the best beers I've ever had, but I figured then that to drink beer wasn't why I was there. I sensed that the fewer distractions I had to deal with, the more likely I was to complete the trail. So, I swore off beer and stupidity and continued on. Not drinking beer proved far more doable than avoiding doing stupid things - - At least in the first month or so.

When it was over, I weighed 30 pounds less than when I started, but I was a whole lot smarter about a whole lot of things.

On the day I finished, I had no clue about the value of what I'd just accomplished. Understanding that completely would require years and years of thinking about the million or more little episodes that comprised the whole experience.

But not much of that matters.

What does matter is that thirty years later -- which happens to be about ten-thousand days -- I can tie every defining and positive part of my life back to thru-hiking the Appalachian Trail. That includes a happy marriage, healthy well-adjusted kids, career success, overcoming health challenges, and generally feeling comfortable in my own skin wherever I am.

I'd be remiss at this point if I didn't acknowledge my parent's role in those things, too. They blessed me with a pretty good start, too. Thanks, Mom and Dad.

I have few regrets about the Appalachian Trail. Often, when faced with challenges or decisions I don't want to make, I still remind myself with the words, "No regrets." Because of my AT experience, those words are steeped in meaning.

I have built valuable and enduring things since my thru-hike. Most are built upon the values and lessons collected along the Appalachian Trail. Thirty years later, I can link who I am to five particular choices that became the foundation of my successful AT experience:

(1) Taking the initial risk to set off on an adventure.
(2) Living each step of the adventure – not just enduring them.
(3) Not quitting when things got tough.
(4) Intentionally thinking about and learning from my experiences.
(5) Continuing to embrace lessons and values learned once I got home.

Sticking to these five choices while hiking has made all the difference in the last 10,000 days. Had I not embraced any one of them fully, my life's trajectory would have been very different.

These same five choices are essential to harnessing the transformational power of an adventure. If you don't take the first step, your adventure will never unfold. Often, these first steps that are the hardest, but if you don't start, you'll never finish. Do what you do with gusto. You must immerse yourself fully in whatever you choose to pursue. Giving half of what you've got isn't going to get you where you want to go. Take the leap with both feet. Get wet, get dirty, and be fully present. Be ready for the tough parts when they come because they will arise to threaten your success – that's almost a guarantee. When that happens, you can either push through the challenges or you can quit – and each choice has different consequences. Make your adventure about learning. Recognize that learning takes place when we make it a priority. Embrace your experiences, think about them, and draw some conclusions about what each says about you and your capacities.

It's important to write things down, to voice your conclusions aloud, and to be honest with yourself. Experiences are just experiences unless you make sense from them and explore what each says about you. If you do that, then the result is often an enduring and expanded understanding of who you are and what you can do. Lastly, make sure you don't stop living what you learned when your adventure ends. After all, isn't the point of adventuring to become someone more than you were before? That doesn't happen in the same way it could when the end of the trail is the end of your adventure.

According to the Appalachian Trail Conservancy, twelve thousand have completed thru-hikes since Earl Schafer became the first in 1948. Fourteen-hundred others completed their thru-hikes in the years before I finished mine in 1987.

In the seven years ending in 2017, seven-thousand finished thru-hikes, fifty-thousand attempted thru-hikes, and millions more spent many days and weeks along the trail.

The collective time invested in Appalachian Trail experiences is staggering. So, too, is the positive impact on the health and well-being of those who make such investments. What a wonderful resource the Appalachian trail is and every acre of our public lands. That's something we should collectively never forget.

So, what's the payoff of rearranging your entire life for a thru-hike or even a several-week sojourn? I only know my story, but for me, six months on the Appalachian Trail has paid dividends ever since.

Getting the most from a thru-hike is not a random occurrence. The magic unfolds as one thinks about their experience both as it happens and in the months and years that follow. I don't believe we ever stop learning from a well-lived thru-hike or a 3-month trek across Europe or sailing from the Caribbean to the coast of Africa.

After we log an incredible adventure, everything after that is colored by the experience forever. Learning continues just as long as you keep thinking about your experiences critically and don't stop searching for new insights contained in them.

The best place to start a thru-hike – or any significant adventure – is to ask yourself, "What do I need to be different as a result of this experience?" If you can answer that question honestly and re-form the words into a clear and simple understanding of why you are setting out on an adventure, then you are ready to start.

Nobody hits a target without first having a target. I believe those who head out on an adventure because it sounds fun or because they couldn't think of anything better to do are at a distinct disadvantage. Once you know what you're after and set your sights on that thing, then you're more likely to achieve what you're after -- whatever it may be.

In 1987, I had no intention of writing a book, but the memories of hiking the Appalachian Trail have sustained me for 30 years -- and not in a sad, tiresome sort of way. I still tell stories, and people tend to listen. Occasionally, some come for advice. I still find strength in the lessons learned; laugh at memories; and though I don't see them anymore, I still find t the people with whom I hiked is still relevant. I've never been at a loss for a story since the Appalachian Trail or lacked something to daydream about.

That's one of the things I was looking for when I decided to thru-hike – I wanted a story to tell. I found that and more and gained perspective on many things -- especially on how to live well and live strong.

If you are looking for tips on how to hike the Appalachian Trail like what to carry and how far to hike each day, this is the wrong book to read. If you are looking for tips on why to hike the Appalachian Trail and how to get the most from your experience years and years later, then reading this might be time well-spent. This is not a "How to" book. It is more a "Why to" book.

The Appalachian Trail made me a better man and a more interesting person. I'm more resilient and self-reliant as a result. Completing my thru-hike on Springer Mountain became the foundation for 10,000 better days and plenty of opportunities since. What gave the experience meaning? Lessons learned about who I am, about the greatness and generosity of people along the trail, and the hefty serving of humility I was force-fed along the way.

I'm sure one part of the thru-hike experience is similar for every individual at the start of a thru-hike. Whether standing at Springer or Katahdin, as excited as you are about getting started, thru-hikers are gripped by the enormity of the challenge ahead. The awareness that the only way to complete the journey is by doing the work a little at a time over a long period is almost overwhelming. You can't magically wish yourself to the end; to succeed, you must do a little each day. Those who can stick with the routine of getting up, lacing your boots, strapping on a pack and pounding out ten or twelve or sometimes twenty or thirty miles each day, will eventually find themselves at the opposite terminus.

There's nothing glamorous about a thru-hike. It's sweaty and smelly and painful now and then. Burps and farts and blisters and unfamiliar but ever-present odors are part of the experience. It's hard work, too. It takes slow and steady effort all the way to the end without compromise. At least that's the way it is for most of us. Most of us don't make our experience about speed. Some do, though, out of necessity or to satisfy their own passions. I'm content to let the runners do their thing. Their accomplishments are impressive, yes, but speed is not for me. It never was and never will be. And that's okay for the rest of us.

Finishing a thru-hike is not what determines success or failure. And while not completing a planned thru-hike may rank high on a list of regrets for some, three-hundred or eight-hundred or a thousand miles is enough for anyone to reap a life full of benefits -- as long as you leave the trail free from regrets.

The Appalachian Trail is the heart of a million stories about people growing up, getting healthy, healing, and moving on to bigger and better things. This book is just another story, typical in many respects of any thru-hike. What follows is my collection of stories -- none too exceptional. They unfolded as I hiked. Each shaped my experience, and each continued to influence me for thousands of days after. I celebrate my openness to learning from each little experience. Thirty years later, learning from my experiences matters far more than how much I ate or how far I hiked each day.

While it may sound trite to observe what so many others have already said about grand adventures, I'll repeat what they've said because it's that important. It was never the destination that mattered, it was the journey, and surprisingly, thirty years on, the journey continues still.

The first part of this book recounts the people and experiences encountered through fourteen states and over 2,100 miles. They include near death on an icy mountain, surviving a kidnapping attempt, and brushes with war heroes, beautiful women, oddballs, characters, and a suspected serial killer. There was a ghost one afternoon, too. Maybe. In the final chapter, I share a few regrets -- which miraculously are mild and minimal. I also share reflections and advice I think might have value for any adventurer.

Remember, this is a "Why to" book not a "How to book."

Thirty years later, the value of investing more than a year in preparing for and completing a southbound AT thru-hike is more apparent than ever.

GEORGIA

My story starts in 2017, about a year after heart surgery.

It was raining and uncharacteristically cold and gray in North Georgia; green was the prevailing color of the hillsides thanks to pines that hid hardwoods that had already gone brown or dropped their leaves. It was late fall, and I was stuck in traffic.

Above me, in the surrounding hills, I could see nature's nearness, but I wasn't part of it, and I wanted to scream. I was mired in traffic outside Atlanta, disconnected and staring off into distant hills. I wished more than anything I stood among them, but I wasn't part of them, and I had no way to get to them.

I was going nowhere fast, trapped like everybody around me – in cars, on phones, oblivious to all but the pressing crap that had to get done that day. It was a sad state of affairs, and it was the way of most mornings. I was just one of many the thousands speeding along in multi-ton killing machines trying to get somewhere I didn't really want to go. At least half of us on the road that morning were paying more attention to texts and e-mails and phone calls than to the road.

The stress of the new day was already crowding me; I could feel it taking a toll on my spirit. Still, I squeezed out a few more texts and cursed the cars around me. That's when the semi swerved and stopped directly ahead. I looked up from my phone by chance and hit the brakes hard. The tires screeched, rubber burned, and smoke from the skid filled the car. I braced for the crash, knowing I was likely to be crushed in the next nanosecond or so and prayed a lifetime of prayers in that instant that the last sounds I'd hear on earth wouldn't be twisting metal and shattering glass. Or my own screams. The impact seemed imminent, but instead of a loud smack, there was silence. And stillness.

Was I dead? No. Somehow my car had stopped near enough to the truck that a pencil could not have slid between them. The front of my car was even slightly beneath the semi's rear step. It was the closest of calls, less than a quarter of an inch from likely death. Or serious disabling injury.

The car in my rearview mirror was equally close as I was to the truck and the car behind it was damned close, too. That driver still held his phone to his ear. He was pale and staring, but not speaking. He looked like he was going to throw up. I was sweating, surprised and relieved not to be dead. My heart pounded like a freight train. I was unable to think of much else but the call my wife almost got. And for what? A few more e-mails squeezed out to people who were in the scope of the lives that really mattered to me – mine, hers, and my children -- pretty unimportant?

As I drove on, I thought, "How did life devolve to this? How had my smartphone become the center of my universe?" I felt sick to my stomach and as far from the freedom of hills and rivers than I'd ever been before. It wasn't right, I knew. It wasn't natural. It wasn't me. It wasn't the least bit healthy for mind, body, or spirit. I couldn't shake the sensation that something was amiss and quite out of balance.

I tossed my phone on the seat next to me and vowed never to text again while driving. I pledged to get outside more, too. Later that evening, though, I was again cranking out texts on the drive home in the dark – having stayed at the office once again longer than I should have. How soon we forget promises and how hard old habits tend to die.

But something happened that morning, something that stirred things deep within. Just as I started to drive on, I began remembering things I'd lost touch with. The memories came from out of the blue and at light speed. Mostly, they were memories of wild places and the feelings that went along with traveling in remote spots. The memories fueled a sense of being alive and well.

I found myself dreaming of working in my garden at home and quick escapes down the Chattahoochee River. And hiking in New Hampshire. And Maine. And along the Missouri River in Montana. I pledged to get off my ass and get outside as I'd always done before. It had only been in recent years that I'd fallen into bad habits and quit regular visits to the wild and remote places that infused my soul with energy.

My mind wandered to places I'd been – mountaintops and streams and secluded spots in the thickest of woods. The memories awoke something in me. I missed the scents and sensations of being in the middle of nowhere, immersed entirely in wildness. It had been too long since I'd ventured into the forest or swam in a mountain stream.

Separate from natural places isn't who I'd ever been. Now, though, in my fifties, escaping the city and even the suburbs wasn't so easy. My kids were in high school. Getting them to lacrosse games, band concerts, SAT prep class and taking them to visit colleges were more immediate priorities. Taking care of a house and a yard and teaching teenagers to drive took precedence over almost everything else.

And I realized I was the one suffering from not getting outside and not keeping in touch with adventures of old.

That morning, I found myself lost thinking about everywhere I'd rather be and driving very cautiously. That's when the voice on the radio announced that it was November 7th, 2017. Any other date would have meant nothing, but that particular date landed like a hammer upside my head. I nearly slammed on the brakes and caused another accident when I realized that precisely thirty years before, likely at almost the same minute, I'd taken the final step of my Appalachian Trail thru-hike.

Thirty years before, I stepped onto Springer Mountain, my life more in balance than at any other point before or since. That day, in 1987, I fell to my knees and cried and laughed and prayed and gave thanks.

"Holy shit," I thought, "Thirty years." It was a hard-to-wrap-my-head-around milestone. I couldn't help but wax philosophical and feel a little old. Thirty years is a lot of days, nearly 10,000. I was no longer the young man I was then. I was now neck-deep in raising three teenagers. I owned a house, had a mortgage, and was paying off two cars. I'd survived several major health threats. Now, I worried about such different things. Instead of dreaming about freedom and adventure and wildness, I was stuck thinking about mortgage rates, insurance, home repairs, five-twenty-nine college savings plans, 401K's, cholesterol, and blood pressure that was higher than it should have been. "What the hell happened?" Life was so different. And me? Well, I was most different of all.

I wondered if I was any better off than I was in 1987. Had thru-hiking amounted to anything measurable or lasting? That question burned in my head. Had it been worth the effort? I knew the answer to those questions because of my heart surgery experience. But what about beyond that atypical situation. Had it appreciably affected the rest of my trajectory?

I'd thought about my Appalachian Trail experiences a good bit in the prior thirty years. Almost daily to be honest. So many of them were crystal clear like the faces of those who made times special or the warm aroma of fresh-baked pies and homemade breakfasts eaten in obscene quantities in trailside diners. Thirty years is roughly 10,000 days, I calculated. "Shit," I thought. "That's a Hell of a lot of days."

"Time will tell," I used to say to those who'd ask if hiking the AT was worth the effort. I couldn't say that anymore. There was no choice but to face that question. What difference had hiking the Appalachian Trail made? In 1987, I quit a job, dropped out of graduate school, spent most of my savings, and said goodbye to a girlfriend who went on to make millions later in her life. In exchange, I hiked 2,139.5 miles, mostly on my own, and came home to face a good bit of unfinished business.

On November 7, 2017, I went on to work and returned home after a few stops along the way. Nobody knew it was the thirtieth anniversary of something so important -- not even my wife or kids. But I knew.

It seemed a day worth celebrating, so in the spirit of a thru-hiker, I bought a Snickers bar – something I hadn't done in years – and choked it down. It tasted like plastic and made my heart race a million miles an hour. I thought I might throw up. Or die. Had I really eaten hundreds of these things as I hiked from Maine to Georgia? For thirty years, the memory of eating three-hundred Snickers bars as I hiked through fourteen states surrounded by nature's bounty, had been a good one. All those days later, though, eating even one was distinctly unpleasant, even nauseating.

For a month or so after the close call on the highway, I obsessed over the thought, "Was it worth it?" I lay awake thinking about that question on quite a few nights. This book is the result of my reflections and my efforts to reconnect with my experience.

For weeks following, I couldn't clear my head. I was continuously distracted by thoughts about the Appalachian Trail and whether strapping a pack on my back and hiking 2,139.5 miles had amounted to anything really. Maybe the Appalachian Trail was just a great distraction? Just a long vacation. Maybe even wasted time? Perhaps I should have stayed in school, finished a Ph.D., stuck with Lori, and accepted the lot I was dealt in life -- to listen to the stories of others rather than to be a teller of tales.

Doubts crept in as I remembered the pleasantries and the challenges of hiking. Most made me smile. Some made me cringe.

Remembering became a near-obsession. I pulled out stacks of letters and my old trail journal and photos and slides I'd not seen in thirty years. Finding a working slide projector proved near as challenging and nowhere near as satisfying as climbing Katahdin. It turns out, as a species, slide projectors have not weathered the last decades well – only about as well as dinosaurs dealt with ice ages and meteors. Not meaning to, a local kid made me feel like both an ancient and an imbecile when he looked at my slides and the broken projector and said, "This stuff's got to be fifty years old at least! Why didn't you just use a digital camera?"

The next day he came back with a few hundred digitized images neatly stored on a tiny flash drive. I felt even older.

I dived into the photos. They were mostly pictures of pretty places and a surprising number of people, who, for the life of me, I couldn't remember ever having met. I busied myself getting re-acquainted with my thru-hike, especially the people I'd encountered. There was one among them, I realized, who I'd encountered in a profound and more meaningful way than any other on that trail. It was me.

I wondered if I was an improved version of who I might otherwise have been because I'd thru-hiked the AT thirty years before. Or would I have been better off to have stayed in school, stuck with the girl I was seeing, stayed employed, and not spent the bulk of my meager savings? Who would I be, I wondered, had I not taken that risk and set off on an epic journey? I questioned how life might have turned out differently had I quit after the 100-mile wilderness or tossed in the towel that day in New York when the heat and loneliness got the best of me.

Looking for answers, I sought the input of "old" thru-hikers I knew. I asked specifically about their experiences since completing their thru-hike. How had the many, many days since been influenced by the relative few invested in hiking the Appalachian Trail?

While our trail experiences were vastly different, not one disagreed that most days since finishing at Katahdin or on Springer were, they believed, somehow better than they might otherwise have expected them to be. Not

I've met a lot of thru-hikers. I've yet to find one who regrets their investment. In fact, the opposite is true. More than anything, based on conversations with thru-hikers from many generations, an Appalachian Trail thru-hike is a probable game changer. And the impacts endure.

That's when I decided to write this book. My motivation? There were two prime reasons. The first was to preserve what memories of my experience I could still remember. Time takes its toll on anything committed to memory. The second, and the more critical, I think, is to perhaps tip the scale more in the direction of success for anyone who decides to shoulder a pack and start walking or to embark on an adventure of significance.

I pledged to never forget names and places like Frye Notch, Rausch Gap, Cosby Knob, and a hundred others. Thirty years later, though, they're mostly words on a page with little meaning except that one night, long ago, I slept there. I'm pretty sure I slept there, at least, because of the notes scrawled in the margins of the trail guide I carried in the now-battered pack that hangs old and faded and unused in my garage.

It's nothing to look at now, that pack -- Wilderness Experience, early-design internal frame, so less sexy than packs these days. No bells. No whistles. No frills. I'm sure it wouldn't make it through another weekend trip, but back then, at least for a few months, it was sturdy and right-sized; and everything I needed fit inside. My life revolved around that pack and that trail guide and those experiences became the foundation of a better life.

Thankfully, I wrote a few things down, mostly in letters that I sent home to family and a few friends. My mother collected those letters in a binder and that she gifted back to me when I returned home. It was a priceless gift. Without those letters, so much of my thru-hike experience would have been lost to time.

There were other names, too, nearly forgotten now -- Gorham House Inn, Upper Goose Pond Cabin, Cass Cassady in Harpers Ferry, and Hightop Hut. I barely remember now, but I know I rolled into each spot late in the afternoon, exhausted and exhilarated, dropped my pack, pulled out the essentials of a thru-hike -- sleeping bag, Therm-a-rest, stove, iodine tabs, pen, paper, and food -- and lived the uncomplicated life of an end-to-end hiker, 159 nights in a row.

Very few days have passed in the last 10,000 when I didn't re-live some moment or reflect on some insight I stumbled upon between Springer and Katahdin. I may have forgotten names and faces and places, but I haven't lost touch with what mattered. A student of mine marveled at a draft of this book, "You wrote this book from memory? But there's so much detail."

"Too powerful to forget," I told her. I guess that's mostly true, but I had to work pretty hard to recover a lot of detail. As I studied photos and letters and had conversations with people who were essential to my experience, I remembered more and more. I guess this book is part fiction, but only because memory isn't exactly infallible after thirty years. If any part is exaggerated, it's not intended to be.

What's included is accurate as far as I remember. Much was chronicled as it happened in a collection of thirty-year-old letters and journal entries. Memories have faded here and there, mostly around the edges, though, but never at the center. Hiking the Appalachian Trail was truly remarkable and unforgettable.

It took 160 days to hike from Maine to Georgia. 10,000 have passed since I guzzled a bottle of champagne on Springer Mountain. What was the value of those 160 days so many days later? An intriguing question, I thought, and found myself thinking about who I am and who I might have been had I started at Katahdin but never reached Springer Mountain. The memories were fuzzy at first, but the more I perused old letters and my trail journal, the easier it was to drift back to a simpler time when I stood at what turned out to be a most-important crossroads. 1987.

Postage stamps were a quarter then; gas was a buck; candy bars were forty cents. There were no "King-sized" versions of anything. A Big Mac was a dollar-fifty, a can of Coke from a vending machine was thirty-five cents, and a blue plate special in a small-town diner – usually served by a cigarette-smoking waitress in a crisp uniform -- was four bucks including a tip. You could still buy a gumball for a penny from a bubble-shaped machine in most gas stations or grocery stores, and the minimum wage was $3.35.

There were a few high-end outdoor stores then, but not many. Most quality equipment had to be purchased by mail. Quality gear cost about the same as it does now, only wages were much lower. What one paid for a quality pack was comparably far more expensive than it is today. Concepts like waterproof, breathable, and ultra-light were new and novel and cost-prohibitive. Most thru-hikers got by with what they could afford which was a mix of army surplus, high-end rain gear, and a few items begged or borrowed from friends or purchased at Wal-Mart. A high-tech rain jacket was $120; quality boots, mostly leather, were about the same, and a decent sleeping bag set you back $100. I paid $125 for the Wilderness Experience pack I carried. It was an awkwardly designed internal-frame pack. Other hikers took an interest in it as we passed, "What the heck is that?" Most carried traditional frame packs.

In 1987, Ron Reagan was in the White House, Platoon won the Oscar for Best Picture, and the St. Louis Cardinals would lose to the Minnesota Twins in game seven of the World Series.

I remember that last fact because I listened to game seven on a Walkman radio in Apple House Shelter somewhere in North Carolina. Baseball was a big thing in St. Louis where I grew up, and I was a loyal fan. That year, I missed nearly every bit of the season and didn't much care except that it was the last World Series my father would ever pay attention to. It was just one of those things I gave up to hike the AT

While my family raised glasses to the hometown team and consoled one another with hugs and another beer, I stood alone and stared at a million stars and listened to a whippoorwill sing. There was no one to share the agony of a World Series loss with that night, so I downed a Snickers bar, chugged a quart of Kool-Aid and lay awake missing home. I might as well have been a million miles from most things familiar, but I wouldn't have traded it for the world.

As small as they were, moments like those were life-changing.

Staying connected wasn't easy. Cell phones and laptops were still sci-fi fantasy. Payphones and phone booths, things you can hardly find anymore, were commonplace in trailside towns and critical lifelines to home. In 1989, Apple released its first portable Macintosh. Like everything technically advanced back then, it was fifty times more cumbersome and expensive than anything now. It weighed 16 pounds and sold for $6,500. Hikers in 1987 were not connected to anything but the trail except through letters and occasional collect phone calls.

Folks back home only knew where I had been or where I was supposed to be; they never knew exactly where I was except in those rare moments when we were actually on the telephone.

Hitchhiking wasn't as ill-advised then as it is now. I caught many rides trailside to little groceries and out-of-the-way hostels without fear. Only once was one of those experiences a bit unnerving. Even then, I never thought the woman who picked me up might filet me or locks me in her basement forever.

Times were different. They were more straightforward, less connected, wilder, and maybe a little less dangerous. Or perhaps they just seemed so because there was no internet, and we only knew what we experienced or read or saw on TV. Or heard around the dinner table. Don't get the wrong idea about 1987. Sure, there were no cell phones, laptops, Wi-Fi hotspots, or Starbucks, but it wasn't exactly the dark ages. We had flashlights, even headlamps, cable TV, newspapers, and radios. And books.

One recollection is as sharp today as it was 30-minutes after it happened. Early November 1987 was cold and overcast. I woke in Gooch Gap shelter and stuffed my sleeping bag into my pack one last time. I was sixteen miles from Springer Mountain. It was November 7th, and it was the first day in one-hundred and sixty that I knew without a doubt that I would finish the Appalachian Trail. That last day, that final stretch, was the first time I could leave the fear of quitting behind me. That's when I was finally sure that I would complete the end-to-end journey. Even if it killed me. Thru-hiking wasn't easy; pitfalls and potential pitfalls were plenty. Before that final day, I was never confident that I'd join the ranks of thru-hikers – about fifteen hundred strong by 1987, a hundred or so who had been Southbounders. That day -- the last day -- was the first time I knew I'd crawl the final few miles if I had to.

Those last miles were effortless until it came to the last few steps.

The southern terminus was just a brass plaque embedded in rock, and the mountain was much less grand than where I'd started in Maine five months before. That brass plaque and the final 2"x 4" white blaze, though, brought me to my knees. On top of Katahdin, June 1, 1987, I remember thinking Springer might well have been the moon; impossible to reach anytime soon and months and months away even with luck and hard work. And then I stood almost dumbfounded on Springer, "How had it happened so quickly?" I was a little lost. I seriously considered heading back north.

I had plane tickets leaving Atlanta in two days and hadn't seen but a handful of people I family and friends for almost six months. If not for that, I'd likely have turned north for another few miles, at least. Or gone back to Katahdin. As scared as I was to give up the balance of trail life, I sensed it was time to go home, and I knew it was time to start building something of substance. Against my better judgment, I made my way from Springer Mountain to Hartsfield-Jackson Airport in Atlanta.

It was the right choice.

Years later, when I look at my wife and children, my dogs, and career success, I am entirely sure that bouncing back north for another round would have been as wrong as wrong gets. At least for me.

If I would l have turned around and continued on for another round, I'd have betrayed one of the more important lessons learned. The trail had often whispered, "You can take breaks, sure, but you can't stand still. Otherwise,

27

you'll stagnate. And the dream of finishing will be lost." That wisdom applies as much to living as it does to hiking the A.T. "Stagnate and the dream will be lost."

A man can climb to the summit and enjoy the view, but he can't stay there forever. Oh, how I wanted to though when I reached Springer. Eventually, a man at the summit will need to descend from that glorious high point for whatever reason. If he dallies too long on the mountain, when he does descend, he'll return most likely to a world he doesn't recognize and one that no longer has much of a place for him. I guess I knew that even though I didn't want to accept it. Begrudgingly, I embraced that wisdom and headed for Hartsfield-Jackson Airport.

Balance is a beautiful thing, and so is living in a state of comfort and security, but moving towards something is vital to a well-lived life. It was a central lesson gleaned from my trail experience. To get somewhere, you must keep moving towards something. And when you get where you're going, don't stop for any longer than it takes to celebrate what you've learned, and then move on to the next great thing. Failing to build anything of permanence, well, that's a hard thing to reconcile when you wake up one day perhaps long into the future empty-handed and alone.

There were more than a few temptations to quit or at least to take shortcuts along the way. I fought them daily with the simple reminder, "no regrets," whispered over and over. It was my mantra with each step. I reminded myself frequently that when I stood on Springer and looked back over the 2,100 miles I'd traveled from Katahdin, I would either see an unbroken line or one fragmented and fractured with shortcuts and skipped sections. I knew I'd experience satisfaction or regret if I ever reached Springer. I also sensed that the choices I made along the way would dictate how I felt about my efforts and even about myself. I sensed whichever choice I made – either hiking every step or completing a half-assed hike -- would define a starkly different direction for the rest of my life. One path would brand me as a guy who quit the AT; the other would brand me as someone who didn't. Drastically different life-long consequences, I was certain, would follow either decision.

I remember thinking at the top of Springer Mountain, just moments after tagging the brass plaque embedded there in the rock that never before had I ever been better-adapted for any role in my life than that of "thru-hiker". That's a tough thing to abandon – being at the top of your game. I

28

knew, though, that "the game" wasn't exactly reality. For a short time, the Appalachian Trail was my safe-space, my comfort zone, and the pinnacle of my competence – especially those brief moments on top of Springer Mountain. That is the moment in my life when everything seemed to hang in perfect balance. On that day, the temptation to continue along the trail was almost more significant than the temptation to quit which had plagued me at previous points.

Pushing through temptations to quit and sticking to the task of finishing what I started have made all the difference. I sometimes wonder what might have happened if I'd surrendered to the temptation, caught a bus home, and re-started life with the identity of a failed thru-hiker. I don't believe it would have been good. In the end, I climbed onto a plane and headed home with my new identity. I was a thru-hiker.

That choice – to push through the tough moments even though I wanted to quit -- has made all the difference in the thirty years since.

MISSOURI

July 31, 1986

"… When there is too much coarse stuff for everybody and the struggle for life takes the form of competitive advertisement and the effort to fill your neighbor's eye, there is no urgent demand for either personal courage, sound nerves or stark beauty, we find ourselves by accident. Always before these times, the bulk of the people did not overeat themselves because they couldn't whether they wanted to or not, and all but a very few were kept 'fit' by unavoidable exercise and personal danger. Now if only he pitch his standard low enough and kept free from pride, almost anyone can achieve a sort of excess. You can go through contemporary life fudging and evading, indulging and slacking, never really hungry nor frightened nor passionately stirred, your highest moment a mere sentimental orgasm, and your first real contact with primary and elemental necessities the sweat of your deathbed."

– H.G. Wells

I set out in May 1987 to hike every step of the Appalachian Trail; there were roughly five million of them. It was described then as a long, green tunnel that stretched from Mount Katahdin in Maine to Springer Mountain in Georgia. It was a 2,100-mile long work-in-progress; a national park, more or less, just a couple thousand feet wide. The official length of the trail changes by the year as sections are re-routed from roads to public lands.

Planning my trip started almost a year before, in July 1986. It was hot and dry that summer. It seems so long ago. It wasn't before cable TV or VCR's, but it was before the Internet and cell phones. It was when the best then in video game graphics was blocky and unconvincing. Everything electronic was archaic and bulky and so little of it was part of everyday life.

I was optimistic, ambitious, naïve, twenty-four and not all the way grown-up. I had a broken heart and a head full of dreams, and I needed a break from graduate school. I wasn't trying to get anything out of my system or find myself. I was neither lost nor searching for anything but a story. At least that's what I told myself. Though mostly happy and on-track, I sensed there was more to life than I'd found so far, and the AT seemed as good a place as any to start looking.

I wanted to be able to pull up a stool at the bar or a chair at the dinner table or sit down next to a stranger on a park bench and have something to add to the conversation. In a lot of ways, that was my motivation to set out on an adventure.

In those days before the trail, I wanted to fuel my daydreams with something of substance, I suppose, and so I found myself inexplicably in places that others might not go. And I probably shouldn't have been.

Rusty was my best friend and drinking buddy; he had been for years. Cheap beer and half-assed adventures were his things. He was rough-cut and charismatic, the sort who could talk anybody into anything. I may have been a dreamer, but he took that to extremes. His apartment was littered with Readers Digest books about Bigfoot and ancient mysteries, dinosaurs and old west gunfighters. He was easily romanced by the unknown and things-never-before-done. His cabinets were stuffed with things advertised on late-night TV that his curiosity just couldn't resist. Rusty was blue-collar as anybody, but that wasn't a role he was relegated to for life. He could have been anything -- a corporate lawyer or an art dealer or a mechanic. He grew up in taverns and tight spots, though, and he introduced me to things like tequila and the salty-earth sides of God and faith. He'd seen a tougher side of life; something I might not have known much about if not for him. If not for his influence, I'd never have stepped inside a strip joint, slid bare-chested across a frozen pond, thrown .22 caliber shells into a campfire to see what would happen or been baptized in a creek one drunken night. Because of him, I came not just to love old-time country music but to understand it.

He was a wholesome sort, faithful to girlfriends, pals, and employers. His passion for simple things made him a favorite of most who met him. We drank a lot – too much, probably– but we laughed lots, too. I'd have followed him anywhere. It was his idea to hike the Appalachian Trail.

You couldn't hang around Rusty without collecting stories. Most were the kind you wouldn't tell your mother, but none were the sort you'd run from years later. I was looking for stories and not quick to judge. He was drawn to people and places you weren't likely to find along a beaten path. I found something fascinating in the experiences of walking into backcountry bars, one-room cafés, and mixing with the up-after-3 a.m. crowd in all-night diners.

We were a good match in that way, not exactly made in heaven, but still a pretty good pair.

He had a way of talking me into things that thirty years later still make for good stories. As my children have entered their teens, I share more of those stories than I ever thought I might. I find them valuable tools for teaching about good judgment and thinking things through -- something I didn't always do back then. Often, when using those stories to teach, I have to add the caveat, "Do as I say, not as I did."

It was a wintry night in 1986 -- months before we'd first broach the subject of thru-hiking -- that left me seriously wondering if we were living as right and as well as we believed. It was a few weeks after we'd wandered into a biker bar and the guy ten days out of prison pulled his jacket aside to show me the pistol tucked in his waistband. "I'd just as soon shoot you as look at you," he said, "but I like you. You remind me of me twenty years ago."

"Is that supposed to give me some sense of security?" I asked him. "That I remind you of a guy who spent time in prison? It doesn't do much for me." I was as honest as could be. "I hope I don't wind up like you in twenty years."

He laughed. "Prison wasn't so bad," he said. "Except when I got out, my woman wasn't the fresh young thing she was when they sent me away. Still full of fire, though." He grinned at me to show he was missing a few teeth most of them, I think. They were probably knocked out in some prison uprising or a long-ago bar fight.

He invited Rusty and me to join him after the bar closed for a little "off-the-books fun" as he called it. "Might even be a few bucks in it for you," he said. "If things go well," he added and winked. I didn't ask what might happen if things didn't go well. I was pretty sure I knew. He laughed and nodded when I told him the woman waiting for me was far prettier and far meaner than he was. I didn't dare tell him the woman waiting up for me was my mother, and she was expecting me home before my curfew.

Later that night, lying in bed, I wrestled with the encounter. "What the Hell was I doing in a place like that? And what about me reminded that guy of who he'd been twenty years before?" I was generally wholesome and well-raised, not the sort likely to wind up with my picture on a post office wall or bleeding in the street with a cop's bullet lodged in my lung. I started questioning a lot of things that night.

But old habits are hard to break. A few weeks later, Rusty and I wound up in a strip joint in a bad part of town. It was not the sort of place either of us aspired to spend much time or to ever call "home." It was the sort of place, though, I'd never been before, and those were the sorts of places that made me feel alive. And filled my head with stories. I followed Rusty in telling myself it was worth just one more tale to tell.

A smoky haze filled the place, the music was loud and driving, and characters more entertaining than the pretty dancing girls sat in every corner. I pulled up a chair sat next to a guy staring at the bare-breasted dancer on the stage above him. His mouth hung open, and he breathed heavily as if he'd just run a marathon. A tiny line of drool ran down his chin. He was too easy a target to resist. I sat next to him, leaned in and whispered in his ear, "She used to be a man."

"What?" His eyes were huge. He looked a little deranged.

I almost walked away, should have walked away, but I couldn't resist the fun.

"That woman," I nodded towards her. "She used to be a guy." I was as matter-of-fact as I could be. "Yep. Played football with him all four years of high school." Of course, my story was a complete fabrication. I was never big enough or tough enough to play football.

"No way," he said.

"Yep," I told him. "He – uh, she – was a helluva wide receiver. All-state, as I remember. Fast as lightning." I nodded emphatically and took another swig of beer, so pleased with myself and trying not to launch into a laughing fit that would send beer spewing out of my nose. Of course, telling him so was just good-natured fun – at least for me. Anyone with a speck of sense should have known I was lying through my teeth. She was five-feet-nothing and petit – hardly the makings of a champion wide-receiver. He thanked me profusely for the inside information, jumped up and raced off to tell his friends -- and the rest of the bar apparently.

I was basking in self-amusement, quite entertained with myself, sipping my beer, until I noticed him moving from table to table, repeating my story, pointing to the stripper and then pointing at me each time. He told nearly everyone in the place, "It's true," I could hear him say over and over. "That guy told me."

"This is going to get out of hand," I mumbled under my breath and went to find Rusty.

It took a while, but I found him chatting with a pretty waitress. "We gotta go," I told him and explained what I had done.

He laughed. Joy and pure amusement sparkled in his eyes. "You started that rumor? Some guy with spit running down his chin told me the story and pointed in your general direction. I didn't think you'd be so stupid to make up a story like that."

"Yeah, yeah, yeah," I said. "We'd best be getting out of here," I tried to get him to budge, but it was too late. The young woman moved across the room towards us, nearly buck-naked. A bartender flagged her down, whispered in her ear, turned and pointed at me. There was no mistaking her reaction. Her eyes blazed fiery red. From across the room, I could see her boiling like a teapot. She wasn't the slightest bit amused and damned-near ready to burst. This would not end well, I knew. I looked for an escape. I turned to Rusty.

"What should we do?"

"Ignore her," Rusty said. "Maybe she'll go away."

"That's the best you got?" I shot back. "Ignore her?"

He shrugged and flashed that winning smile.

I wasn't convinced, and it didn't bring the slightest comfort.

She picked her way through the crowd, a Pyrex coffee pot filled with ice water in her hand. Rusty and I held our ground as she advanced. Half the bar at least was aware as the drama unfolded. Steady, "Rusty said. "Steady." I could tell he loved the excitement. Hell, it wasn't him, who was fixed in her crosshairs.

We kept talking, eyes locked on one another as if nothing was about to happen. She was hollering like a crazy woman when she got to us, barely dressed, quite attractive, and madder than hell or a hornet or both or some never before seen beast. Now, there might have been an opportunity to stand and apologize, but I'll never know. We sat there like statues without the slightest acknowledgment that she even existed. What idiots!

Rusty's advice proved as misguided as could be. Not paying attention only made her madder. She emptied half the pitcher over my head and the rest over Rusty's. Then she reared back and smashed the pot over my head. It exploded into a billion slivers. Glass went everywhere. People froze, others jumped out of the way, and others just stood and stared and shouted. Suddenly, I was the focus of just about every person in that place. Now, I learned something that night, when someone hits you hard enough with a Pyrex coffee pot, they explode into pieces. Fortunately, there's not quite sufficient blunt force behind it to cave in your skull. Had she chosen a beer pitcher instead to smash over my head, I'd likely be dead. Or worse.

So, I didn't flinch; it didn't hurt much, and I guess I must have looked tough as nails as I stood in slow motion, calm as could be, turned to Rusty and said, "We're leaving."

Now, it's a pretty bad sign when you're surrounded by pretty women dancing without shirts on but most people are looking straight at you. A swarm of bouncers moved in our direction. They were either well-trained or not very clever. If they wanted to bust us up, they made a big mistake. They came at us with the door at our backs, leaving us a convenient escape route. We backed out the door, calmly as I remember, and raced like madmen across the parking lot to the car. Rusty did a "Dukes of Hazard" slide across the hood of the car, dropped in behind the wheel and peeled out in a hail of dust and gravel, my door swinging out widely and me hanging on for dear life. Both of us were laughing like idiots -- scared idiots -- which, of course, we were.

For the next few days, I picked glass slivers out of my head. "I need to grow up," I told myself. "I'm a good kid from a good family. I go to church. I have prospects. I wasn't raised to get a pitcher smashed over my head by a bare-breasted stripper or to be chased out of a strip joint by a band of bouncers. How the Hell did I get here?" I made some promises to myself. I promised I'd get back on track.

Maybe that blow to the head knocked some sense into me -- and Rusty, too. The tone of our conversations changed, at least a little, from then on. We talked about growing up and getting serious and being husbands someday and fathers. It was the last time I ever set foot in a place like Roxy's but not the last time I ever did anything stupid.

A few months later, it was still 1986, and I was stuck in the dead of a helluva hot summer. Rusty and I sat in my office at the university readying to leave to hike the Ozark Highlands Trail in Northern Arkansas. It was a hundred and twenty miles of rugged trail, most of which as it turned out was not well marked and maybe only existed in some mapmaker's head. We didn't know what we were doing except that we'd have to eat and sleep and find our way. We loaded packs with food and maps, ponchos and other stuff we figure we'd need. We had two weeks off and the name of a guy who would ferry our car from one end of the trail to another for fifty bucks. Buried deep in my backpack was an unloaded .22 pistol; something I figured might just come in handy.

We checked and double-checked roadmaps and trail maps until we thought we knew what lay ahead. Still, we knew from experience that once off the well-traveled roads, we'd be at the mercy of gas station attendants and random folks who could be flagged down and who might be able to point us towards trailheads and such. It was a before GPS and Google Maps and when there were few guarantees trail maps and backcountry roads were precisely where they appeared on maps drawn twenty years before. Even the advice of weathered locals wasn't likely accurate once you pushed beyond trailheads and parking turnouts at the edge of old logging roads.

We took it on faith we'd find what we were looking for. That, however, turned out to be a naïve assumption.

Another few minutes and we'd have been on our way to Hurricane Creek, the Buffalo River, and the Boston Mountains. The only things left to do were to pee once more, check to be sure doors were locked, and be sure wallets were where they were supposed to be. I was about to shut my office door when the phone rang. I answered it against my better judgment. An unshakeable feeling deep in my guts wouldn't let me ignore it.

Rusty told me to let it go. I couldn't. After ten rings worth of hemming and hawing, I answered the phone. In many ways, it proved to be the call that changed my life forever even though it had almost nothing to do with me directly. It was Rusty's mother. His father – a man he'd not known so well the prior ten years -- wasn't likely to live beyond the next few days. He hung up, shaken and torn. "I have to go," he said.

In 1987, news traveled more slowly from here to there, and people who rambled with a loose itinerary did so at the risk of missing big news. Had she not caught him then, in the last seconds of the last minute before we left, it would have been another week before he'd heard about his father. That's the way it was then when it came to staying in touch. You did your best. That's about all you could do. Immediate news about what was happening at home was rare when you traveled.

So, the Arkansas trip was over before it started, at least for the two of us. I told Rusty I felt an obligation to still go. I figured I had demons to wrestle and my soul needed the challenge. It would be good for me, I told him, and I told myself, "To push some boundaries." The prospect of traveling alone through Northern Arkansas scared the hell out of me, but I couldn't tell him. While it was 1986 everywhere else, it was still the 1930's in parts of Northern Arkansas -- the parts I was now heading to on my own.

I hid my fear, told him I was sorry about his father, threw my pack in my 1980 Toyota and turned towards Arkansas. I needed to clear my head, I told him; I had some thinking to do.

Rusty stopped me as I started out of the parking lot. He stood baking in the sun; I sat behind the wheel, air-conditioner blasting. When he had something important to say, he spoke it without the least hesitation. "We need to hike the Appalachian Trail," he said.

"What?"

"Next summer. Yeah. It's two-thousand miles long. Starts up in Maine somewhere and goes down to Georgia." He'd read about it in National Geographic – about a couple with young kids who made the two-thousand-mile trek in the 1970s. "Took them eight months," he said. "I bet we could do it a lot quicker." He didn't know much more about it, but he was sure we should do it. And that we'd be better for doing it.

I'd heard of the Appalachian Trail, had seen a sign in Newfound Gap when hiking in the Smoky Mountains earlier that spring. I'd even spent a cold, snowy night in Icewater Spring shelter listening to mice scramble around my pack and across my sleeping bag while I slept. I was skeptical, but Rusty wasn't, and he made believing easy.

So, that's all we knew about it -- that the AT was the longest marked footpath in the world -- 2,100 miles or so; and that a family with a little boy and a baby had completed it in 8 months a few years before. It stretched north to south or south to north depending on where you started, and it was lined with shelters filled with mice. We knew the trail passed through the Smoky Mountains and ended in Georgia. We knew the half-way point was likely somewhere in Pennsylvania, but that was about the extent of our knowledge. Neither of us could have named Katahdin or Springer as the terminuses. Names like Earl Schaffer, Benton MacKaye, and Grandma Gatewood were as unfamiliar as any others. We knew nothing of the Appalachian Trail Conservancy or that only about one in ten of those with the intent to hike end-to-end typically did so. Nor did we understand that relatively few chose to start in Maine and follow a southbound route.

Five minutes later, he had me committing to thru-hike the following summer. We shook hands on it, dramatically spit in our hands and clasped them together roughly like we'd seen guys do in Clint Eastwood westerns and like Mel Gibson in "Mad Max Beyond Thunderdome". It was as if doing so made our agreement more solid. He stood sweating in the street, I sat behind the wheel of a beat-up Toyota; neither of us was quite aware that we'd just committed to change the trajectory of our lives from that point onward.

With that dramatic handshake, life seemed suddenly infused with a spark of excitement that hadn't existed even seconds before. The decision didn't seem the slightest bit reckless. Without much thought at all, to have committed to dropping out of grad school, quitting my job at the university, and setting out on a twenty-one-hundred mile journey. Arbitrarily, we set a date for departure: June 1.

Heading to Arkansas by myself without much of a plan suddenly seemed purposeful. Life as a whole was more engaging then, and the future bright as could be. I felt new-found energy, and the most exciting story of my life developing.

Adding a dash of purpose to life changed my outlook on most things considerably -- especially in the short-term. I was then on a research mission to Arkansas not setting out on a generic hike. I remembered knowing then that something was instantaneously different, and though, not exactly sure what it was or how things would play out, I was a little more alive.

Rusty left to tend to his father; I headed south to Arkansas. Excited and oblivious to what lay ahead. Planning for my thru-hike started then and there, nothing more than daydreams really. I didn't have a clue what any of it that meant or what it would require, where I would start, how much it would cost, or if it was even possible or advisable. None of that mattered in those early stages. What mattered, it turned out, was that I had a sense of direction, and that sense of purpose made me a different person altogether.

I didn't know where to start looking for information. There was no internet; few books on the subject – at least in local bookstores, and living in the great state of Missouri, there wasn't exactly a surplus of thru-hikers to turn to. I did know, as I drove out of Columbia, Missouri, that my first stop when I got back from Arkansas would be the card catalog at the university library. There were few options for conducting research.

For the next 11 months, Rusty and I found a way to work the fact that we were hiking the Appalachian Trail into the first couple minutes of every conversation we had regardless of who we were talking to. That trip to Arkansas became an essential part of preparing for my thru-hike. Mostly, I came home from that trip knowing considerably more about how not to go about making a long-distance trek.

Against all likelihood, the following May, we boarded a plane in St. Louis bound for Baltimore. From there we flew to Bangor, Maine where we spent the night in the closed airport, concealed behind a bank of display cabinets where we scared the piss out of a maintenance man who tried to vacuum behind them where the four of us lay sleeping in a space barely right for two. From there we took a bus to Millinocket and a taxi to Baxter State Park where we hiked a few miles to the base of Mount Katahdin. Then we climbed four-thousand, five hundred feet to the summit of Katahdin and the start of the Appalachian Trail.

On June 1st, 1987, I took the first of five million steps that would eventually lead to Springer Mountain and the thirty years beyond that.

A lot happened before we took those first steps -- a lot that mattered and ultimately contributed to a successful AT hike. That's what this book is about -- the stuff that mattered and lessons learned not just about hiking but about life in general. 10,000 days later, those lessons continue to give significance not only to the one-hundred-sixty days along the AT but also to lessons learned leading up to and immediately following them.

ARKANSAS

Slow me down, Lord. Ease the pounding of my heart by the quieting of my mind.
Steady my pace with a vision of the eternal reach of time.
Give me, amid the confusion of the day, the calmness of the everlasting hills.
Break the tensions of my nerves and muscles with the soothing music of the singing
streams that live in my memory.
Help me to know the magical restoring power sleep.
Teach me the art of taking minute vacations, of slowing down to look at a flower, to
chat with a friend, to pat a dog, or to read a few lines from a good book.
Slow me down, Lord, and inspire me to send my roots deep into the soil of life's
enduring values that I may grow toward the stars of my greater destiny.

-- Unknown

Rusty went to bury his father; I set out along the Ozark Highlands Trail,
alone, more inexperienced than I knew, and less prepared than I wanted to
be. It was my first significant solo hike, multi-day and in the middle of
nowhere. I expected to be physically challenged, but the uphills and the
heat proved to be the easy parts. Being alone, even for five days, was far
more mentally taxing than I could have imagined.

Nothing was what I expected. Parts were gorgeous, and it was easy
enough to follow the trail through the Hurricane Creek Wilderness. On
less-traveled stretches, though, the trail had been obliterated by logging and
forest road construction or never even completed at all. At one point,
finding where the path crossed a clear-cut expanse of once-beautiful timber
wasted half-a-day. It was evident that a mile around a running track wasn't
remotely similar to a mile along a rough and broken section of trail. One
backcountry mile, it became clear, was rarely equivalent to another.

I tried to call the man who was to shuttle my car from one end to
another.   His line had been disconnected. That proved to be a stroke of
good fortune. As it turned out, hiking the whole route which proved in
exceedingly poor condition in places, would have taken twice the amount
of time I'd allowed.

An so, with a sense of confidence bolstered by my new-found identity as a "thru-hiker," I set out with a vague sense of direction and little specifics about where I was going or how far I needed to travel. It turned out hope and optimism are good things, but without direction and purpose, they aren't enough.

A day into the hike, I found myself as alone and as far from anything familiar as I'd ever been. There was no one near to provide answers or input. There were no cell phones, and the car was miles behind me. And it was hot as hell. Going was slow, and though I managed well-enough with map and compass, frustration and lost time ate my energy. The heat took its toll, too, as temps burned north of ninety and humidity hovered near ninety-five percent. It was like moving through soup, thick and close, and the world burned like a furnace. It's then I stumbled on a swimming hole along Hurricane Creek, serene and secluded, shaded mostly, and water so refreshing. It was a lifesaver, a place of salvation, and it was the kind of spot that might have spawned romance if I were other than alone. Instead, it was a lonely place, still beautiful, that amplified the lonesomeness of the moment. Being alone was both everything I needed then and nothing that I needed to be reminded of.

I'd only been away from home seventy-two hours but going alone was tough. I hadn't spoken to another human for at least twenty-four hours, and that wasn't easy. I stayed for a day and a night along the creek, left at dawn, lonely and a little sad, even after a last refreshing dip at first light. I hoped to camp higher in the mountains by nightfall. The swimming hole turned out to be the last water for miles. By mid-afternoon, my Nalgene bottles were empty, and my throat cracked and tortured. A crisis was brewing. No water behind me for five miles, no promise of water for who knows how many miles ahead. Most of the streams on the map had been bone dry when I found them. Everything became then a quest for water, nothing more. It didn't exactly make sense to push further forward. If there were no water in the next mile or two, the situation would only be worse -- me further from the swimming hole and still nothing to drink. I gambled, though, and pushed on.

I started wondering if I'd made a fatal mistake, limping on without water. The heat was blistering, and I felt like my vision was blurred by more than sweat running into my eyes. Then, I saw it. It was at the bottom of an eroded streambed, five feet or so below me. Water. It was nothing spectacular, just a long, shallow puddle, a few feet wide, twenty feet long, and ankle-deep at best. It was a beautiful sight, though, one that rivaled the coolest, bluest, clearest freshwater spring I'd ever seen or even imagined. I dropped my pack, jumped to the streambed below and knelt at the water's edge to fill my bottles from the puddle there. That's when a splash at the opposite end of the puddle nearly scared the life out of me.

I looked up to see some manner of creature coming towards me at an unhurried pace. It was huge and ugly. I didn't know what it was. A sea serpent, maybe? Some mythical beast? It was more a monster than a snake, massive and ugly, and coming straight for me. It was as long as I was tall, big around as my leg, with a head larger than my clenched fist. Its size and confidence rendered it more substantial and more lethal – at least in my brain. I dropped my half-filled bottles without having taken a drink, gave ground, and retreated up the bank. The snake kept coming, then stopped, half-out of the water, six or maybe eight feet from me. Still too close. So near, he was even uglier and reeked of evil intent. My heart pounded. He rushed at me, a feigned rush, fortunately, intended clearly to strike fear into my heart, which it did. And then he flashed the cotton-white inside of his mouth which was as big as the whole of my palm and fingers. Two hooked fangs, like needles of death, were prominent in that defiant, still-open mouth. He lay there absolutely still, intent on not giving even an inch of his territory.

He blocked my access to the water as completely as if he'd drained the creek.

The inside of that mouth was whiter than any white I'd ever seen. "White as snow?" I remember thinking. The whitest of whites, in my mind is still, would better be described as, "White as the inside of a water moccasin's mouth."

I scrambled to the top of the bank above the puddle, safe enough from those fangs and the deadly venom they were designed to deliver. I used a long branch to retrieve my water bottles from within the snake's reach. He didn't flinch; he just stared at me and my stick, his mouth wide-opened and bright, turned his head slightly and curled slightly that he might spring with those teeth if I should present a target.

He was perhaps the most at-peace creature I'd ever encountered in the wild or anywhere else. And the most terrifying.

This indeed was now a crisis. I hadn't had a drink for hours, it was a hundred degrees, and I could feel the impact of encroaching dehydration.

A cold, clear drink was within easy reach except for that accursed beast. I collected my bottles and walked to the far end of the puddle. The snake swam next to me as I moved along the elevated bank, his eyes fixed on me all the while and mouth wide as it would go. At the far end, he cut off access to the water and lay at the pool's edge taunting me. Like a billboard, his wide-opened mouth advertised, "Come any closer, and I'll kill you." I suspected there were no falsehoods in his advertisement. I toyed with him some, walked end to end, stopped mid-way and reversed direction to see what he'd do. The snake, determined to keep me from the water, followed every move I made. I suspected if this was to be a war of wills only, he would win.

I needed water, but he refused to give even an inch. My choices were limited, and I could feel irrationality creeping in. "Desperate situations require desperate measures," I remembered telling myself. I unpacked my backpack rather haphazardly -- sleeping pad and food, stove and rain gear, clothing and toiletries. Finally, I pulled from the bottom of the pack the hard-shelled gun case. "Wow," I thought, "This thing is ridiculously heavy." I pulled the pistol and the box of shells out, slipped nine cartridges into the revolving magazine, gave it a spin like a gunslinger in a western movie, pulled the hammer back until it clicked twice, and stared at the snake with a renewed confidence. I was ready now to take control. Like Clint Eastwood or John Wayne.

I marveled, I remember, how getting ready to defend myself with what was really the equivalent of a pop-gun. It took forever. I was lucky that it was a slow-witted snake threatening me instead of a fast-acting pack of marauding monkeys or worse. They'd have absconded with my backpack and its contents before I could have mounted the feeblest defense or even decided to pull and load my nearly worthless pistol. Carrying a loaded gun was illegal, though; and strapping it to my hip for all to see, while legal, wouldn't have gone far towards making friends should I ever cross paths with another human again, something I wasn't at that point sure would ever happen again.

I walked to the far end of the puddle, the snake followed, never closing his cotton-white mouth. "Last time for that," I told him, even as my heart skipped a few beats. I drew a bead on the center of his open mouth; my finger twitched on the trigger. I felt a sense of power. "Go ahead, make my day," I told him. In a moment, he'd be dead, and my water bottles would be full, and I'd be on my way. "Last chance," I said aloud and sharpened my aim dead-center on that perfect bright, shite target. I steadied the pistol with both hands, "See you, Sucker!"

But a few minutes later, the snack was not dead. The last chance I'd given him wasn't his last chance. I never pulled the trigger. It didn't seem right. Or fair. As ugly as he was and as scary, I had no stomach for killing the snake who defended his territory so well. I unloaded the pistol, buried it in my pack with all my other trappings, swung the load onto my back, and moved on, thirstier than before and not sure how I felt about not killing the snake. I searched for the next puddle, starting to believe maybe, just maybe, I didn't have the demeanor for this kind of work. When push came to shove, I feared, I might not be prepared to manage my own survival.

Not far ahead, though, I found another puddle, not as deep or as clear as the previous one but unprotected by a mythical beast like the other. I drank unchallenged and filled my bottles full as I could.

That night I bedded down in the middle of the forest near enough to the creek for a morning drink. I lay under a million stars at least. I was pleased not to have slaughtered the snake just because I had the power to or because I was impatient and thirsty and put my own needs above that of another living thing. Life, I remember thinking, was more valuable than that, and killing the snake would have been an unnecessary shortcut. And wrong. Shortcuts, I told myself there on the banks of that creek under a canopy of lush treetops, become a way of life if you let them. They rarely lead to anything good. Not killing the snake, I decided, wasn't an act of weakness, but the act of a man capable of understanding his place and what was most important. In subsequent months, I figured out that the snake was merely hiking his hike while I was hiking mine.

Maybe I'd taken shortcuts more times than I should have in the past, I considered. What might life be like if any of us resorted to taking fewer shortcuts?

That night, I slept under a million stars or so. My sleep, surprisingly, wasn't tormented by images of serpents and creatures with exploding heads. I'd made the right decision, I figured, sparing that beast. There would have been no pride in splattering his head and leaving his ugly carcass to rot. Since then, I've wondered, now and again, how life might have been different if I'd have had to carry with me for the last ten thousand days the image of that snake with an exploded head. Instead of rising the next morning with the soul of a killer, I woke refreshed and satisfied that I was a man of patience and mercy who respected even small lives that stood between me and comfort. Hmmmm.

I headed back to the swimming hole the next morning, mostly at peace. Lonesomeness, however, was getting the best of me, though. It had been four days since I'd left my car at the trailhead. The single conversation I'd had since with another human wasn't near enough to sustain me out there. I'd met him at a crossroads looking across the Boston Mountains. He leaned on a truck piled with tree trunks, smoking a home-rolled cigarette. He was missing two fingers, three teeth, and an eye. "Never been further than Little Rock," he said. "Not sure why I'd want to. All I need is here." He was certain. But I was equally sure that everything I needed was not there. I needed people and meaning and vision and a sense of where I was going, and I needed to know why and how all the pieces of the puzzle fit together. I thought more about the wisdom of chucking it all and heading out on a two-thousand-mile journey. The more I thought about it, the harder it was to find any reason why not to do it. Especially on my own.

I don't mean to pass judgment on anyone, especially on that hard working man in outback Arkansas. I'm a firm subscriber to the thru-hiker HYOH philosophy -- "Hike your own hike, let others hike theirs." I'm sure the world would be a better place if more of us embraced that philosophy outside the context of the A.T. That man's "hike" was not the hike for me.

I came home from what I initially thought of as my less-than-successful foray along the Ozark Highlands Trail. The more I thought about it though, the more I realized I'd gained two valuable lessons, in particular. They were embedded in my brain when I returned, and even deeper in my heart, it turns out.

First, it was clear that no matter how strong we are, we are not meant to go it alone. That's a lesson that doesn't apply just to hiking the A.T. As humans, we are not intended to live life alone. At least not the vast majority of us. Going it alone now and then is a good thing, that's for sure, but it's no way to live life for the long haul. At least not for most of us.

Beginning then and there, I formulated what I believe to be among the most critical advice that can be offered to any person. The most significant decision any of us will ever make is choosing who to spend the bulk of our life with. Humans tend to be wonderfully resilient in moments of great challenge, by design or by accident, but going solo is never as satisfying as pitching in and working and growing and building alongside others. Surrendering to another person and following them because it's convenient isn't the same as choosing that person with whom you'll share the road. Or the trail.

Along the A.T., there were times when I wanted to quit – lots of them – and each came when I was traveling alone. Time and again, it was camaraderie and companionship that made the difference in the toughest moments. Five days of hiking alone in Northern Arkansas was enough. I headed home, anxious to get on with life.

The second lesson from my foray into Arkansas came compliments of that snake. Not killing him left me feeling weak, deflated and inadequate. It was only after I thought about it some and looked for a more profound meaning in the encounter that I came to realize it meant something totally different. Not killing the snake revealed in me strength and patience and the value I placed on things like fairness and life. The more I thought about it, the more satisfied I was with the outcome of my tangle with the snake.

Thinking about our experiences is essential to reaping the most benefit from them. In the end, and 10,000 days later, some of the smallest experiences proved to be most significant in their enduring importance.

John Dewey, early twentieth-century educational philosopher, wrote that we don't learn from experience alone but instead learn from thinking about our experiences. That's something I embraced early in the process of preparing for the Appalachian Trail -- thinking about my experiences and what they said about me. Writing helped. So did spending long hours by myself thinking. Being somewhat aware that I was a flawed creature and accepting that there was room to learn and grow served me well. So did having a reasonably clear vision for what needed to be different as a result of my adventure. Taking time to think about the many little adventures experienced on the way to Springer Mountain added meaning to each one.

I made one stop on the way back to Columbia – to see an old girlfriend. She never knew it, but I was there at her door because I'd learned something from not killing that snake. She'd tried to rescue me from my broken heart and got burned in the process. I thanked her for trying to save me and tried to explain why I had not given more.

I told her about hiking in Arkansas but left out the part about not killing the snake and how that had reminded me that I wasn't as hard and cold as I'd come to think I was.

I told her about my plans to hike the A.T. She smiled and nodded, "That'll be good for you."

I was excited to get back to Columbia. Rusty and I had a journey to plan.

MISSOURI

September 1986

From my Pre-trip Journal:

"It would be impossible to sum up anyone's reasons for mounting such an ambitious project in less than a good-sized book. The Appalachian Trail is a challenge. It's an opportunity to slow the pace of life, to focus on the self and one's relation to man and God and the natural world. Most of us have dreams of traveling or writing a novel or being a singer or living some other fantasy. Hiking the trail is living a dream. It's taking a risk and doing something that on the surface looks crazy, but underneath is a sound venture. A thru-hike is not an exercise in survival; it's one of building a lifestyle. This adventure is meant to be so much more than a walk in the woods. There's so much to learn about things like balance, focus, wholeness, unity, determination, and spirituality. 5 months along the Appalachian Trail is not unlike a semester in school. It's a chance to gain understanding and develop some direction. It's an opportunity to grow."

In early September, when I told my father my plans to quit my job at the University, drop out of grad school, and hike the Appalachian Trail, he lost his cool. "That's the stupidest thing I've ever heard," he shouted and stormed from of the room. He didn't give me a chance to explain.

I turned to my mother who stood nearby, tears in my eyes, and told her, "I need to do this."

Ever faithful, she smiled and traced a cross on my forehead, "Then do what you need to do." She wasn't wild about the idea either, but she understood about letting children make their own choices. "Your father will come around," she said, and she touched my hand with the tenderness only mothers wield and wiped a tear from my cheek. "Your dad's ways are not your ways, and they don't need to be. He just wants what's best for you."

"This is best," I told her, hoping I was right. God, I hoped I was right. The last thing I wanted was to come home a few weeks after leaving and admit, "I was wrong, Dad. It was the stupidest thing ever."

Thirty years later, I don't wonder who was right, my father or me. Hiking the AT wasn't the stupidest choice I've made. It was, I know, among the best. That's what this book is about -- How 10,000 days later, I still benefit from those few months.

Rusty and I didn't have a clue what we were doing. We began planning in earnest. We agreed to meet each week to lay out a plan. Every Tuesday night, we did so without fail, always over a beer which almost always became two, and typically three, and often enough four.

In the heart of Missouri, in 1986, veteran thru-hikers were not exactly plentiful. We found ourselves pretty much on our own when it came to planning. Until an envelope stuffed with miscellaneous information from the Appalachian Trail Conference -- That's what it was called then instead of the Appalachian Trail Conservancy as it's known today. We pored over a copy of The Philosophers Guide until it was dog-eared and the cover was coming off; we studied maps and talked of "what-ifs" and the things we heard and wondered; and talked about the few books we could find on the subject. More often than not we worried more about things like trail names and boots because that seemed rather important.

And then the beers would kick in, and our excitement would bust beyond the seams. By the end of our "meeting," we'd have announced plans to anyone near enough to listen. "We're hiking from Maine to Georgia." Often, if the bar was small enough, and not too crowded, everyone in the place would raise their glasses in our honor. And the barkeep or waitress, given they were pretty enough or curious enough or attentive enough, would get an invite from one of us or both to join us the following summer.

Accidentally, we almost recruited an army to join us. Through the course of our Tuesday meetings, more than a handful of people -- most whom we'd only just met -- their imaginations sparked by our drunken enthusiasm, got swept up in our excitement. The prospect of chucking it all and pitching in with the two particularly good-natured drunks with a dream and a promise of something better was apparently more exciting than whatever their immediate prospects were. The next time we'd wander into that particular bar, they'd seek us out, greet us with a hug as if we were family, and tell us, "I've been thinking about your offer," they'd say, "And I'm seriously considering it."

"What offer?" Rusty and I would whisper to one another with a mix of shock and confusion. "You know her? I don't." We'd stare back at the pretty girl who neither of us recognized, dumb looks plastered on our faces, too polite to admit that neither of us had any recollection whatsoever of having met her (or him) or inviting them to join us. We were too polite to say things like, "Who are you?", "Have we met?" and "What the Hell are you talking about?" So, whenever that happened -- and it happened quite a lot -- we'd note in the meeting minutes, usually written on a napkin and lost after every single meeting, that we could no longer hold planning meetings in that establishment.

By October, there were 6 or 8 places where we could no longer hold our meetings for fear of running into someone who thought they'd been invited to hike the Appalachian Trail with us.

A month or two into planning, we had a heart to heart talk. "No more invites," we agreed. There'd been too many near misses, and if we didn't change our ways, we'd likely leave for the AT with a small army in tow. That wasn't the plan, but Joe and Jim did throw in with us. Jim was a 187-pound nationally ranked college wrestler with a bad knee, and Joe was a principled kid with time on his hands between college semesters. Jim was crazy; Joe was not. Joe was a dreamer. Jim, well, I never got to know him much. He was just a guy open to "whatever."

Our hike was never about sticking it to the man or dropping out of a society that had lost its way. We weren't rebelling against anything or protesting or trying to change anything. We were just adventure-bound and looking for a story. At least I was. I figured I had room still for growing up; Rusty had some living to un-live and things to sort through; Joe was pushing personal boundaries, killing time until school started in the fall; and Jim, well, Jim kept his reasons to himself if he had any. The four of us were a mismatched bunch.

We were like kids who couldn't contain our excitement. The quality of planning was piss-poor mostly until the last month when a sense of urgency crept into our planning. We had talked about the same things over and over for months, and thanks to the beer, forgot most of what we talked about before the next morning. But the meetings kept us on-track, and in the end, with a bit of last-minute scrambling, we wrapped up our logistics planning in that last month before we left.

Thoughts of hiking the Appalachian Trail, though, occupied my thoughts almost continuously, and well they did. Otherwise, I likely would have found myself wholly ill-prepared mentally and emotionally.

It was my friend, Paul, whose wisdom tipped my chances of succeeding as a thru-hiker towards the positive. I had the same conversation with him five or six or ten times in the spring of '87. It turned out to be of critical importance. I feel bad years later, sort of, that each time we had that same conversation, I wanted to punch him in the nose. I thought he was playing with me. It turns out he wasn't.

"What are you going to do out there?"

"Hike the Appalachian Trail."

"Okay," Paul would say, "but what are you going to do out there?"

"Hike the A.T."

"Sure," He'd say, "I get that. But what are you going to do?"

At that point, I'd get frustrated, call him a pain in the ass, tell him to get the crap out of his ears, consider popping him in the nose and storm off to find something better to do and someone less challenging to talk to. After a long while, me convinced Paul was just an ass, he sat me down for a serious talk.

"Six months is a long time," he said. "You can't just go out there and hike and expect that to be enough. That's not going to sustain you or get you anywhere but a few miles further along. It might get you to the end of the trail – but I doubt it. That's a long time to hike without anything more. You need a reason to stay out there; otherwise, you'll get lost and bored and have no reason to push through the hard stuff. And I'm pretty sure there's going to be hard stuff. You need to think about why you're doing this and what it means if you make it or what you'll do if you crash and burn. Something's got to keep you going when it stops being fun. You gotta have a purpose."

"I won't crash and burn," I said defiantly.

"Not if you have a reason to work through the hard stuff."

"You're an ass," I told him, but he was right. I was discovering that on my own, too. Without purpose or vision or reasons that made sense, there was nothing substantial to anchor to when storm-force winds started to blow -- literally and figuratively.

When I'd talk about my plans, plenty struggled to understand why a young man would quit a job, strap a pack on his back, and walk through the woods for the better part of six months, especially those with lives that seemed narrow and planned. Older folks -- relatives and people who'd known me since childhood, especially those who'd settled into comfortable lives, would often lean in sympathetically and in a hushed tone whisper, as if talking about cancer or mental illness, "So you're going out there to find yourself?"

"Nope," I'd tell them. "Absolutely not. I never lost myself."

"So you're going to get it out of your system? Sow some oats, maybe?"

"Nope," I'd tell them. "Absolutely not. If anything, I'm going out there to put something into my system".

By hiking and quitting your job?"

"Yep." Few understood that.

Some would be bold enough to ask, "Is this about that girl?"

"Which girl?"

"Good point," they'd say. "There were a few, weren't there?"

I never thought they noticed.

To them, I'd say, "Absolutely not. This is about me. No one else."

At the start, my father seemed to understand the least. When I announced I was quitting my job, dropping out of grad school, and heading out to hike the Appalachian Trail, he didn't hesitate to blurt out, "That's the stupidest thing I ever heard." I'm pretty sure he felt that way until we met in New York and took a short walk together. He didn't say much, and neither did I. I think he sensed changes in me. Changes he liked.

By the time I called from Gatlinburg to tell him I'd be home in two weeks, I think he knew hiking the AT had been a game-changer.

Thanks to Paul, I accepted that the Appalachian Trail had to be more than a walk in the woods. In the months before I left, I often thought about why I was going and what I needed from hiking the AT. I figured I owed people some sort of explanation. More importantly, I owed myself an explanation beyond my tired line, "I'm looking for a story." Sometime before I left, I sat on the banks of a quiet stream outside Columbia, Missouri, and wrote these thoughts:

Why a Man Picks Up and Leaves

"Because the grass may be greener on the other side, a man leaves to look, and if it isn't, well, at least there was a chance that it might have been. And there is satisfaction in searching and in knowing what's on the mountain's other face. If it's not what he seeks, then that's alright, because he knows he gave his all, and it's hard to find fault with anyone for that. When a man gives everything to learn some secret, even though his quest fails, he uncovers some

part of himself yet unseen, and he is stronger and better and purer because of it. A man leaves because the grass might be greener on the other side, because the air might be cleaner, and the waters more calm. He leaves, too, because his troubled heart might find solace and his thoughts might clear. He leaves to find balance, a place in the great circle, an understanding of who and what and why he is and was and will be."

"This man doesn't leave because he's lost or unhappy. He doesn't leave because his spirit is broken or his soul decrepit. He leaves because he is strong, because he believes in himself, and because he has surrendered faith to the greater powers. Somewhere there may be more and there may be better and there may be greater; there's no assurance that there is, but there's no assurance that there isn't. And not to look for what might be because it might not be is failure, plain and simple. A man searches because he might find, a man looks because he might see, and a man leaves because he might not come back."

"Maybe the grass is more green and the ground more fertile on the mountain's other side. Unless a man picks up and leaves and sees and smells and tastes and feels and fully touches the other side, his life will be plagued by wondering and guessing and pretending and wishing. And that's a hard thing to live with. Questions like that linger and smolder until they breed feelings of helplessness and a sense of life having been wasted. And so this man picks up and leaves so that he might lie on his deathbed and look forward with childlike glee, never questioning where he has been."

I always knew Lori wasn't the one. She knew it, too. I warned her not to get too close because I might bite, but she stuck around in spite of that warning. We became friends in the fall and learned to exist in the present without giving the future a second thought. I never called her my girlfriend; I don't know what she called me. She never understood my Appalachian Trail obsession, or maybe she understood it too well and accepted it was an impenetrable barrier between her and me and any sort of future. She recognized there were no guarantees beyond the day I would pick up and leave without a promise of ever coming back. Still, she hung around, and I appreciated her tolerance. She was the kind of friend any man mired in indecision or committed to chasing windmills would be fortunate to find.

I left Columbia on a Thursday without fanfare and little acknowledgment of the years spent there. I locked my office, keys inside, checked out of my apartment and signed some papers at the HR office. I met Lori for breakfast. She was the closest thing to a steady girlfriend I'd had for a while. We stood in the parking lot trying to make our goodbye more than it was meant to be. I tried to kiss her like a soldier tramping off to war. I dipped her way back trying to recreate that famous Times Square photo of nurse and sailor celebrating war's end, but we stumbled and nearly fell.

Instead, we hugged and shared a last lingering look. "I'll miss you," she said. I didn't say anything back. I was flying to Maine in less than a week and didn't honestly know if I'd miss her. I suspected I might. She'd been a good friend, but I didn't know if there'd be room for her in my head or heart as I hiked or afterward. And I wasn't sure if I'd be back.

Honestly, I was scared. I was excited, sure, to be setting off on a new adventure, but I felt like I stood at a great roulette table with more than I could afford to lose piled on a single number. The ball and the wheel were spinning, and I was watching and knowing if my number didn't hit, I'd be dead-broke spiritually, financially, and personally.

The enormity of how much life must be rearranged to accommodate a thru-hike is staggering. It's a massive investment of time, resources, and opportunities. The risk to relationships and one's identity is significant. Almost overwhelming. Mostly, I hoped I'd never need to look my father in the eye and be forced to say, "You were right." Money was the least of my concerns. Time was what mattered. I had put everything stable on hold for a while and to do what? I wasn't entirely sure.

I still find it offensive -- as I did then -- when someone looks me in the eye and says, "God, I wish I had time to do that!"

"Had the time?" I usually snap back, "You think I had the time? I made the time, buddy, and it wasn't easy."

I drove out of town singing at the top of my lungs to the Eagles, "Take It Easy. The words strangely paralleled my life.

Well I'm a-runnin' down the road try'n to loosen my load
I've got seven women on my mind

Four that want to own me, two that want to stone me
One says she's a friend of mine
Lighten up while you still can
Don't even try to understand
Just find a place to make your stand, and take it easy.

Running down the road trying to loosen my load? Yep, I thought, that's me. Even the math added up. Seven. My four siblings were married or had at least found the loves of their lives. Not me. I wasn't even close.

Despite an undergraduate degree, an unfinished graduate degree, and a satchel full of stories, I was hauling out somewhat less than I'd hauled into Columbia five years before. I sold most of what I owned or gave things away. I felt good about leaving. I was on my way to find a story, something I needed. I suspected more might be waiting for me than I bargained for, but there was no way to know. I guess in many ways, I was on my way to make my stand along the AT.

MAINE

From my Journal:

"The first two days have been filled with frustrating and expensive delays. First, the plane arrived in Bangor after midnight. We missed our bus connection and ended up sleeping on the airport floor. At 5:30 a.m., we were up and hiking 5 miles to the nearest truck stop to look for a ride north. No luck. Fortunately, a gentleman drove us to the bus stop about 15 miles further on where we waited almost 7 hours for a bus which took us to a small gas station in the middle of nowhere, 16 miles from where we wanted to be -- Millinocket. Then it started to rain. Now joined by two other hikers, we faced a 16-mile hike in a torrential downpour. Again, Providence provided. We caught a ride to the nearest hotel. My share of a room for the night was eleven dollars; dinner cost five more. Expenses continue to mount, but we're still dry. Seven hikers plus seven backpacks crammed into the back of a covered pickup truck for the ride. Tomorrow we have a taxi cab scheduled to take us to Baxter State Park. Thirty-five dollars more. It's raining, and unfortunately, permission to climb Mount Katahdin is given only on clear days. The forecast is for continued rain. We may need to camp at the mountain's base for a couple of days or so. Twelve dollars per night. I need to start moving, I'm going crazy."

"You won't hear from me for a while after this. If all goes well, we'll be on the trail the day after tomorrow."

AT hikers adopt trail names, not nicknames exactly, but personal monikers likely chosen for some highly personal reason. They're a way to uniquely identify oneself as a thru-hiker among the sea of day users and weekenders. Sometimes they're awarded by others as a result of something that happened. Sometimes people assume their own. Trail names are adopted so thru-hikers can maintain anonymity mostly, a safety consideration really, and because remembering a name like "Missouri Express" was easier than remembering the given names of those you might meet once but read about for months in registers left in trailside shelters and hostels.

Hikers might call themselves by their trail names, but few others did -- except easily impressed people at trail crossings or shelters who wanted to fit into your adventure without doing the work. Hugh was a hiking partner who in the end figured quite prominently in my experience. We met in Harpers Ferry and climbed Springer Mountain together. He was an unflappable Brit, a barrister by trade, who came to the U.S. in search of adventure, stumbled upon the AT and got sucked in. We accepted he was for whatever reasons the White Rabbit, but when we wanted his attention, we just called him Hugh.

Thru-hikers most likely grow to be somebody different than they expected to become. Trail names are the outward embodiment of who they are – or were at the start. They are the initial step in building an identity and an external brand. Two-thousand miles down the trail, they hold almost sacred significance, but only for the hiker who owns the name and other thru-hikers who remember him or her for some significant contribution to their experience.

The night before we took our first steps along the Appalachian Trail, Joe, Jim, Rusty, and I, lay crammed in a Millinocket, Maine, hotel room like so many bums. Choosing a trail name seemed somehow more urgent than any other single thing. None of the names any of us threw out resonated in the slightest, and the longer we sat, the more outlandish and non-serious the suggestions became.

It was Rusty who suggested, "Mack and the Boys?" It was a name based on characters in John Steinbeck's novel, Cannery Row, specifically from this passage:

"What can it profit a man to gain the whole world and to come to his property with a gastric ulcer, a blown prostate, and bifocals? Mack and the boys avoid the trap, walk around the poison, step over the noose while a generation of trapped, poisoned, and trussed-up men scream at them and call them no-goods, come to bad ends, blots-on-the-town, thieves, rascals, bums. Our Father who art in nature, who has given the gift of survival to the coyote, the common brown rat, the English sparrow, the house fly and the moth, must have a great and overwhelming love for no-goods and blots-on-the town and bums, and Mack and the boys. Virtues and graces and laziness and zest. Our Father who art in nature."

"No-goods, come to bad ends, blots-on-the town, thieves, rascals, bums," That pretty-well described how we were felt at that moment. From then on, except for the brief "procedural" debate about whether four guys could share one name, we were Mack and the Boys. It was a moniker that had nothing whatsoever to do with mac and cheese, as so many assumed, but was instead a tip of the hat to the ne'er-do-wells of Steinbeck's Cannery Row and to other such folks wherever they might be found.

We were green as the mountains were tall and misfit for the adventure. Joe was a city boy whose notion of a trail was paved and through a city park. He was the kind of guy who dropped his head and powered through anything that got tough. Jim was a genuine blue-collar badass who in the movie version of this book might best be played by a young Sylvester Stallone. He was Rocky Balboa in the years before he became champion of the world. He was as physically dominant as any man, loose around the edges, I'll admit, and came close to scaring me.   I never figured out why he'd signed on with us or what he was looking for. It didn't matter, though. He wasn't around for long. Rusty was a dreamer, cut out to be a hard-drinking, life-loving cowboy. It's too bad he couldn't sing and wasn't born in the last century in Texas; otherwise, he'd have had it all. He looked like Rowdy Yates from the 1960's series Rawhide, played by a boyish Clint Eastwood. He was handsome and sturdy but soft at the center. And me? I was just a guy who wanted someday to be able to kick back in a bar with a surplus of stories to tell about life and adventure. I was a boy at heart, very much afraid of letting my father down.

Two days later, we started the 5,000-foot climb up Mount Katahdin. That was the last day I was fooled into believing there'd be anything glamorous about hiking the Appalachian Trail. After that, it was hard work. Fortunately, it was hard work mixed with an ample dose of laughter.

Everything about the climb up Katahdin was gorgeous, breathtaking, and overwhelming. It rained, it snowed, the sky cleared and somewhere in the crystal clear distance we imagined we could see the ocean. We probably did see it, in fact. But standing at the summit and looking south was life-changing and nothing near what I expected. Emotion crashed over me.

I'd invested a lot, almost everything, to be there at the summit of Katahdin. I had risked relationships and respect and identity, and then, after a year of dreaming and hard work, I found myself at the beginning of something humongous. The idea of Katahdin had been the focal point of our lives for nearly a year. It had been just a dream. It was our destination, and now that we'd arrived, we found ourselves only at a starting line, not a finish point, and Katahdin, the spot we'd been working so hard to get to, wasn't even close to where I wanted to be. It was nearly overwhelming. Springer Mountain was so far from the top of Katahdin that wrapping my head around the distance was impossible. It might well have been the moon. There was no way to get there, at least not fast, and not without doing a little bit every day for a long time. I missed everyone and everything I knew.

It was like the rest of anyone's life journey, I realized. Getting anywhere required just what the Grateful Dead sang about, "You got to mellow slow, take time - you pick a place to go and just keep truckin' on."

The first real doubts crept in there on Katahdin. I was excited, sure, and physically prepared, but standing at Baxter Peak, knee-deep in sweat and snow, the enormity of what lay ahead was overwhelming. 2,150 miles was a long way to walk. For the first time, I entertained the possibility of not doing what I set out to do. What a terrifying prospect that was!

For a solid year, I'd told every human I knew that I was going to hike the Appalachian Trail. I'd been so confident and sure and inspired and inspiring. I'd accepted plenty of free beers from people who wanted to be part of the dream. I hadn't allowed a single person, most of all myself, to consider even the slightest possibility that I might, for whatever reason, never reach Springer Mountain. Or even New Hampshire. The reality was that I'd never entertained the possibility of not finishing until I stood there on Katahdin. That was a mistake. And now I started to wonder. What would it mean to go home without doing what I set out to do? I faced either making good on my pledge to every person I'd talked to for the last twelve months or failing to live up to the hype I'd created. The stress was mounting. What if I didn't finish?

It was before the days of Facebook, thankfully. Otherwise, I'd have boasted about my intent to finish the Appalachian Trail to a hundred times more people than I already had.

Success waited at the end of five million steps -- nowhere else in my mind. Failure, though, could happen anywhere in between. Standing in a half-foot of snow, a million miles from anyone or anything familiar. I remember being so aware that failure meant a hell of a lot more than success, and the prospect of failure was a million times bigger than the likelihood of success. Self-imposed or not, the first thousand steps or so were more pressure-filled than I was prepared for. I'd quit a job, spent a pile of money on a plane ticket and gear I couldn't afford, told my father I didn't care that he thought hiking the

AT was the "stupidest thing he'd ever heard," and said goodbye to a good woman who was a good friend.

I realized then that I'd set myself up for failure by telling everyone I knew that I was going to finish the Appalachian Trail. I'd left no room in my experience for learning or adjusting my plan or quitting because I'd gotten enough. That was an awkward place to be so early in the experience.

A poster of the Appalachian Trail hung in my parent's basement. The 2,150-mile route through fourteen states was marked with a long, red line. That image was indelibly etched on my mind – It still is. I knew that one day, no matter how close I came to reaching Springer Mountain, I'd look back over the length of that long, red line that came to symbolize my journey and experience one of two things -- contentment or regret.

At that moment, there on Katahdin, I understood more than at any other point what Paul was getting at every time he asked, "What are you going to do out there?" Hiking the AT has to be about the journey, not the destination. There on Katahdin, I committed to being a purist; no shortcuts, I told myself. I knelt and prayed next to that weathered wooden trail sign at the top of Katahdin, the one every thru-hiker knows so well, but most know as a finish line rather than a starting point. A tear slid down my cheek as I swore there'd be "no regrets," and I took my first steps southward. After a whole year, finally, I was an Appalachian Trail hiker.

The Appalachian Trail Conservancy's pamphlet, Step by Step -- An Introduction to Hiking the Appalachian Trail, describes starting in Maine in these terms:

"A few thru-hikers start in June or early July at Katahdin and finish in Georgia in November or December. Southbound thru-hikers must wait to start the AT when Katahdin opens, usually by June 1st, but sometimes later. June starters can expect swarms of black flies and high stream crossings in Maine, but waiting much longer means additional weeks of winter hiking on the southern end. Hiking southbound is considered the toughest way to hike the Trail: you should be in seriously good shape before attempting this. A Southbounder starts his or her journey with the toughest mountain on the entire Trail on his first day, and spends their first month in the hardest state on the Trail."

I wish I had read that excerpt before we started. Then again, we were probably too enamored with ourselves to heed the warnings.

The 100 mile-wilderness stretches from Baxter State Park to Monson, Maine. It's fifteen million acres of inaccessibility so thick that a man who loses the trail and keeps wandering might never be found. Steep, rocky slopes, exposed roots, long stretches above treeline, lakes, wild streams, bogs, and trees -- billions of trees-- and not much else. Expect to see God there in the unending raw expanse of nature -- unspoiled, uninhabited, and unforgiving to the ill-prepared. You just have to look.

These days, I've heard, a sign at the start of the 100-mile Wilderness greets Northbound Hikers. It reads:

There are no places to obtain supplies or get help until Abol Bridge 100 miles north. Do not attempt this section unless you have a minimum of 10 days supplies and are fully equipped. This is the longest wilderness section of the entire A.T., and its difficulty should not be underestimated. Good hiking.

I don't recall a similar sign at the northern edge of the Wilderness in 1987. If there had been one, we probably wouldn't have paid much attention. We were stupid and optimistic, overconfident and loving the identity of being AT hikers, even though by then – just a day into our hike -- we didn't understand what it meant in the least.

Considering the inexperience of most Southbounders by this point, a more appropriate sign would have been like the one Dorothy, Toto, Tinman, Scarecrow and the Cowardly Lion encountered on the edge of the haunted forest. It read, "I'd turn back if I were you."

Most AT hikers pass through the 100-mile wilderness as Northbounders. By then, their bodies and minds have been strengthened by two-thousand previous miles of hiking. Jim, Joe, Rusty and I weren't so prepared. We'd come just thirteen miles from Baxter Peak when we reached the edge of the Wilderness and plunged in. That's when the rain started. It rained at least a little on every day after that for the next thirty until three of us crossed into New Hampshire a month later as different men altogether.

The black flies, mosquitoes, and no see-ums were relentless. They tore flesh from arms and faces without mercy. No see-ums were the worst. I remember tangling with a mess of them one morning. They burned like fire, but there was nothing to see or swat or crush between my fingernails. I ripped my clothes off and ran screaming into a lake that a week before had been solid ice. I was lucky the shock of the cold didn't stop my heart, but at that point, anything was a fair price for escaping the fiery assault of no see-ums.

The call of a loon next morning echoing over the water and everything entirely still left me awed and filled with peace and mostly re-focused. It took a long while to pack that morning and get on the trail. We weren't good at this -- yet. By the Smoky Mountains, packing each morning would take just a few focused minutes.

Perpetually wet boots and the constant dampness of everything else took its toll. Nothing was warm, even slightly, not even the rare sunshine that cut the clouds. The bone-deep chill continued until the morning when I lay unseen in tall grass, close enough to hear the soft suckling sounds of a near-newborn moose calf nursing at his mother's teat. It was the way mother moose nuzzled her calf, as tender as any mother ever, that finally warmed me through and through despite the chill air. The ranger at Baxter State Park had said, "Don't worry about bears; steer clear of moose, though. They'll cause the most problems." Mother and calf, though, were the ones who pulled me into nature's embrace. It only got better from there, and I only got stronger.

Through Maine and especially in the Wilderness, the trail climbed straight up each mountain. There were no leisurely switchbacks. Maine was no place for sissies. Even the surefooted could count on falling once or twice or ten times on the way to the top and back down from each mountain. Bog bridges, which were felled logs laid across swampy patches, made crossing otherwise impassable stretches possible with still-dry boots. If you were lucky. Still, the wet logs were slick as ice and a fall from a bog bridge meant getting soaked or worse.

Some bogs were deep, like the one I sunk into clean to the bottom of my pack. Had I not been wearing it, I'd have sunk deeper. Even so, I was mired hopelessly in the muck almost to my waist, completely and utterly stuck. I struggled 20 minutes to free myself, then 10 minutes more -- Nothing. Jim, Joe, and Rusty were ahead, and I was falling further behind by the minute. It was rainy and windy and cold. Conditions were getting worst. Shit. And then I saw them, off a bit in the distance, a group of identically outfitted young people, probably an Outward Bound group, trekking towards me.

They'd reach me soon enough and save me, but I'd forever be a story they'd tell about the hapless hiker who might otherwise have died if not for them.

I was in danger of becoming Outward Bound lore, I figured – part of a story to be told and re-told forever illustrating what happens when ill-prepared sorts venture where they shouldn't be. I didn't like that prospect one bit. I struggled harder, lay on my side, rolled to and fro and half-swam through the mud. The sucking sound of the mud giving way hinted that perhaps I was about to win freedom. And then, suddenly, I was free – soaking wet and muddy -- but at least I was loose from what I thought would be my watery grave! I rocketed to my feet and did my best to make myself presentable -- something nearly impossible after you've been soaking in a bog for 40 minutes. In the nick of time, I met them at the opposite end of the bridge -- none of them the wiser about my near-miss. We exchanged pleasantries in passing, and I cautioned them about the slickness of the bridge. I hurried passed and stepped up my pace. I was far behind the rest of "Mack and the Boys," darkness wasn't far off, and I was starting to shiver.

Near miss, I thought. One of a hundred more, as it would turn out. Most in Maine.

The next day, we came to the edge of a small but spirited whitewater stream, waist-deep maybe or a little more. Rusty and I stared across in disbelief. On the other side was a tree prominently marked with a white blaze. "They want us to cross this stream? What the Hell?" Rusty was indignant. "Couldn't they have built a bridge?"

He sat down, took his off boots and stuffed a sock down inside each one. "I'm not hiking with wet boots for the rest of the day. Or getting my camp shoes wet."

I was skeptical and tended to be a bit more cautious than him. I kept my mouth shut. "You hike your hike, I'll hike mine," I thought. I knew when editorial comments were not likely to be helpful. I sat back on a rock to watch.

Rusty reared back and pitched the first boot across the stream. Boot and sock landed softly on the other side, a little close to the edge for complete comfort, but high and dry enough. He turned and flashed an "I-told-you so" kind of smart-assed smile then reared back with the second boot. He let it fly, putting a little extra into his throw this time. His aim, unfortunately, was off, the throw trended high, the boot smacked a branch above, and splashed into the middle of the stream. In less than an instant it was swept downstream, still bouncing on the surface but fast disappearing.

"Nice shooting, Tex!" I hollered out joyfully, not at all cognizant in that instant what a lost boot in the middle of the wilderness meant to the four of us. But barefoot Rusty was paralyzed to move, and the gravity of the situation clicked suddenly in my brain. I tore like a madman down the bank, whipped with briars and low-hanging branches as I did, nearly panicked as reality took a deeper hold. It didn't take an expert to figure that getting stuck halfway through the 100-mile wilderness with one boot and a tattered camp shoe with soles worn thin as paper would have been bad – real bad. I ran harder and faster, bounced off trees and stumbled over rocks as I did, and then the boot was gone, and I stood alone and out of earshot of Rusty's urgent inquiries.

The situation was bleak. I walked downstream, praying while I did, even reciting a poem-like prayer from my childhood, "Come, St. Anthony, look around, something's lost and can't be found." But neither boot nor sock was to be found. I was a half-mile downstream from Rusty when I turned back to break the news to Mack and the Boys -- that we were in dire straits.

Even if we re-distributed Rusty's load between the three of us with solid boots, we'd be moving far slower than planned. At a slower pace, we'd likely run out of food before reaching Monson, and we'd be in pretty rough shape when we did. I prayed a little harder, mostly, that I wouldn't be so stupid the next time there was an important decision to be made. And then I saw it, the boot, laces hung up in a submerged branch within easy reach. The sock, though, Rusty's expensive Norwegian hiking sock that had been a gift from his mother or some other special soul, was gone. I fished the boot out of the stream with a stick.

I sat on a rock to catch my breath. "Holy cow, that was a close," I told myself. "Too close." There were scratches on my face, and my knee was bruised from a minor fall. Though Rusty had chosen to throw the boot across the stream, I knew I was complicit in nearly disabling the whole of Mack and the Boys. Despite the churning in my guts as Rusty reared back to throw the boot, and the internal voices warning, "This is going to end badly," I stood idly by and watched. I knew better – and I knew I knew better -- but I did nothing. "That's not how you get where you want to go," I lectured myself, "by letting things happen when you know they're wrong or likely to be wrong." I sat for a while thinking, oblivious to poor Rusty's plight a few hundred yards upstream where he anxiously awaited news of his boot.

There was a lesson in all of this, I knew. Finishing with no regrets wasn't going to happen if I merely stood by and expected things to go my way. Or if I made hiking the Appalachian Trail only about hiking the Appalachian Trail. No. Success was only likely to happen if I made it happen. And worked to get better most days.

A stupid decision on my part almost derailed the entire experience. I took stock of what it would have meant for the four of us to have had to limp the next fifty miles, one boot short and food supplies dwindling. It wasn't pretty. All I had to do was speak up, and I could have interrupted a lousy situation even before it unfolded. I should have taken a stand, and I knew it. Internally, I pledged to be a better member of the team from that point on.

I was a bit smug as I handed the wet boot to Rusty. "Guess that's why you're hiking for a living and not playing ball."

"Shut-up," he said, his smile becoming an ugly grimace as he slipped his bare foot inside his dripping wet boot. That's when we broke into uncontrolled laughter. He knew, like me, that we'd dodged a big-ass bullet.

I couldn't pass judgment on Rusty for his error. There was no need to preach. He knew and I knew what had almost happened. Sure, my boots were still dry – but they wouldn't be soon enough. And though I was still wearing two socks, deep down I knew it might as easily have been me sitting there desperately hoping somebody would rescue my boot. I was not above making stupid choices, I knew. I also knew that finishing the Appalachian Trail could only happen if I minimized the number of stupid decisions and learned from the ones I did make. How does one stop doing stupid things? My boots were wet and squishy. You trust your instincts, I told myself. You slow down. And you focus on the things that matter most.

An hour later, Rusty and I walked unsuspectingly into an ambush. It was terrifying and out of the blue. She was alone and came at us from nowhere, suddenly in front of us, behind us, and all around all at once. She wasn't the slightest bit frightened. Rusty bolted down the trail screaming like a little girl, I fell back into the woods, turned and ran headlong into a tree. I hit the ground hard, bounced back up, and turned to face her. She was like a thousand attackers, screaming and drumming her wings. No, she wasn't human; she was a ruffled grouse protecting her chicks.

Like a torpedo, she came straight for my head. "Oh, shit! Oh, shit! Oh, shit!" I hollered. "She's coming right at me!" There was nowhere to run. A foot short of my face, she exploded into a thunder of wings, feathers, and commotion. My heart nearly stopped. And then she hit the ground and ran to the left dragging one wing useless behind her. "She's hurt," I hollered to nobody in particular. Such a brave creature, my heart went out to her. She ran into the woods to the left; the chicks, ten of them at least, scrambled to the right. It turns out, that's what grouse do to safeguard their young. First, they charge like banshees, drumming wings and squawking and exploding in their attacker's faces to disorient them. Then, once they've scared the piss out of their attacker, they feign a broken wing, luring them in the opposite direction while their young escape in another.

It sure felt like a close call, though there'd been little danger. We were a bit embarrassed to have been bested by a bird, sure, but more so, we were thankful no one had witnessed our less than courageous response to the momma bird's more than heroic defense of her brood.

The bird was nearby still. We watched from afar as the grouse crossed back over the trail to collect her brood beneath the safety of her wings. What an impressive and altruistic creature, the ruffed grouse. Who'd have thought that? We walked a few yards down the trail, found a vantage point where we could conceal ourselves and sit and watch as Joe and Jim approached without a hint of what was about to happen to them.

Their encounter did not disappoint. "Better than TV," I said aloud as sat back and enjoyed the show.

Later that night, four days beyond Katahdin, the Wilderness nearly killed Rusty and me. Ironically, it was a lack of water that almost did it -- that and an abundance of stupidity. We were slow learners.

The two-thousand-foot climb up Chairback Mountain was tough. The temperature dropped quickly, fog set upon us like a blanket, and visibility was down to thirty feet at best.

In 1987, few trail shelters offered much comfort. Most were solid enough. In Maine, there were still a few holdovers from the 1930s, three-sided "baseball-bat" shelters that forty years later provided less comfort or protection than sleeping on the ground. "Baseball-bat" shelters were built long before. Just two or three of them remained in 1987. They were relics. The floor was constructed from 3-inch diameter rough-cut poles lashed together to form an elevated and impossibly bumpy sleeping surface.

There was nowhere nor no way to lay that was close to comfortable even on a Therm-a-rest pad and piles of clothing. Near the end of its life, the roof of the shelter leaked almost as if it wasn't there.

Northern Maine in early June, it's cold and wet, and it gets dark early. The rain left little reason not to be in bed by 7:15 pm and asleep by 7:20 pm. There was little choice that night but to stay in bed until daylight. Even after a full night's sleep, the urge to get up and pee or at least drink some water is strong. Drinking leads then to having to pee a little later.

It was hours before dawn. Deep in the middle of the night. The four of us lay awake laughing at each other's discomfort and pissed about our own. Sore muscles on a bed of baseball bats don't make for a good night. I flopped from side to side, front to back, rolled this way and that, groaned as I did. At first, my companions found it entertaining. Then it bred frustration. Nobody slept. Had I not already embraced the trail name "Mack & the Boys," I might have from that night been burdened with a name like "Flap Jack."

It was damned cold and wet. Instead of hiking the few hundred yards down to the nearest spring to fill water bottles before we went to bed, the four of us bedded down with barely full bottles. At 3 am, when you swallow the last bit of water in your bottle, and it's not enough to slake your thirst, you lay thinking about how thirsty you are, and dream about how refreshing a long, cold drink would be. Mild cravings become torturous and threaten to drive you mad. "Water," I remember thinking, "I must have water." In the distance, thunder rumbled faintly. The more I thought about water, the more I couldn't stop thinking about it. Or talking about it. The more I talked about it, the more Jim, Joe, and Rusty thought about it, too. The four of us lay awake, mad for one single swallow of cool, fresh water.

Rusty and I slipped on camp shoes without socks, threw on cotton sweatshirts and started down the hill with flashlights. The fog was encroaching on everything. We couldn't see much, not even the trail, but we pushed on. How long could it take to hike a few hundred yards down to the spring and back? Far longer than we imagined, as it turned out.

In the distance, the thunder was less faint and rolling in slowly. There was no moving quickly in the fog. Locating the spring wasn't so easy as it was in daylight. Nothing was familiar, and we stumbled on the spring only after wandering a good bit and only with some luck. We filled water bottles and started back up the slope. Where was the trail? The mist was colder now. Little chunks of sleet occasionally stung our faces, and shoes intended to be dry "camp shoes" were no longer dry nor did their worn soles provide no traction up the slick slope. The temperature dipped five degrees then ten. All quite suddenly.   The fog got thicker, too, and obscured the trail even more.

Shit. I wasn't one to cuss often then. After four days in the wilderness, my language had deteriorated.

We followed what we thought was the trail until it disappeared, and whatever path we thought we were following became indistinguishable from the rest of the wet, now sloppy forest floor. A little more wandering and we were lost – irretrievable so. That's when Rusty dropped his light, and it broke into what seemed a million pieces -- it just as well might have been. It was beyond repair. In frustration, he kicked a tree and hollered. Now, a steel-toed boot might have been a match for the tree, but old tennis shoes were not. Now, we were in real trouble – one working light, four wet and inadequate shoes, one of us was limping. We were lost, temperatures were dropping, the storm was picking up, and I was shivering in my wet cotton shirt.   The odds were not in our favor.

We knew we were downhill from the shelter, so we headed up. "Joe!" I hollered. No answer. "Jim?" No answer. Over and over and over, we yelled their names, not quite panicking, but not exactly calm either. We understood the seriousness of our situation. And still, there was no answer from our companions. The storm was about to break on us. As we pushed higher up the mountain, we knew we were in trouble. And then we heard the faintest of calls. It echoed from below us on the mountain. It was a mocking tone. "Joe!" came the retort, followed by something unintelligible. And then there was silence; a long, protracted silence.

"Jim?" We yelled, and the voices echoed back, "Jim!" accompanied by far off laughter and more silence.

"Keep yelling," we hollered desperately. "Keep yelling!" -- came the echo and the laughter. They were oblivious to our plight. Or maybe not. The storm closed in, things looked bleaker, their voices faded away, and then we stumbled onto the path that led to the shelter. Salvation! We were beside ourselves and pissed when we got to them. "You bastards! What the hell is wrong with you?" They just laughed. "Hell if we're sharing any water!"

As we ducked into the shelter, the sky opened with a tremendous crash and wild downpour. It was barely above freezing. A moment after that,

Rusty and I were in sleeping bags warming rapidly, pissed off, sheepish, and thankful to be exactly where we were even though the roof leaked without shame.

Joe and Jim were highly amused. Rusty & I shivered in our sleeping bags, sipping cold water. Unwilling to share. They laughed at us for being idiots. We knew they were right.

Moments later, almost asleep, Rusty uttered in total disgust, "Crap," he said. "I have to pee." The rest of us broke into uncontrolled laughter.

"Another close call," I thought as I drifted off to sleep. Day five on the Appalachian Trail hadn't been easy. Lots of learning, though, I thought. I wondered if I could keep this up.

Whether on the trail, at home, or in a hotel, I've rarely spent a night since without a bottle or glass of water at my head. It was the closest of calls that night on the side of Chairback Mountain. The situation was brought on because of laziness. Had I done things the way they should have been done -- put on the right pants, a warmer jacket, and the right shoes -- the trek to the spring would have been a non-issue.

Lessons like that endure for ten-thousand days. Thirty years later, I tend to carry what I need. And not just when I'm hiking.

Like some grand metaphor for life, we emerged from the 100-mile Wilderness changed men, though I question if we deserved a title like "men" at that point. We were more like boys who had faced a lot and survived by accident and luck. The lessons were pretty obvious.

From then on, I approached hiking the Appalachian Trail with a different perspective, one that would contribute significantly to reaching Springer four months later. People so often dismiss trials and tribulations and near-misses with a curt, "oh, well, live and learn." From that day further, I embraced the deeper meaning in that wisdom as "If you live, then you learn."

I was far more intentional about decisions.

Maine was a good teacher. We survived misfortunes to learn unexpected lessons big and small. As we learned, we got better and stronger and smarter. In the last thirty years, close calls like those on the secluded banks of a rushing stream and on an icy hillside during a thunderstorm have spared me wasted time and effort more times than I can count.

If only for those few lessons about the importance of weighing risks before acting rashly, hiking the AT was worth the effort.

The 100-mile Wilderness ends in the town of Monson. We rolled into Shaw's Boarding House and ate over-done steaks at the kitchen table with Mr. Shaw and his family and drank so much milk that Shaw had to get up mid-meal and run to the store down the street for two more gallons.

Not only was it one of the best meals of the 5 months along the A.T., but it was a rare display that went way beyond excellent customer service. What's missing in America? People who will open their homes to you, feed you a decent meal and give you a warm and cozy spot to sleep for a fair price -- about $10 bucks or so in 1987. And what else is missing? People who will graciously accept what others offer without judgment or complaint. We were happy to be there, and part of the Shaw family for the evening.

The Shaw's weren't as impressed as I imagine we were with ourselves. It occurred to me later that they'd seen plenty of southbound hikers. Most of them were relatively fresh and new and lightly-seasoned. We were nothing special. The Northbounders they'd met were no doubt beaten by wind and burned by the sun; were well-seasoned with two-thousand miles of experience; sported months of facial hair, and were prepared with much better stories.

When asked, "Where'd you come from?" we could only say, "Katahdin." It was a hundred miles from there. I'm sure that was hardly interesting to Mr. Shaw who'd spoken to almost every northbound thru-hiker for 10 years or more. In comparison, we must have seemed like children. I'm sure they had their doubts about us ever seeing the top of Springer.

Jim limped nearly every mile of the last one-hundred. He hated being wet and cold and far from home. Later that night, he broke the news we expected. He'd be heading home in the morning. Hiking the Appalachian Trail wasn't his thing. He'd lacked a vision from the start. At least that was my take. I was a bit shocked the next morning when he asked to borrow thirty dollars for a bus ticket home.

Watching him walk in the opposite direction the next morning wasn't exactly sad, but as his silhouette got smaller and smaller, Springer Mountain seemed to get further and further away. "Twelve days in," I remember thinking, "and just one-hundred-thirteen miles along." There were 2,023 trail miles to go. Everything warm about home seemed to be getting further and further away. I thought about my father. How soon before I'd need to admit to him he'd been right all along?

Mack and the Boys were now three. Joe, Rusty, and I looked at things with a bit more seriousness. Jim was the most physically prepared among us. If the trail could victimize him, then how vulnerable were each of us? Maybe finishing wasn't something that happened just because you said it would. I started to wonder about the consequences of not finishing. Could failure on the AT break a person's spirit in a way from which they could never recover? I hadn't entertained such possibilities, and then, rather suddenly, I needed to. I could at least feel some of the strands attaching me to the trail starting to fray.

Through the years, I've wondered what not finishing might have meant to my life's trajectory. Though I was fortunate not to ever have known, I sense the toll might have been unexpectedly high.

Maine was a long, hard, wet two-hundred-seventy-nine miles. It rained at least some on twenty-six of the twenty-seven days it took to cross the state. Maine-liners -- or whatever people from Maine are called -- don't believe in switchbacks. Trails went straight up one side of a mountain and down the other. If not slogging up a mountain, one was picking their way through the bogs and swamps that lay between the mountains. "R and R" in Maine referred not to "rest and relaxation" but to "roots and rocks." There were plenty of them, and falls were frequent. Nothing about Maine was easy except sitting above treeline and admiring God's handiwork or swimming in the crystal clear, icy lakes within sight of moose and loons and an occasional eagle. I remember playing with a cow leach somewhere up there. It was fascinating, like a giant non-offending worm. Maine was full of wonders small ones like that and huge ones like every mountainscape.

Now, you may not be a believer in God, and that's fine, but Maine will predictably leave anyone with a soul wondering about creation and Creator. The beauty is spectacular.

We reached the Kennebec River too late in the day to cross. The Kennebec was dam-controlled and could be safely waded at lower levels, but it could be quite fatal at higher levels. Mack and the Boys, reduced now to three, stood debating our next move. Camp at the river's edge or backtrack a mile or two to a more secluded spot. The tendency to think rashly, like pushing across the river despite the high water, now after brushes with almost disasters in the wilderness, was much less a part of our repertoire then it might have been just days before.

Thirty years later, details are hazy about how things happened precisely, but without effort or planning, we wound up in the back of a pick-up truck heading to a house owned by a young man trying to get a rafting company off the ground. We slept in beds there for the next couple nights, enjoyed free meals, and made a few bucks nailing shingles onto the roof, painting and doing other odd jobs. It was one of the first examples of the deep kindness that often dwelled in the hearts of many living along the trail. I wish I could remember the man's name or the name of his fledgling company. We turned down the invitation to stay longer, maybe even to spend the summer as raft guides there, and turned south again, not so much smarter or stronger, but yes, more confident in humanity -- at least the small slice that lived along the trail.

If I'd been better about keeping a journal, maybe I'd know more names of people and places that defined my experience. I found the process of writing at the end of the day laborious. I wrote a good deal, though, but between writing letters and journaling, I always chose letters. I asked that those I sent to family and friends be forwarded on to my mother who collected them in a binder. That binder became my journal. Most letters miraculously made it back to my mother.

Despite having prepped for a year and hiked two-hundred miles from Katahdin, I'd never met a thru-hiker before the kid at Speck Pond. For more than a year, I'd waited to meet someone who could confirm my suspicions – that a thru-hike was a good thing with enduring benefits. I sensed thru-hikers might somehow stand out from a crowd and even be better prepared for life than most, but so far into my hike and my preparations, I'd never met anyone who could confirm or dispel those ideas.

The kid was eighteen or so but seemed much younger. He hung in the shelter of his father's shadow, who himself chugged beers and smoked cigarette after cigarette there amidst Maine's incredible beauty. The kid was thin and pale -- scrawny even, irritating, distant, and socially awkward. He didn't fit my idea of what a thru-hiker was supposed to be. Or what I was supposed to be when I completed a thru-hike. Where was the unbound confidence and uplifting persona of one who'd accomplished something remarkable?

There was nothing spectacular or inspiring about the boy. In fact, even the opposite was true. Not once did he utter anything slightly resembling wisdom or insight. Were my ideas about the impact of a thru-hike wrong? Was hiking the AT just a long walk in the woods? Maybe even the stupidest thing ever? I'd already discovered thru-hiking wasn't a cure for all ills but was it even something worth doing? The boy cast doubts on whether it was.

With now slightly less than two-thousand miles to go and more than I could afford to lose invested in my experience, I wasn't sure dropping out of the world and retreating to Maine had been so wise.

Crap. Maybe you were right, Dad. After all, he'd been so right so many other times in my life.

I tried to assure myself that odds were in favor that at least one of the fifteen hundred previous thru-hikers would likely be less than impressive. That thought brought little solace, though. What were the odds I would run into that one less-than-impressive thru-hiker in the middle of nowhere in Maine?

I'd like to say reminding myself of the essential importance of letting others hike their hike eased my concerns. It didn't. I guess I wasn't quite ready to embrace that philosophy fully.

My fears didn't last long. Soon after, we began to meet Northbounders and thru-hikers from past generations. To my relief, they were an impressive bunch, even those years and years beyond their thru-hikes. They struck me as sturdy, tested, and wise. They moved at an unhurried pace and existed easily in the moments we shared discussing conditions of water sources and shelters we'd passed in recent few days. That's when I learned there were four or five southbound thru-hikers ahead of us. No more.

I'd heard others say hiking southbound was a lonely road. Thankfully, I thought, I was blessed with steady companions. Would that last, I wondered, though. As amazing and beautiful as all things were, the strain of the first four weeks was more than any of us imagined. And not the physical strain.

I sat on a rise overlooking a lake in Maine. It was bright and cold and like everything else, beautiful. I was thinking about a ham sandwich -- White bread, lettuce, American cheese, big slabs of meat carved from a bone, mayonnaise, and potato chips crushed on top of the whole thing. Joe appeared out of nowhere, breathing heavy. He was more like a tank when he hiked than a man, strong and determined. If you didn't get out of his way, he would likely bowl you over and not even notice.

He plopped down next to me and sat without speaking for a while. There was no need to say anything. We both stared across the lake. I thought of my grandmother. She used to make sandwiches like that. I'm not sure what Joe was thinking about, probably my well-being. He did that a lot.

"You miss her?"

"Who?"

"Lori."

"Nope."

"What's on your mind?"

"A ham sandwich."

And Lori?

And my grandmother.

He smiled. He was as perceptive as anybody; he knew my answer meant more than the words. He knew I was at finding peace and adapting well to trail life. He knew what I'd invested entirely in the experience. Mostly.

Joe never planned to thru-hike; he always expected to go back to school in August. He didn't need a thru-hike, though. School for him was his thru-hike, I realized. He had no regrets and had never tasted the bitterness of losing his way. He lived life as he hiked. He always had a destination in mind. Joe was the kind who set goals for himself and then found a way to achieve them even if they killed him -- which they never did because he was hard as nails and laughed a lot. If his goal were a thru-hike, he'd have reached Springer or died trying. He'd have lasted ten-thousand miles more if he'd set his sights on doing so.

In the last thirty years, I've often told anyone who'd listen that everyone needs to figuratively hike their own "Appalachian Trail." Doing so, I have preached, makes for a better life in so many ways. For me, my "Appalachian Trail" was conveniently the Appalachian Trail. For most, though, their "Appalachian Trail" is along another path altogether.

Joe was hiking another A.T. at the same time he clocked five-hundred miles that summer. He built his life on principles and ambition and faith. That path -- his true Appalachian Trail -- led him to a Ph.D., a happy marriage, two kids, and no regrets, I'm sure.

I wish I'd paid more attention to the example he set. Though I learned a lot from him, I could have learned more.

NEW HAMPSHIRE

<u>June 28, 1987</u>

From my Journal:

"I left Joe and Rusty early because I was beginning to shiver violently and feared hypothermia. To keep moving was the only way to ward off a chill. I crossed two and a half miles above treeline, across the three peaks of the Mahousic range. It was raining and cold, and the higher I climbed, the more apparent it was that conditions were worse on looming Goose Eye Mountain and Mount Carlo -- even worse than those on Baldpate Mountain a few days before. There was a pond on Goose Eye Mountain. I never saw it. Unless one stood within a few feet of the banks that day, you'd never know it existed."

"I was alone, an hour ahead of Joe and Rusty, and mired in the worst weather I've ever come into contact with. I struggled across the peaks, whipped by rain and wind, stiff from the cold, unable to see much, praying with each step, and conscious of how unprepared even the best-prepared man is to deal with the whims of Nature. I pushed on, surprised to find myself more at peace than fearful. I survived the crossing, settled into the shelter and basked in the confidence that comes with overcoming struggle."

"I'm infinitely more familiar with my own strength and stamina and so much more clear on my ability to stay focused even when panic might have been more natural and maybe even more appropriate."

The three of us crawled more or less out of Maine through Mahousic Notch, a mile-long maze of boulders that required crawling, scrambling, and at times pulling off packs and passing them forward through spots too narrow for pack and person together.

It's known as the hardest mile of the AT, and except for a stretch along the James River in Virginia where I was mauled by more mosquitos than I knew existed, I can't argue.

It was wet and muddy, and even in late in June, there were pockets of ice in spots that never saw the sun. We spent a final night in Maine at Carlo Col shelter and crossed into rugged, unforgettable New Hampshire the next morning. As we crossed the first state border -- something that was an important milestone every time -- each of us was steeped in a sense that we'd been tested through Maine and were somehow stronger and better because of it. Physically, we were, for sure, despite the reminders of the tolls paid by knees and feet and places where pack straps had rubbed for hours and hours. Were we emotionally or mentally strengthened? Maybe. We knew the jury was out on that.

Something was apparent, though. The confidence that came from the first two-hundred and seventy-nine miles was not something you easily purchase or find without effort.   It had real value.

A mile further south, I came upon Rusty sitting on a rock, looking disgusted.

"What's wrong?"

"Soles are coming off my boots." It looked pretty bad. He was trying to fix them with a meager supply of duct tape, and things weren't going well.

Then Joe walked up. "What's up?"

"Rusty's boots are falling apart."

"Yeah, mine, too." He pulled one of his souls back from the toe a few inches. He looked at me accusatorily, "Didn't you say these were the best boots you could get? They aren't gonna last much longer."

I looked closer at my boots. "Crap. Mine are separating, too."

We may have been goofers in the early days, but we hadn't skimped on boots. We'd finagled a deal with a local outfitter. 25% off the best boots he carried. We purchased leather boots assured to be top-of-the-line. "They'd even received accolades in Backpacker Magazine," the salesman told us. There may have been doubts about our preparedness here and there, but we were confident that we were well-equipped when it came to boots. And after all, didn't everything step start and end with the soles of your boots?

But Maine was wet and brutal, and there'd been twenty-six consecutive days with at least some rain. Our boots had taken a beating beyond what they could bear, and now they were giving up at an alarming rate.

At Gentian Pond, we did our best to salvage them with string and duct tape and some sort of shoe patch that never hardened. We made it to Gorham House Inn and laid our hands on a supply of duct tape and wrapped our bad boots liberally. We needed twenty more miles from those boots. If we could make Pinkham Notch in the White Mountains, we could hole-up and find some help getting our boots healed up or head to North Conway and buy new ones.

The White Mountains were hard. They were steep; rugged and breathtaking. Without the prior three-hundred miles through Maine, we never would have made it.

That's when I started worrying about Rusty. Sometimes I imagined hearing his knees scream with each new step. He'd developed a significant limp which was much more apparent when he walked barefoot and without a pack. Though we poked fun at the hunched over and stiff gaits with which each of us limped to the nearest tree each morning for the first piss of the day, there was little humor in it really. We weren't the superhumans we imagined we might be after the first few hundred miles. Walking before you were warmed up was anything but pain-free. Or graceful.

Coming down Wildcat Ridge into Pinkham Notch from high in the Whites was excruciating. If the pain brought tears to my eyes, I could only imagine Rusty's agony. I came upon him near the bottom just as a kid of eighteen or twenty passed him heading up the ridge. He was not a thru-hiker.

The kid was too damned happy. The pounding that knees take on a two-thousand-foot descent is far worse than what the heart and lungs deal with on the same uphill. We were near the flatlands at the bottom, thirty vertical feet, maybe, and Rusty was in a bad way. The tears in his eyes from the pain came from deep within. I could see the questioning in his eyes. And the anger. I was smart enough not to say anything and to keep my distance.

That's when the kid skipped by with his tiny pack, clean-scrubbed face and combed hair. He reminded me of Peewee Herman, the purposefully irritating comedian from the 1980s. The kid said the wrong words; he sang them more than he spoke them, "At least you're going downhill."

I wanted to spit on him. Had he been within reach, I might have grabbed him by the throat and throttled him, but I couldn't let loose of the hand-cable at that particularly treacherous spot without tumbling the last thirty feet. Fortunately, for Rusty and his knees, he was off the last steep part of the descent and among the gentle forested floor below.

Had the boy been within his grasp, he'd have done far worse than I wanted to, I'm sure, but he couldn't let the boy's words pass. He mocked his cheerful, sing-songy tone, not caring if the kid heard. Probably making a point to let him hear. Rusty got madder and madder as he did until the anger boiled over and he lashed out and kicked a river birch. He got the worst of the encounter.

The tree was fine; Rusty wasn't. He hollered in pain; fell against a nearby tree, barely catching himself from falling flat. Fortunately, no bones were broken, but his limp and his outlook were a good bit worse for the next few days. I held my tongue. Nothing could be gained from lecturing him about the importance of self-restraint, I was sure. The time wasn't right, him on the ground nursing a toe that was already turning purple. He'd likely have killed me then, and there had I not kept my mouth tightly shut. And I probably would have deserved it.

"You hike your hike," I thought. "I'll hike mine."

The mile into Camp Dodge, the work camp at Pinkham Notch, was brutal. Bad knees, poorly made boots, and now a toe that was likely fractured. Mack and the Boys did not present a particularly flattering representation of Southbounders when we rolled in.

Still, we were received warmly with bowls of soup, hunks of homemade bread, cots to sleep in, and a place to shower. It was the sort of hospitality we needed.

We stayed at Camp Dodge for five days waiting for new boots to arrive. We'd have been happy to join a trail crew but battered running shoes weren't acceptable backcountry footwear, so we stayed at camp and read and slept and helped out in the kitchen.

The manufacturer was hesitant to do anything about our boots until I threatened to change our trail name from "Mack and the Boys" to "Three Guys with Bad Boots" and to leave a carefully-worded indictment of their product in every shelter from Pinkham Notch to Springer Mountain. That got the job done.

Of course, I didn't tell the rep that the likelihood of me or any of my partners making it to Springer seemed to be less and less likely all the time.

The climb to the top of Mount Washington wasn't easy. 4,300 feet up, up, up from Pinkham Notch through Tuckerman's Ravine. It was brutal, especially in the heat. There was a chunk of ice at the base of a headwall, tucked back in a hollow that seldom saw the sun. It was big as a battleship. I stopped there to splash my face with the bracing ice melt. At the top, there was a visitor center and a million people, or so it seemed. It was more people than I'd seen in a month. My aching muscles threatened rebellion when they saw the parking lot filled with cars. "What?" They seemed to cry incredulously. "We could have driven up here?"

The bulk of the million people, it seemed, stood in line at the snack bar, clean and groomed. More than a few could have stood to lose a few pounds. I stood there drenched with sweat, thighs burning from morning's long uphill, glad I'd climbed myself. I felt somewhat higher and mightier than the weekenders. If I hadn't been so tired, I might have patted myself on the back. I doubted many of them could have patted themselves on the back even if they'd tried. "But for the grace of God go I," I reminded myself. It's simple to stay fit and trim when you have no other choice.

At the top of Mount Washington on the wall of the visitor center are two plaques. Instantly, each in some way made me a better thru-hiker. Hell, both practically made me a better person.

Outside the building is a monument dedicated to the 10th Mountain Division; soldiers, tough-as-nails, who did spectacular and heroic things to ensure our freedom.

This is the text on the monument: "Dedicated by the New England Chapter of the 10th Mountain Division in memory of comrades who gave their lives in the Aleutians and Italy in WWII."

"This elite division of alpine troops spearheaded the victorious Fifth Army against the mountainous Gothic Line fortresses and across the Po Valley to shatter the German defenses in Northern Italy."

"It was their love of New England Mountains, coupled with their dedication to human freedom that inspired hundreds of young New England Patriots to join the 10th Mountain Division. Many returned to their beloved mountains. Those heroes who did not return are still fondly remembered as brave men whose souls rest forever amid these mountain peaks. -- Sempre Avanti"

Two men stood to the side of the plaque, one older, the other younger. Their closeness suggested they were father and son. Perhaps the younger was a grandson. They intensely discussed something of significance, their conversation clearly not for anyone else's ears. The young man listened like he heard something startling for the very first time. The older man spoke with some difficulty as if the words revealed a painful truth. I couldn't hear that; I could just see it. He stared into some faraway world and spoke just a few words at a time. I guessed he might be back in Italy in 1944 remembering the last moments of a friend's life or some heroic deed he witnessed that went unrecognized. I wanted to know so much from that man, but I could see there was no room for me or any other in their conversation. I'd not earned any right from anything I'd ever done to invade their privacy.

I watched without letting them know I watched. I felt the man was a glimpse into history. A brush, perhaps, with greatness.

After two-hundred miles of straight-up climbs and straight-down descents through Maine, my lungs, my back, and my legs were rock solid. I could do more then than I ever could with a pack on my back and do it with less pain. I felt like a growing super-human. To that point, I'd congratulated myself on each new summit and marveled at what I could do. No more, though, after reading that plaque. And watching that old man.

The boys of the 10th Mountain Division put toughness in perspective, and I wasn't even close to their league. While I could outpace almost any weekender along the trail, not once was anyone shooting at me as I did. And a sixty-pound pack was nothing compared to a hundred pounds plus a rifle, cartridges, shovel, and grenades. That day I downed a hefty shot of humility. And I grew up some. That day I came to understand even more that we stand on the backs of true heroes. And perhaps even more importantly, I began to see that there's nothing ordinary about heroism.

Thru-hiking was nothing heroic. Clearly.

Sempre Avanti. Ever forward.

A student I knew who thru-hiked in 2017 as an 18-year-old, told me that the number of stoners and young folks out for a good time had swelled in recent years. "Especially in the first few hundred miles," she said. "Most didn't last, though, unless they got a clue at some point later, and then they did alright." To would-be thru-hikers reading this, here's some advice: hike your hike, sure, but don't miss the opportunity to make it so much more than an ongoing party along a thin slice of America.

What an opportunity a thru-hike presents to embrace values like simplicity and humility and to understand who you are and who you might one day become. Hiking two-thousand miles isn't really that big a deal. Lots do it; lots have done it. What does matter is that it provides an unparalleled opportunity to glean insights into how the world works and where you and others fit in. It's those who take advantage of opportunities to learn who reap the benefits of a thru-hike for the next 10,000 days or so.

I have rarely met anyone who in response to being asked about their end-to-end adventure has said only, "It was a good time." All have had something much more to share. Most eventually acknowledge, "It was far harder than expected, but God, I sure learned a lot."

I wonder if those who hike the AT as if it were a 2,000-mile long party ever make it to the end. And if they do, what's left when they get there? I don't know the answer to that. I believe that those who start with that perspective but then experience a sort if awakening along the way, ultimately finish more grown-up and ready for future challenges than when they started. Even the over-fifty crowd.

Heroism isn't commonplace it would seem. Stupidity, on the other hand, well, that's another story.

There is another plaque inside the visitor center atop Mt. Washington. People call it the "death list." It lists causes of death for nearly 150 hikers, adventurers, skiers, climbers, and goofers who have perished on the mountain since 1849. Most died from falls and exposure, avalanches and heart attacks, and a good share died in car wrecks on the mountain, too. I can't help but wonder what role stupidity played in many of those deaths. It was a factor in quite a few cases, I would guess.

I remember my own near miss-during the fast-moving storm that caught Rusty and me ill-prepared on Chairback Mountain. "But for the grace of God go I," I thought as I reviewed that list.

I imagine few of the people on that list got up the morning of the day they died and said, "I think I'll be reckless on the mountain today and see if I can get myself killed." Most died, I'm sure because they charged into something without thinking or because they were careless in a particular moment. Those behaviors weren't always beyond me, I knew. But I also knew I'd come far since that morning in Columbia, Missouri, when I shook Rusty's hand and committed to quitting my job, dropping out of grad school and setting out on an epic adventure.

That had been more than a year before, 4 months before and I was not the same man.

If I'd read the "death list" in the salacious spirit which I might listen to a radio broadcast about a disaster -- without connection or much other thought -- it might have done little to influence my behavior.   Instead, I crossed the Presidential Range thinking about how important it is to think about our experiences if we want to be more than we are. So, I thought some of who I was and even more about who I wanted to be, and I took it all to heart.

Because I took a moment to think about that plaque and the one-hundred-fifty tragic stories there, I don't do as many dumb things as I might have done. And before I do anything rash, I'm far more likely to think about consequences first. That commitment made so long ago has proved decisive most of the 10,000 days since.

Southwest of the Franconia and Presidential Ranges, we crossed Mount Moosilauke in our brand new boots which were barely broken in since they arrived by overnight courier after my threat to change our trail name to "Three Guys with Bad Boots." The three-hundred-sixty-degree views from the summit were spectacular. It was the kind of place I might have chosen to stay if I could have figured out how.

South of there was the Sugar House at the base of Mount Cube. Theirs was a fascinating set-up involving what seemed like miles of plastic tubes channeling gallons and gallons of maple sap – one drop at a time -- from a thousand tapped maples trees, down the mountain, and into a huge evaporator. From the millions of tiny droplets eventually came maple syrup and sugar and all sorts of candies. It was a pretty cool operation and like so many things those days, a reminder that almost nothing happened on its own or automatically. A drop or two of sap from a single tree was insignificant, but a drop or two of sap every few minutes from a thousand trees over an entire spring was enough to fuel a prosperous livelihood.

Later that evening, we sought refuge in a barn belonging to a former governor of the State of New Hampshire.   The Governor -- I believe his name was Thompson -- was a kind man who warmly took interest in our stories. The barn seemed like the Hilton compared to some places we'd stayed – high ceilings, stacks of hay bales to sleep on, everything neat and orderly. A friendly dog and a few cats added to the homeyness of the place. It had rained much of the day and we were looked forward to a good night's sleep in a warm, dry, and secure spot.

Nope. That's not how the night turned out.

Many lessons were learned that night. None came easy. First, there's nothing soft or warm or snuggly about sleeping on top of a stack of hay bales. When one lay on top of them, he or she sinks into the softness in about the same way he might sink into the surface of a slate pool table. But at least most pool tables – at least any I've encountered -- aren't infested with spirited mice scurrying in and out of cracks and crevices. That explained why the cats hung around with such interest. It apparently wasn't our fellowship they were

82

seeking. And then, as dusk settled in and a light rain started, the birds came home to roost, hundreds of them.

Now, pigeons have a low muted cackling that isn't at all shrill or offensive as long as you're not trying to sleep, and as long as there is just one or two of them. If, however, you are trying to sleep, and there is a mob them agitated by an approaching storm and the presence of a bunch of cats, then it's like seeking peace in a high school cafeteria the day or so before summer vacation starts.

The three of us lay on our less-than-comfortable beds grumbling about the mice. Little did we understand that they were but a minor concern compared to what lay ahead that evening.

The first splat was soft and innocuous. It was the quiet smack of something soft falling from above. The first was followed by another and then another, unevenly spaced and relatively infrequent. Splat. Splat. Splat. Initially, the sounds failed to set off alarm bells, but as the sounds of things falling from on-high picked up in frequency, we understood their origins. The birds in the rafters, having had a satisfying supper just before dusk and now settled in for the night, were doing what we should have predicted. Splat! Splat! Splat! Splat! The noxious stuff came down like rain. And it would continue to come down all night long. Joe, Rusty, and I were quick enough to cover up with a tent fly. Unfortunately, we forgot our packs. That was a mistake.

Next morning, they resembled the bottom of a parakeet's cage.

There was a hose available, fortunately. We scrubbed what we could from our bodies and packs and set out from the Governor's barn soaking wet, feeling unclean and like we hadn't slept in weeks, and a little less heartened by whatever lay ahead. One can only laugh so much about being shat upon all night long by a hundred million pigeons – at least it seemed like so many. Ever since that day I've harbored a burning hatred for pigeons. Is there any wonder why?

Thirty miles or so we hiked into Hanover, NH, and stepped onto the Dartmouth University campus feeling like we didn't exactly belong. It was middle-July. The campus was deserted. I can't remember where we slept, but I do remember eating in the dining facility there. All you can eat. Everything you could want. Our behavior that day bordered on obscene. I'm certain each of us downed six- or maybe ten-thousand calories shamelessly. Leaving that place, I'm sure we made it no further than the nearest shade tree where we collapsed and slept off the afternoon's excess.

By that point, I knew times had changed.

Rusty waited until the morning we were about to cross into Vermont to tell me. He was wearing a ridiculous pair of Hawaiian shorts when he did. They were anything but flattering and in ways softened the blow of what he was about to tell me. He was plain and honest when he said it as was his typical way. "I'm going home," he said.

"When?" I didn't let on that his words felt like a mortal blow to my thru-hike, to my relationship with my father, and maybe even to the course of the rest of my life.

"Now."

"That's sudden." I'd never really considered what solo hiking the last fifteen hundred miles would mean. Joe would be heading back to school in a few weeks, and there were few Southbounders to throw in with. The writing on the wall was pretty clear. This would be my hike soon enough, in less than three weeks, and if I weren't mentally ready, it would end shortly after that. I was about to become the totality of that misfit bunch once known as Mack and the Boys.

"I have things to do back home," He said. There were no apologies.

I knew he was done before he told me. His knees were a wreck and the spark I'd known for years was gone. I'd watched him spiraling away from who he was for a few weeks now. He wasn't the man who'd left St. Louis in 5 weeks before or the guy I'd drank so much beer with in college. He was somber and satisfied and impatient to get on with life.

In the last few hundred miles, I knew my thoughts had wound far further through the pathways of my brain than my legs covered along the trail. I'm sure he wrestled with just as many big life questions. Maybe more. He didn't know my thoughts, and I didn't know his. I just nodded. I didn't need to know more. There was no reason to convince him to stay. I figured getting on with his life was more important than anything along the AT and that moving on in the right direction was as good a reason as any for going home. Now the rest of the AT was my challenge.

The mental strain of a thru-hike is more than the physical burden. That's often said. Too much time to think about unfinished business undermines a hiker's focus, and an unfocused thru-hiker isn't likely to last much longer. Once you feel like there's someplace more critical you need to be and that things you need to get done aren't getting done, then staying just delays the inevitable.

"You gonna quit, too?"

"Nope."

"Why not?"

"Things to do."

He knew the truth; I didn't need to tell him. I couldn't quit because I'd re-structured my entire life to be there. I'd bet everything that I would be successful and on the assumption that it was worth doing. Though I was beginning to doubt both, going home would be an admission that my father had been right and that the whole thing had been stupid from the start. Quitting for me, I sensed, might be a bad decision. A really, really bad decision.

He nodded, and we turned in opposite directions. I don't know if he looked back at me, but I looked back and watched him walk away in those goofy Hawaiian shorts, hoping he'd be alright. Also, hoping I'd be alright. He seemed happy enough; I tried to be happy for him. I turned south towards Vermont and whatever lay ahead, thankful Joe was still at my side.

Mack and the Boys were now just two.

With Rusty gone, I'd be alone soon and that was something I had never bargained for. Joe hadn't signed on for a thru-hike. I hoped early on he might be swayed to stay, but I knew that wouldn't happen. He had other priorities. I always knew that wasn't even slightly possible. He'd leave somewhere in Massachusetts to be back at school in just three weeks.

I had bad memories of the five days spent alone in Arkansas the previous summer. Traveling solo wasn't easy, I knew. Knowing that lay in my future, I continued on defiantly and in a lousy humor. I remember thinking that when Joe left the trail name "Mack and the Boys" would be pretty ridiculous for just one guy. Would I need to change my name?

VERMONT

July 16, 1987

From my Journal:

I regret never having learned to play the guitar.
I regret not having put more effort into high school and college.
I regret letting that woman walk out of my life.
I wish I had saved more money.
I wish I had developed my writing skills. And gone more places.
I wish I had made more stained glass windows and carved wooden figurines.
I could have been a good high school wrestler if I hadn't gotten distracted.
I wish I'd never stopped weightlifting.
I used to go to daily mass and read the Bible? Why did I stop?
I wish I would have asked Angie Hampton out on a date.
I probably shouldn't have drunk as many beers as I did.

I refuse to add the Appalachian Trail to this list. I will not say, "I wish I would have finished" anymore. That's why I keep walking -- to break the chain.

Joe and I crossed into Vermont, weathered and tested; "beat to hell" was probably a better description of how we were feeling. And how we looked.

Sweet and gentle Vermont provided a welcomed respite from the physicality of the prior four-hundred and fifty miles. Maine and New Hampshire were rough; Vermont was soft by comparison.

Raw determination and self-deprecating humor, the kind that allowed us to laugh at our own naivety and keep trudging on in spite of it, had pulled us through to that point. We crossed into Vermont different men, no longer greenhorns, but neither were we experts. It was toughness, not artistry, that got us that far, and it showed, I'm sure, in our faces. We rolled into the shelter that night, rough and tumbled, looking as much like pirates as hikers, shirts stained with sweat, sunburned, and in need of showers. That's when we met Bill and Laurie Foote.

Meeting a Northbounder is a unique experience. An instant bond exists, and there's immediate respect. There's a natural but friendly spirit of competition. Northbounders and Southbounders search one another to find their own destiny. By Vermont, Northbounders may have traveled sixteen hundred miles and the Southbounders slightly more than five hundred, but the southbound hiker has crossed the White Mountains, the Mahousics, and the State of Maine, and the Northbounder knows only by reputation that those are a formidable proving ground.

By the time thru-hikers near the end of their journey, most are impressive in their own ways. They're equipped with capacities and confidence beyond the ordinary. They are perfectly prepared to do what the AT requires. Almost all bear the look of one who's traveled hard and far. They're gaunt and haggard, tattered some around the edges, and each would stand out in any crowd except one made up entirely of thru-hikers.

Bill and Laurie were different. They were the leanest, tallest and by far the cleanest thru-hikers we met. Everything about them was picturesque. And tidy. Their trail name, The Happy Feet, fit them more perfectly than any trail name ever fit another hiker or band of hikers. They were pleasant and welcoming and did everything in an organized, unhurried fashion. They were polite, almost to a fault, and their manner almost dainty. Joe and I powered through whatever came our way, but the Happy Feet seemed to have danced their way to where we met, probably even holding hands and skipping now and then as they did. They were, it seemed, a fresh, young couple in those early sickeningly-sweet polite days of a budding relationship. Instead, they'd shared a long and prosperous life together.

Joe and I were suspicious of them from the start. How could anyone so clean and relaxed and happy have traveled so far? They watched us prepare and eat dinner that night with the kind of horrified interest one might watch a lion kill then devour an antelope. Joe and I scarfed down a ton of instant mashed potatoes swimming in instant gravy with cans of tuna tossed in and crumbled cheese melted on top. We then slurped chocolate pudding that failed to thicken from the same pot like two unruly dogs. In contrast, they dined on neat and tidy freeze dried suppers and measured quantities of this and that. At the end of the meal, which they finished long before us, we were left with a mess; they were left with a few neatly folded bags.

While they sipped tea, Joe and I swallowed Snickers bars nearly whole and stuffed ourselves with handfuls of granola. We talked about the trail and our experiences, about people we'd met and why we were thru-hiking. They were there, it seemed because they'd done most of what they'd wanted to do in the other world. The AT was for them more reward for a life well-lived than a stepping stone to something bigger. Joe and I were still goofers at that point – both in life and a little less so as thru-hikers. We were trying to figure things out. That was fairly obvious.

And then, out of the blue, Laurie announced, "We made up a song to help us remember the people we've met. Want to hear it? We made up a verse about you guys, too." She was so damned happy. How could we refuse?

"What?"

"We made up a song. Want to hear it?"

"Okay." What other choice was there? All I could think was, "When the hell could you have made up a verse about us?"

Too many years have gone by to remember the particulars of their performance. It was a happy tune, as one might expect, sing-songy, recognizable, rhyme-y, and bright. As they prepared to sing, they perked up -- as if that were possible – and leaned in a little closer to each other in a way reminiscent of great duos like Sonny and Cher, Donny and Marie, or Nancy Sinatra and whoever she sang with. And then they let loose in a style reminiscent of the many camp counselors I'd know in younger days. I half expected backup singers to step out of the woods, bluebirds to fly around their heads and bunnies and baby deer to venture out of the woods to watch.

The song was cute; the tune was recognizable. There were verses about Northbounders who we'd crossed paths with as they headed north and Joe and I pointed south. Most songs on the radio last three or four minutes; their song continued for what seemed ten times that long.   Probably was. There were twenty verses, at least, and more likely hundreds or thousands, it seemed.

While they sang, Joe tried to hide in his water bottle but then choked on whatever he was drinking, red Kool-Aid probably, which drizzled out of his nose in a sputtering fit of coughing. Joe was the sort who freely quoted Dirty Harry, Josey Wales, Rooster Cogburn, Monty Python, and Peewee Herman, once in a while, but he was not the sort who thrived on "cute." I smiled patiently through the endless performance, not sure if I wished I were drunk or glad that I wasn't because of what I might have said. Joe wandered off – to vomit, I guess. He wasn't exactly the sentimental sort.

Rarely, in the thirty years since, when I've seen or corresponded with Joe, have the Happy Feet gone unmentioned. It wasn't a game-changing meeting, but it was memorable.

I should have paid closer attention to Bill and Laurie's example. It was wonderful. I saw them once again in Roanoke two months later, but never after that. In the years since I've come to understand they likely lived their lives much the way they thru-hiked the AT For five million steps, I repeated the mantra, "No regrets," but I think I stopped saying that with such conviction once I finished my thru-hike. Bill and Laurie, I trust, in their own way, repeated that mantra or one similar to it, each day and each step of their lives, both before, during, and after, their hike.

Initially, I found it impossible to imagine how anybody could hike without wrestling with the inner demons swimming around in their head. The Happy Feet had time to memorize a million verses of a silly song because they had no demons to wrestle. That was, I believe, the product of a life well-lived from the start.

If I did anything wrong as a thru-hiker, it was that I stopped living like a thru-hiking after I reached Springer Mountain. Not entirely, but more than I should have.

While writing this book, I learned that Bill Foote passed away in the spring of 2000. Crossing the James River used to require a somewhat precarious trek across an interstate bridge. It now crosses the James River on a footbridge that would not exist if not for the labors of Bill and Laurie. The bridge was completed and dedicated, unfortunately, a few months after his death. But thanks to his nine years of wrangling to get the job done, thousands of hikers will cross in relative safety and solitude instead of risking their lives crossing on the old interstate highway bridge.

Maybe the building of that footbridge is one of the great examples of what can be accomplished when thru-hikers continue to live by the lessons learned along the AT

Back-to-back-to-back twenty-mile days take their toll on a body. I was limping a little when I met Reese Lukel at a crossroads just north of Winturri shelter. He was a middle-aged accountant and a section hiker who for fourteen years, beginning in 1973, had been piecing together an end-to-end Appalachian Trail thru-hike, one section at a time. He was also a member of the Appalachian Trail Conference Board of Directors. He was poised to complete the AT in just 4 weeks. For good reason, he was particularly proud of that accomplishment. We walked and talked for sixteen miles. He was as pleasant as any man I'd ever met. At Stony Brook shelter, he shared the lunch packed by his wife, Melinda -- Fried Chicken, grapes, and Hershey bars.

I didn't know Reese well at all, and I've never seen him since, but I sensed he was a wise man, especially about the Appalachian Trail. He talked about the soul of the Trail and its power to heal and strengthen. His wisdom and commitment impressed me much. On the outside, he was just a middle-aged man, but inside he understood so much more.

We came upon his RV in Sherburne Pass. Reese handed Joe and I each a bowl packed with a near-obscene pile of ice cream – vanilla bean with blueberries and strawberries left over from a fourth of July celebration. We sat in lawn chairs in the shade of an awning on the side of the RV, ate ice cream, and shared stories. And feeling quite civilized.

As we turned to leave, Reese called after us. "One more gift," he said, smiling like a kid, almost embarrassed, and handed Reese's peanut butter cups to each of us. Joe and I walked on feeling tough-as-nails and loveable as puppies. The next three and a half miles didn't hurt in the least. We settled in at Pico cabin, with a thunderstorm brewing in the distance.

Later that fall, I came upon a copy of Appalachian Trailways Magazine in a trail shelter down south. Reese was on the cover. He'd completed his section hike. He was one of the great volunteers who's played an unheralded role with the Appalachian Trail Conservancy and the trail clubs that maintain sections along the way. His legacy, with those of so many others who work so tirelessly, has given the nation an essential resource that benefits the physical, spiritual, and mental health of millions. That's a worthwhile way to spend ones' time.

More of my time seemed devoted to thoughts of the future and of building things of substance like a family when I got home. By the end of Vermont, my dreams were taking shape. The "story" I was seeking wasn't along the trail, I sensed, but back home somewhere. Whatever the outcome of this great journey, I started to think, the more significant challenge would be to build something back home that might outlive me.

I often thought about the "death list" on Mount Washington and wondered if those men and women had left legacies beyond their name and cause of death on a plaque? If I'd thought about that list in the same spirit one might listen to reports of a distant tragedy on the radio, with neither connection nor much other thought, the example might have done little to influence my behavior. Instead, I embraced those examples as lessons and as possibilities for me if I allowed them to be.

I was capable of doing stupid and rash things, I decided, the consequences of which could easily be my name on a plaque like that one. I decided then to be more intentional about most things. With each step after that, I pledged to take a little more care and to add a measure more caution. That, of course, proved easier for the next sixteen-hundred miles but not quite so much so for each of the next ten-thousand days.

I've taken my share of missteps since then, but because of hiking the Appalachian Trail, I've taken more deliberate steps than I ever might have. Those purpose-filled steps have surely tempered the impact of the more-stupid ones I have or would have taken.

MASSACHUSETTS

<u>July 24, 1987</u>

From my Journal:

"I've invested 600 miles worth of time, energy, resources and physical strength. I'm satisfied that I have wasted nothing. Hiking the Appalachian Trail has been worthwhile, meaningful, and educational. I'm better, stronger, and understand much more deeply because of it. There are no regrets. I'm tired, though, and I miss home, and I feel like there are other things I should be doing. Sometimes I feel like I've learned where I need and want to be. It's then, when I think of those things, I find myself questioning, 'What am I still doing on the Appalachian Trail?' It's confusing, but mostly it's assuring. I feel as if I've finally found direction and hurdled the obstacles that have kept me from settling down. Things like stability and security are suddenly appealing. Neatness, cleanliness, organization, even fashion, are all a little bit more appealing. Maybe I'm growing up."

We cruised into North Adams, Massachusetts, Joe and I, like men with a purpose. It was Joe's last night. We needed a place to stay, but the hotels were booked or ridiculously expensive. We'd have to head back into the woods to camp on the outskirts of town unless some good fortune befell us. Next day he'd catch a Greyhound Bus to the Midwest, and I'd continue on my own. 1,457 miles to go. "Damn," I thought; "That's a helluva long way." I wasn't in good humor. I seriously wondered if I'd reached the end of my Appalachian Trail hike, too. I hadn't prepared mentally to hike solo, and at that point, I only knew of a few other southbound hikers. Where they were, though, I didn't have a clue.

North Adams was an upscale community, at least the part we wandered through looking for a post-office and a cheap place to stay. We must have looked like bad-fitting hairpieces. People tried not to stare, but couldn't help but steal sideways glances at the unkempt and not-so-recently showered trespassers. We smiled back and offered falsely enthusiastic nods, tried genuinely to assure them that we weren't there to steal their daughters or eat their pets but most put their heads down as they passed or crossed to the other side of the street.

A young man, neatly groomed and well-mannered, approached us and asked, "You guys hiking the trail?" Quite surprised to be recognized as humans, we nodded.

"Let me buy you an ice cream soda," he said. He was dressed to play tennis later or maybe to have dinner at the club; his hair was perfect; his clothing expensive. Joe and I and the young man were clearly from different dimensions, though a sense of duty to offer kindness to others had not escaped him. "What a nice kid," we thought.

Who could refuse such kindness? We followed him to a quaint apothecary where we ordered sodas and settled into a booth. Our new friend, Pat, dominated the conversation.

"How are your sodas?" He was enthusiastic and filled with positivity. He seemed the sort destined to be a U.S. Senator or at least a small town mayor. He gesticulated wildly like a politician, a drunk, or a guy high on the wonders of life. He was fascinating and all over the place.

"Admirable kid," I thought. "I wish there were more like him. The world might be somewhat better if there were."

"I've lived here my whole life," he said; "But I can't wait to go somewhere where people have more open minds. The world is such a wide open place. I really envy you and your freedom and your spirit. God, I wish I could go with you. Someday I'm going to do it, too, the Appalachian Trail. And someday I'm going to travel in space."

Nothing in his manner caused the slightest uneasiness until he announced, "I've been in a mental institution for the last 21 months." He spoke quite plainly about it, then added, "But I'm all better now." He took a long slurp from his soda, "Been out since last Tuesday. That ever happen to you guys?"

"Um, get locked in a mental institution? No, not me. What about you, Joe?"

Joe looked at me sideways and shook his head at Pat, saying as he did, "Um, no, at least I don't think so."

I shook my head, too. What had we stumbled into?

"There were voices in my head," he rambled on. "Mostly in code, though, so I couldn't understand them. Nobody else could either," he said. "People didn't think they should be there, so they sent me away." He paused to take a few more sips of his soda. "Man, that's good, he said."

"The voices are mostly gone now, and I don't really miss them, but I feel bad that we couldn't help the senders. They chose me to call out to for help.

Turns out my brain receives messages from a civilization on the backside of Pluto. Or somewhere. Nobody can figure out why. I think I was wired that way for a special purpose, from the beginning of time, probably, but who knows? I always knew in my guts they were calling for help, but since I don't understand their language so well or their codes, I couldn't fully explain what they were saying or where their base was. I think it was on the backside of Pluto. It could have been Neptune, though. That's why NASA couldn't see it with their giant telescopes."

He smiled expectantly at us. We just stared without knowing what to say.

"They gave me lots of drugs while I was in there. They quieted the transmissions, but I do think the government should look into doing their part to help that civilization. Don't you guys think so? If their messages start coming through, I'm going to mount a rescue operation – that is if asteroids haven't destroyed their base. I think that's what they were most concerned about."

Joe and I nodded with growing uneasiness.

"After all, they could become taxpayers and help solve debt issues in this country. We could at least ship them supplies on our next shuttle to Uranus or Saturn. I always forget which one the space shuttle stops at first. I hear it's pretty up there -- on Uranus, not Saturn. Saturn looks like Nevada; Uranus is more like California. Do you like the Beach Boys? I love their music, and I want to learn to surf. I hear Elvis Presley was a pretty good surfer. Man, that guy could sing, and he got the chicks, didn't he? I think he's dead. What do you think? People still say they see him. Do you like dogs? I can hear what dogs think. It's just like they're talking when they walk by. It's surprising that they think in English. You wouldn't have thought that, would you? I always thought dogs would have thought in smells, not words. I can't understand cats, though. I don't really like them. I think they're here for all the wrong reasons. I don't think they were part of the original plan. They're likely transplants from another part of the solar system or below ground."

Joe and I just nodded and slurped our sodas in stunned silence. Even if we had wanted to, there was nowhere to slip a word into his stream of consciousness. We thanked him profusely for the sodas, wished him well – really well -- saddled packs and headed for the door as gracefully and as quickly as possible. We laughed for half an hour, shaking our heads all the while, half-singing, half-shouting the Who song, "I gotta get out of this place if it's the last thing I ever do!"

Sometimes I've wondered if that guy was really crazy or if he was just a helluva an actor with a great sense of humor.

It was late afternoon when we noticed the sky growing uncharacteristically dark. We were prepared to deal with rain, but a storm of biblical proportions was a different matter. We stood on the outskirts of North Adams watching everything above us turn black and churn like it was mad as hell.

"Better watch that sky, boys," the old guy said in a tone beyond serious. He wore faded overalls and the kind of battered ball cap you'd expect to see in a Midwest farming town. "Man on the radio says it's gonna get real bad. If I 'uz you, I'd get you down to the Catholic Church and see if you can spend the night there. I'm no churchgoer, but it seems that'd be your best bet. A storm like this might get you killed." He thought a little more, "Or you could hunker down under that railroad bridge down the road a piece."

Seeking shelter at the church sounded reasonable enough. I'd grown up in a Catholic school; Joe did, too. We'd spent most Sundays in church listening to sermons about feeding the hungry, clothing the naked, looking after the sick, and inviting strangers in. I'd dropped plenty of dollars and small change into collection plates. "Do unto others" might well have been burned into my forehead. I'd listened to the Good Samaritan story a thousand times. Like the back of my hand, I knew well that Jesus told his followers, "Verily I say unto you, inasmuch as ye have done it unto one of the least of my brothers, ye have done it unto me." (Matthew 25:40)

How could the church turn us away?

The sky was a nauseating mix of black and green, devoid of any power to calm. I watched the swirls above me fully expecting a finger of twisting fury to reach down and scratch a deep furrow in the earth. 30 minutes or so and the weather would hit full-force. The moment was tense, Storm and dusk were poised to strike precisely at the same moment. It was hard to imagine things getting much darker. We were in for a hell of a storm.

We sought refuge at the Church, feeling very much like one of those "least of my brothers." I knocked on the door and waited. Joe stood on the lawn behind me, two or three stair steps below me. He was a good Catholic boy, too. Better than me really.

The white-haired woman who answered the door listened intently. "Can we sleep in the church garage?" I asked. We are Appalachian Trail hikers, I explained, we hiked down from Maine. The weather was threatening, and we've been unable to find shelter or even a place to pitch our tent.

She just stared. I asked again, "Could we sleep in your garage?"

"You'll have to speak with Father." She said and disappeared inside. She locked the door behind her.

It was a long while before the door opened. As the seconds clicked off, the storm got closer. The man who opened the door was old. He didn't smile.

"We need a place to shelter from the storm," I said. "Could we sleep in your garage? Or pitch our tent behind the church?" I couldn't imagine being turned down, not after all those sermons, and with the sky falling and time running out to get somewhere else.

"I don't think that would be appropriate," the man said. The quickness of his response raised the likelihood his mind was already made up when he opened the door and asked, "Can I help you?"

Feelings of betrayal welled inside me; I was pissed and about to give the hypocritical bastard a theology lesson when Joe's hand touched my shoulder lightly. "Let it go," he said. "The storm's gonna hit. We gotta go."

He had a way of bringing clarity and calm to any situation.

"Could you direct us someplace where we might find shelter?"

"No," he said, and the door closed abruptly. The lock clicked loudly, and the wind, as if on cue, blew harder.

The situation was dire. Joe spoke first, "What's it gonna be?" He was closer to the edge than I'd ever seen him. The weather was about to explode. Hairs were standing up on my arms and on the back of my neck. Pound for pound, though, Joe was tougher than anybody I'd ever known. Things were looking bad for us at that moment. I could see that in Joe's face.

The railroad bridge the old man mentioned was three-quarters of a mile behind us. "That's our option," I said, and we turned into the wind and raced the imminent rains. Shit. The situation was bleak.

Seasoned hikers toting full packs can cover about four miles an hour with sixty-pounds on their back. It would take ten minutes to reach the bridge. We didn't likely have that much time. Joe and I prayed like madmen as we half-ran, half-walked as fast as we could. Somehow, against all odds, we slipped under the bridge just as winds crashed to new violence and the rains let loose a fury. It was the strongest storm I'd witnessed.

Lightning strikes and thunder crashes were continuous and deafening. "Shit," I yelled over the racket, "Bastard preacher could have killed us."

I don't know if Joe heard me. It was too damned loud.

We'd have been in bad shape without the bridge. It didn't offer much protection against the horizontal rains that pelted exposed skin like bullets. Deeper under the bridge was a loading dock of sorts piled with boxes and railroad supplies. It was cordoned off with chain-link, well-lit, neatly swept, with a large sign high on one wall that warned, "Trespassers will be prosecuted to the fullest extent of the law." The rain was now slicing in sideways in sheets. Puddles formed on every previously dry surface except the area behind the fence.

Neither Joe nor I were rule-breakers, but extraordinary circumstances call for extraordinary measures. We pushed through a gap in the fence and huddled back where it was still dry. Even there, though, it was too windy for a tent, and a light mist showered us continuously. We grabbed broken down cardboard boxes from a neat little pile and constructed shelters best we could. They provided a little protection from the blowing rain but not from much else. If not for the raging storm and trains roaring passed every thirty minutes or so, the 1000-watt bulbs flooding the area with near-daylight and the threat of being arrested and jailed for a night or two for trespassing, we might have slept. It didn't help that Joe needed to find a bus back to Missouri next day or that I would start my 1,457-mile solo trek as soon as he had.

It was the worst of 160 nights along the AT.

I lay in my cardboard box thinking of my father's words, "Stupidest thing I ever heard." I was ready to concede he'd been right all along.

To say we woke to clear skies and birds singing would be an outright lie. Neither of us slept so neither of us actually woke. Instead, we crawled out of our cardboard boxes and made haste to get the hell out of there before someone arrested us. Above the bridge, birds were indeed singing, and the skies were bright blue. A few hundred yards down the road a massive oak felled by the storm had smashed a now-useless barn. Debris littered the streets.

Unfortunately, the barn likely belonged to the farmer we'd met earlier.

"Close call," Joe said as we walked past. It wasn't much further to the spot where the trail crossed the road into North Adams. It was the end of the line for Joe.

Saying goodbye wasn't easy. We'd hiked 582.5 miles and been together each night for two months. We'd endured storms and slept in cardboard boxes, fought no-see-ums and learned enduring and difficult lessons together. For those 582.5 miles – plus the months leading up to our departure from Missouri -- we'd laughed often and come close to crying a time or two. But there wasn't much to say at that crossroads. Joe had come as far as he planned to, but I wasn't anywhere close. He had to be back at school in a week, and I was 1,457 miles short of Springer Mountain, a distance about as far as anything I could imagine.

I hadn't prepared for this moment. I had expected to be hiking with Rusty from this point on. The prospect of a solo hike hadn't figured into my plans. With the harsh reality that I was alone roughly taking hold, the game was different then, and the doubts were massive. Joe could see it in my eyes.

"You gonna be okay?"

"I'll be okay." I wasn't sure I would be.

"You could come home with me."

"Not yet. I've got a few hundred miles in me still. I hope."

"I'll see you when I see you."

"Yeah, see you then."

We embraced in one of those uniquely male bear hugs with plenty of back-slapping and grappling that almost turned to full-scale wrestling. If we'd been gentler one or the other might have started crying. Joe turned towards North Adams to find a bus home; I turned south to Mount Greylock where I'd heard a hiker could get a bowl of soup and some bread at Bascomb Lodge for a few bucks.

A hot bowl of soup is good for the soul. That particular day, I was in dire need of good soup and fresh bread. On the way up Mount Greylock, I came to understand what it meant to be alone and far from home.

When you hike by yourself eight-hours or more a day, thoughts race and rattle through your head at breakneck speed. A good number of thru-hikers, I suspect, lose interest amidst the ups and downs and swirling that goes on in your brain. Their leaving the trail has little to do with the physical aspects of a thru-hike. It's the mental drain that gets them.

Some of the thinking that goes on is great and powerful and uplifting, some goofy and inconsequential, and some downright painful. I often had imaginary conversations with people as I walked, conversations I wished

I'd had years and months before with people who'd passed or people I'd lost touch with, or people I had unfinished business with. I also prayed a lot. Sometimes I ambled along trying to remember things I'd learned in high-school French class. By the end of the trail, in the recesses of my brain, I'd rediscovered the days of the week in French and the months of the year, and French words for things like apple, swimming pool, French fries, and shirt. I could articulately introduce myself and ask, "Do you speak French?" Mostly, though, I prayed and thought about people I'd known and dreamed about what I would do when I got home.

The priest who turned Joe and me out into the storm angered me deeply, that's true, but that didn't shake my faith. I found solace so often in thinking about creation and the goodness of the humans I met along the way – even in the crazy young man in North Adams. When it was over, I could look back along the unbroken line winding through 14 states and say that I'd only met two truly unpleasant people along the journey, a crotchety waitress in Hot Springs and the creep outside of Kent, Connecticut, who scared the piss out of me and convinced me that evil – pure evil – is a real thing. The priest in North Adams didn't get an honorable mention, but at least I understood his motivations.

CONNECTICUT

From my Journal:

   "I've traveled a lot of the last hundred miles alone.   I'm not sure if I'm proud of that, impressed or embarrassed. I believe in what I'm doing. I've seen a lot, I've felt even more. I don't know if I'll finish, for now, though, I'll keep walking simply because I'm finding something.   It's not the kind of something I expected or the kind that can be defined. It's more a sense that I am improving. I'll keep walking as far as I need to. Clearly, it's good for the soul."
   "I used to fear that hiking the AT would allow the wild, untamed side of me to take control. I'm growing confident that the quiet, stable, sometimes-practical side of me is becoming dominant. My daydreams are no longer wild or exotic, rather they are simple, settled, peaceful and without glamour. To make these dreams come true, though, I need to fill myself with the accomplishment that will come from completing this journey. And so I'll keep walking until I'm done whether that is at Springer or somewhere nearer to here."

   Kent, Connecticut, had it all -- laundromat, grocery store, payphone, coffee shop, and a post office. I breezed in early enough to enjoy them all. At the laundromat, I put on my cleanest clothes, a cotton t-shirt that didn't smell so bad and rain pants and tossed everything else into washers. Then I went in search of food. Everything from my pack amounted to less than a load, but I needed two. My socks smelled so terrible they had to be washed separately and run through a second cycle.
   I bought bread and a jar each of peanut butter and jelly at the grocery next door, made ten sandwiches and sat on the curb and ate them in less time than 30 years later it takes to make and eat one. I washed them down with a quart of milk and came up thirsty for more, so I ate a quart of ice cream and a few apples. Then, I wolfed down a Snickers bar.
   I called my mother, collect, of course, told her everything was going well even though I was now traveling by myself.   I picked up a food box at the post office, took what I needed from it and dropped the leftovers at a nearby church.

Before we left Missouri, we'd packed twenty supply boxes and addressed each to "General Delivery" in towns along the AT Scrawled across each box, we wrote, "Hold for Southbound AT Hiker." The boxes were stored in my parent's basement, and every week or so, my father took a box to the post office and mailed it.

We'd packed each box with enough for four hungry hikers. Now there was only me. Each was a mini-horn of plenty filled with far more than I could use – oatmeal, mashed potatoes, rice dinners, pop tarts, gravy mixes, sausages, granola, cans of tuna, peanut butter, vegetarian chili, dehydrated refried beans, and drink mixes. Not a single item had been purchased from an outfitter; all were commonly found in grocery stores.

The food was heavy by today's standards, but it was more than adequate. And it was cheap. My father sealed and mailed a box every week or so per the schedule I'd compiled: Caratunk; Gorham; Glencliff; Hanover; Wallingford; North Adams; Kent; Unionville; Port Clinton; Duncannon; South Mountain; Linden; Tyro; Troutville, Bland; Damascus; Erwin; Hot Springs; Fontana Dam; and finally, Suches, Georgia.

Engaging him in the experience was the best choice I could have made. By the time I reached Massachusetts, his tone was different. By the time I reached Georgia, he was unabashedly my greatest fan. Not once did he complain about his job or miss a deadline. He knew mostly where I was and knew what I had to carry.

During our disjointed and drunken pre-trip planning in Missouri, I'd read "research" that tied a long-distance hiker's success to three things: pack weight, personal cleanliness, and the variety of their diet. Most thru-hikers would agree that those things are absolutely important. My interpretation of "variety," though, proved to be poorly informed. Even buried in so much extra food, I got tired of macaroni & cheese, instant oatmeal, tuna, rice, canned chicken, and sardines. Each time I picked up a food box, after taking what I wanted and trading with other thru-hikers who were equally desperate for a little variety themselves, I went straight to the grocery store for things like – zucchinis and onion, carrots and cabbage, cheese and bacon, bagels and Snickers bars. No, you couldn't carry fresh stuff like that for long, a few days at most, but fresh food went a long way to satisfy cravings, and even raw bacon traveled well in cool temperatures and lasted for weeks once cooked.

My love affair with grits and pecan pie started along the A.T., but not until I found myself south of the Mason-Dixon line.

I picked up a packet of letters at the Kent post office; bought some coffee and another quart of ice cream, sat with my back to the wall of the laundry and waited for my socks to dry. She sat down on the sidewalk next to me, the woman with the soft way about her, and made small talk about my backpack and the way I was dressed. She knew some about the Appalachian Trail, recognized me for what I was, and had lots of questions. Hiking the AT, she said, was a dream of hers. Not realistic now, but someday, she said. The conversation was easy; she was close to pretty, soft around the edges, older than me but not by much. She wondered if she could fix dinner for me. "At least I can offer you a place to shower?"

That's not an offer thru-hikers tend to refuse.

I dressed "normally" as I could from the limited options in my pack. At least my clothes were clean even if I smelled of a multi-day trail stint. It was well before there was anything fashionable about backcountry dress; long before the present-day options of nylon trail shirts and pants that tended to be indistinguishable from business casual clothing. Most hikers wore cheap nylon shell pants or army surplus clothing. Or running shorts.

I sat back and watched her fold the last of her laundry, delicate items mostly, lacy bras and such, and listened to her talk about her mother and such. Was I supposed to see those things? She seemed rather obvious about them, and I wondered, "Was this a different sort of adventure unfolding?" My imagination tumbled in and around the possibilities as we walked to her car, she carrying a laundry basket of lacy niceties on top, me toting a loaded backpack.

I was feeling pretty good, quite optimistic, energized even, full of hope, and a little scared. It had been a week since Joe left and I was doing okay, but it was nice to have someone to talk to. I was growing ever more certain this might be more than a typical "yogi," and I mused about how I might start my journal entry about whatever was about to come next: "I never expected anything like this would happen to me ..."

My overwhelmingly positive outlook tanked, however, the second we stopped at her car. As a thru-hiker, I felt worn and ragged, the impacts of high mileage evident in my overgrown beard, wind-burned skin, and tender joints and feet. Her car looked worse for wear than any thru-hiker I'd seen. The paint was faded, one quarter-panel was caved in-in, a side window was repaired with duct tape, and there were just three hubcaps. It didn't quite match the enticing lingerie piled on top of her basket. She opened the door; the squeaks reminded me of the morning groans of a thru-hiker, especially after a particularly hard day. But that wasn't the worst of it. She cleared trash from the front seat and threw it in back, and invited me to lay my pack on the bed of garbage there. It was a foot thick, at least.

While never a sentimental sort or the kind to name or otherwise personify a backpack, I felt nearly-obligated to apologize to mine for the disrespect as I lay it carefully in back.

There was something gross on the seatbelt, chocolate, I think, but old chocolate, and gummy. It was either that or something dead, I reasoned. She apologized profusely, smeared it with an old napkin, and tossed it in back.

The engine roared when she started it. There was either a hole in the muffler or maybe no muffler at all. Now and then the serpentine belt squealed but not with delight.

Oh, God, where had the romance gone? Suddenly, there were a million reasons why not to go with her, but the car was moving, and the prospect of a shower was hard to resist. And she was a pretty woman with a collection of trashy lingerie, though that mattered less and less the more the adventure unfolded.

Kent was a small town, I figured; how far could her place be? I would have left a path of breadcrumbs if I'd had any. Instead, I tried to pay close attention to the way back as we drove. After a quick shower I figured, I'd hike back into town. I could cover eight miles in less than two hours on an open road without getting my heart rate up. I'd be back on a southbound track, fully-loaded and clean in no time, I figured. It sounded like a well-reasoned plan. It wasn't.

The drive to her place was neither quick nor straight nor was it remotely possible to track where we were going or where we'd been. I tried to follow the twists and turns, but thirty minutes into the drive I no longer knew if I was up, down, west, or east of where we started. Fifty minutes later, we pulled into a collection of six or eight old buildings. There wasn't much welcoming about it.

She led me up some stairs to an apartment above an old storefront. Through the window, I could see it was loaded with old furniture and boxes and every description of non-descript crap. Her apartment was an extension of her car, an absolute wreck. "Barely habitable," I thought. "Holy shit." I moved through the apartment afraid to touch any surface for fear I might

103

contract some heretofore unknown disease. It was worse than the worst trail shelter since Maine.

And I didn't have a clue where I was.

Lingerie? What lingerie? All I knew was that I was hopelessly lost somewhere in the Northeastern United States; that I had likely been kidnapped by a lady driving a crappy car who lived in a filthy apartment; and that nobody knew where I was. Nobody.

I forgot her collection of sexy lingerie. What an idiot, I thought; how had I gotten myself into such a mess? Unfortunately, I sort of knew. The worst, though, was yet to come.

She made me a bowl of chicken noodle soup and pointed me to the shower. It was less clean than the sloppiest shower I'd found along the trail so far. The door did not lock. There was mold on the walls. Yuck. I got in, let the water run over me and made absolutely sure not to touch the walls. At least the water was hot.

I remember seriously considering showering with boots on just to avoid the scummy floor.

She knocked, pushed open the door and stepped into the room. I was relieved to see she was not wearing a skimpy outfit. "I have to go out for a minute," she said. "Make yourself at home." She stepped out then back in almost immediately, not bothering to knock. Thankfully, I thought, she's still dressed.

"Can I get you anything while I'm out?"

I wanted to say, "antibiotics," but I didn't. "No, thank you," I managed. Her smile was sweet and gentle. If only she weren't such a slob, I lamented. She was, though, and she was getting scarier by the moment. What the hell had I gotten into?

She told me she kept the chain on the door locked when at home, and told me I should do the same. And then she was gone. I figured telling me she kept the door chained was significant. The front door closed. She locked it from the outside, and then she was gone. I locked the chain as quickly as I could and breathed a little easier. Just a little bit easier.

I dressed in a hurry, packed for a quick getaway, sat on the couch in the only spot not cluttered with clothes and crap, and tried to figure my next move. My situation was anything but favorable. I was alone in the middle of nowhere which wasn't so different from hiking except this was a very different kind of alone in a very different sort of middle of nowhere. That no one knew where I was kind of freaked me out. I looked around the apartment for a phone. At least I could call Joe or Lori and tell them what was happening, but there wasn't one. Even if I could call someone, I didn't know where I was, who I was with, or whether I'd been stolen from the Appalachian Trail or just borrowed by a socially awkward hippie-chick. What was I supposed to tell them anyway?

Things were not looking so good. I began thinking that maybe I was to be the main course of a cannibalistic feast that evening. Or murdered ritualistically. Or imprisoned here for life. I wondered if she'd gone out for salt and spices and a big red apple to shove in my mouth while she roasted me. Maybe, I thought, she'd gone to gather the rest of her cannibalistic clan for the evening's feast, the one that would feature me as the main course.

I started thinking seriously about making a run for it. I was, after all, freshly showered and that was my top priority.

I sat on the couch trying not to touch anything; I waited longer than seemed reasonable, hemming and hawing about whether to make a run for it. That's when there was a soft knock at the door.

Not answering seemed wise. It may have been an early dinner guest, I reasoned. I pulled my pack a little closer and sat perfectly still.

There was another knock, soft still but a little more insistent. I could hear my heart and the clock on the wall that hadn't been reset after daylight savings months before. The clock ticked loudly; my heart pounded as it would later hoofing up the straight side of Priest Mountain a few states later. I sat absolutely still and listened.

I was pretty sure whoever had was knocking had left. My heart was just starting to relax when the man exploded through the door with a crash.

He didn't bust through the door gracefully as James Bond might. He smashed through it like a bull, stumbled halfway into the room, banged his shin on the junk-filled coffee table spilling half the crap onto the floor. He backed into an end table and knocked the lamp to the floor. Bang! He'd pulled half the doorframe from the wall and stood there nursing his bruised shin.

He was short and fat and broad and bearded; chains dangled from his wallet, and he wore leather head-to-toe despite the summer heat.

He looked at me, his face red and hot, and his eyes wild as Hell. He stared like an animal. "Who the hell are you?"

I started to explain with words that didn't exactly flow coherently, I pointed to my pack. "Was hiking. Met the woman who lives here at the laundry. She let me shower. Nothing else." I took a breath, finally came to my senses, at least some. Once the element of surprise was no longer his, I began to see he did not cut an exactly impressive figure. "Who are you?"

"My girlfriend lives here! What the Hell are you doing here?"

Shit, I thought. Could this get any worse? We stood at what seemed a dangerous impasse, staring each other down like characters in an old western. He wanted blood, I just wanted to live. And hike a few more miles. Was I supposed to run? Or beg for mercy or clobber him with a lamp? I'd have yanked the pistol from my holster if I'd have had one. He seemed to be contemplating whether busting a table over my head was his next best move. Then he softened some. I half expected him to break down in tears and wail about his unfaithful girlfriend, though he looked more killer than tender-hearted. And then he was gone through the shattered door frame leaving me shaken and ready to run. I guessed that was my cue to get the Hell out of there.

I collected my things, shouldered my pack and started out the door. She came in just then, stopping to inspect the shattered door. He hung back in the hallway, a few feet behind, squinty eyes focused on me like lasers. "Sorry," she said. "My boyfriend wasn't happy to find you here. We need to take you back to Kent. Now."

"Oh, you think so?" I wanted to spout off all kinds of sarcastic stuff, but I held back. We walked down the steps to where his car sat, engine running, trunk open. It wasn't quite a "General Lee" knock-off, but it was close. It was something I never expected in Connecticut, land of neatly-tailored homesteads and picturesque little towns. The car was a pretty good match for the leather vest he wore and the chains swinging at his hip. The leather pants, though, were a bit too much. I wanted to tell him his look was too contrived for his muscle car and that a Harley might fit his outfit better, but I figured the last thing he wanted from me was fashion advice, so I kept my mouth shut. My goal was, after all, to survive the encounter.

Now, I grew up among plenty of Missouri rednecks. Back then, Missouri had its share of world-class rednecks. I remember being a bit surprised that there wasn't much outward difference between those guys back home and this man from Connecticut. I tossed my pack into the trunk, careful not to get too close lest one of them shove me into the trunk and slam it shut like some animal trap. I was quite pleased to see there was neither a shovel nor a tarp in there.

Against my better judgment, I squeezed into the backseat. The less-than-happy couple climbed into the front seat; the woman scooted into the middle up against him, and we were off flinging a ton of dust into the air. The engine screamed like a race car. If that thing had had wings, we might have flown back to Kent. No one spoke for the 30 minutes it took to fly back to the laundry.

Most corners, he took at near eighty, and I held on for dear life. I don't remember there being seat belts back there. It was a rough ride. He was either a lousy driver or trying to make me sick; either way, it was a white-knuckle ride. He stopped abruptly at the laundry in Kent, let me out of the back seat, pulled my pack from the trunk and set it at the curb with surprising care. She smiled through the window and mouthed "Sorry," and then they were gone.

Thirty years later, I still wonder if she'd gotten what she wanted and if I'd been a pawn in a twisted game. At least I'd gotten to shower.

It was late afternoon. I stood in front of the laundry, my head spinning like one of the washers inside. The map showed a trail shelter a mile outside of Kent. I strapped on my pack. It felt like a warm embrace from a familiar friend and headed there at a quick pace, exhilarated, relieved, shaking my head and laughing. "What a long strange trip it's been," I sang the Grateful Dead classic as I pounded down the road.

I wished there'd been someone to tell my story to, but there wasn't, and that wasn't such a bad thing. I hiked on reciting in my head the long letter I'd write home by candlelight about the day's adventure. To whom did I owe the next letter --my parents, my sister, or Lori?

Shelters that sit close to the main road attract a different sort than those set further back in the woods. An over-used fire pit, fast food wreckage, and empty beer cans are clear indicators that a particular brand of riff-raff might settle there now and then and whose motives aren't likely aligned with those of an average hiker. As a rule, I avoided such places, especially when alone and on weekends.

The shelter outside of Kent was a few hundred yards from the road and easy to get to. It had been a hard day, and I didn't care. It was early evening, the sun was getting lower, and I was done for the day. Wouldn't it be great to hang out with a few thru-hikers or a lovely young couple or even an exuberant Boy Scout troop? The thought of a little fellowship with other humans -- decent ones -- added a little spring to my steps.

The shelter was nice enough. I breezed in like I owned the place, picking up speed as if crossing a finish line. It was good to be back among white blazes, the two-inch by four-inch paint swaths that marked the trail. Life was simpler there. And safer. That's when I surprised the mostly-naked man in the shelter. He yanked a sleeping bag across his mid-section, but I'd already seen too much. He shoved his tattered Penthouse magazine deep into his sleeping bag.

Crap.

AT hikers tend to make a point of respecting individuality. They live by wisdom like, "Hike your hike, let others hike theirs." The near-naked man was indeed hiking his own hike. In a manner of speaking. Still, he was excited to see me – well, not me exactly, and no, not excited like you might think, it was just that he, well … Oh, never mind, let me start again.

I was flustered and off-balance. The man greeted me like an overdue friend. It was as if he'd been waiting for me. He cleared space for my sleeping bag on the shelter floor. His bottom half was thankfully tucked inside his own sleeping bag, and he moved carefully not to expose himself. I appreciated the consideration, but it was too late for that. He rambled about how we should build a fire and cook dinner together and how glad he was to have someone to talk to.

The man gave me more than the creeps. I looked for a sizeable stick with which to bash his head should he come towards me. He seemed, though, to be more the kind of guy who might sneak up on you while you were happily sleeping. My senses tingled, and internal alarm bells blared over and over inside my head.

It was bad enough that I'd caught him in a compromising position and that he was naked from the waist down under his sleeping bag. Even worse was that while there were 10-feet of space to the left of where he lay, he graciously cleared the two-feet between his bed and the shelter wall. He patted the narrow space in a way that no doubt was intended to be inviting but which made me want to puke. I figured if I fell asleep next to him, come midnight, he'd likely destroy my airway with repeated stabs from a fork or smash my skull with a big old rock.

"Thanks," I said. "I'm not staying."

"But it'll be dark soon. There's nowhere else to stay. You have to stay here." His feigned concern was transparent. It made me want to throw up.

"I need to catch some people. There's enough daylight left to make a few more miles."

"Wouldn't you be better rested in the morning? It won't be safe hiking after dark. You really should stay here," he said. If he had been wearing pants and could have gotten out of his sleeping bag without scaring the piss out of me, I wonder if he would have come towards me, even latched onto me. Or worse.

I'd never known anyone to try so hard to get me to stay. Something about this guy wasn't right. Something about the situation wasn't right. It was a more profound fear than I'd ever experienced before or since and in an entirely nauseating sort of way.

I watched every move of his as I carefully made my getaway.

The crazy kid in North Adams made me uncomfortable, as did the woman with the trashy lingerie in Kent, but in both of them, I sensed something fundamentally positive and good and innocent. In this man, this monster, there was nothing positive or the slightest bit redeeming. The danger was palpable. It was clear, present, and genuine. The hairs stood on the back of my neck and goosebumps rose on my arms. All sorts of bells and warning whistles sounded in my head. Together they blared one message, "Run!"

The fight or flight reflex, leftovers from a more primitive time that readied cavemen to take a stand or to run like hell from saber-toothed tigers and pterodactyls, kicked into overdrive. I hit the trail like a madman, almost crazed, driven by an urgency to get away from that creature whom I suspected was a monster disguised as a man. Something was wrong there. I sensed reverberations that I could only interpret to be evil, terrifying and pure.

I took off down the trail at a pace I was confident he couldn't match even after he got his pants on and laced his boots -- unless he truly was some sort of extraterrestrial which truthfully was a possibility I could not totally discount at that point. I raced through the last miles of Connecticut like an animal until I reached Ten Mile River, and then I went on for a bit more. I remember being amazed at the lengths and consistency of my strides, how my heart failed to complain and how generally relaxed and regular my breathing stayed. "What a machine," I remember telling myself, "What a machine!" I must have been clicking along at six or seven miles per hour with a fully-loaded pack of near sixty pounds.

Oh, to be in that sort of shape again.

I glided over uphills and downs and along beautiful stretches of gentle paths, stoked on adrenalin and lost in a hiker's euphoria. I was perfectly adapted for the task at hand, a thing few of us experience regularly. Thirty years later, I remember that time still. "Better than morphine" is the best way to describe it. In ninety minutes, with a fully loaded pack, moving across unfamiliar ground as darkness descended, I eclipsed the nine-mile mark. I came to Ten Mile River, turned up a small draw to an overhanging rock, and dropped my pack. I slept there in the dark. No fire, no flashlight, no stove.

I woke late that night staring straight into a million stars. The fear had settled and dissipated to nothing and in its place was a sense of peace and a comforting presence. The aloneness that had torn me apart in Arkansas the previous summer was gone. By the time I hit New York, I'd found balance along the Appalachian Trail, and even though I was hiking by myself, I couldn't honestly admit that I was alone.

NEW YORK

From my Journal:

"Dear Joan, dear sister, you're my most faithful supporter. Your letters are so important to my feeling I still have a home. I wish I could explain how crucial it is to know that you're thinking about me. Without knowing that, I couldn't -- or maybe wouldn't -- continue. So, Joan, if I finish this trip, and when people say what a great thing it is that I've done, I want you to remember that I didn't do it; we did it together."

"Traveling alone is a good experience and a healthy challenge. Sometimes it makes me realize how little a man is without other people. Unless a man shares his thoughts, his ideas, feelings, efforts, and love with others, he's nothing-- or at least very little. Part of the natural state of being human is sharing and giving. Sometimes it's hard to do these things when you're on the trail alone. That's why it's so important for me to write letters. And to receive them."

Walking through Connecticut is where I regularly started humming the Grateful Dead song "Truckin'." I almost always sang or spoke out loud when I reached the particularly memorable line, "What a long strange trip it's been." Crossing into New York is where I adopted it as a theme song.

By New York, trail mileages were beginning to make sense. Eight-hundred miles traveled was a distance I could wrap my head around. When I thought about the thirteen-hundred miles left to travel, instead of it seeming insurmountable, I at least had a reference for understanding what it was going to require from me. On Katahdin, such a distance was barely imaginable. And two-thousand miles? It might have been the distance to the moon. By New York, I sensed I was different, maybe even better than I'd been before. Some of the ways were obvious, others not so much. I could eat six-thousand calories without thinking; coast ten miles first thing in the morning, catch an afternoon nap in the shade of a spreading tree, and then click off another ten miles by dinner. My head was different, too, for better or for worse. My thoughts naturally gravitated to topics of substance – family, future, God, creation, life, people I'd known and learned from.

By New York, I'd covered far more miles in my head than I'd traveled with my feet. The result of all that time spent thinking was greater honesty with myself and a deeper spiritual connection with most things. By then, on most days, I achieved a certain Zen as I hiked that changed my brain and filled my heart with something nearly satisfying. Now, that wasn't true every day, of course, and everything wasn't perfect. Or easy. And while making progress would never become either comfortable or perfect, by New York, lots was trending "better," -- but not everything.

Through Bear Mountain Zoo, near New York City, the AT passes immediately in front of cages filled with lions and bears. If not for the occasional blaze on the front of an animal cage, I wouldn't have believed I was still on the right route. Through the zoo, thru-hikers thread their way through throngs of clean-shaven, scrubbed, and neatly-dressed picnickers. It's a clash of cultures but not an unpleasant one.

Winding through the weekend crowds that shuffle rather than hike is in itself a surreal and unexpected experience, if not a bit dangerous. It took every bit of grace not to roll over the older folks and smallest children and otherwise distracted people moving at their own speeds. Most were far too enamored by lions and llamas and ostriches than to pay the slightest attention to a single, raggedy hiker. A lady bought me a snow cone. She just walked up and handed it to me with a smile. I think she felt sorry for me. Or I scared her. She didn't say much or even ask about the Appalachian Trail. Little acts of kindness like that, though, went a long way.

I felt quite out-of-place in that crowd and was struck with an intense longing for some overdue family time of my own. There wasn't much that could be done to battle such feelings when they arose but to hike a little faster and dream a little deeper. I found myself having conversations in my head with people I hadn't seen in a long while. They were conversations that those people would never be part of, but they were still quite important to me.

Some miles past Bear Mountain, I remember standing near a turnpike, too near civilization to feel comfortable. The trail shelter was part of a tiny neighborhood. It was a clapboard house converted for hikers' use. There was a grocery down the road and a ramshackle bike with a big basket in the garage for getting there. It seemed a reasonable place to hole up for a day, and it was early enough that just maybe some previously unknown Southbounder might catch up. I stowed my pack and rode down to the grocery, the pedal clicking loudly on the frame with every pass. It was an odd sensation to fly along at fifteen miles per hour. It felt like light speed.

I purchased an Italian sandwich, milk, ice cream, a Coke, and four or five Snickers bars at the grocery. I ate them out front, went in for more, then pedaled back to the shelter, the basket on the front of the bike almost overflowing with foodstuffs that might last another a few days but for me would amount to a satisfying dinner.

It had been days since I'd hiked with anyone, and I was traveling faster than the Southbound pack which was small that year. As far as I knew, it consisted only of Kenny Bob, the Fireman, the White Rabbit, a guy named Peyton and his girlfriend, Susan, a guy named Tall Pall, and some guy who went by the name The Cosmic Yankee. He was just rumored to exist until I finally met him in North Carolina or maybe Georgia months later. He breezed past, we exchanged niceties, and that was it. There may have been others, but I never met them.

I settled in at the shelter with the copy of A Connecticut Yankee in King Arthur's Court a hiker from Australia had given me back in Connecticut or maybe Massachusetts. I found Mark Twain made for great reading along the AT. I learned residents of Connecticut are officially called Connecticuters or Nutmeggers, apparently. Mark Twain characterized them far differently than I would have based on my limited experience of those I'd recently encountered in Kent.

I'd just settled in on the wooden bunk, made it through half-a-page or so when the kid came in. He was nineteen or twenty, maybe, and not a hiker. His clean-shaven, pale skin and neatly-combed hair made that obvious. He wasn't threatening, just a little creepy. He seemed to be trying to gauge me somehow. I guess I was doing the same to him. I tried to project complete and utter disinterest in him or anything about him. I barely looked up from my book.

"You hiking the trail?" He was uncomfortable in his own skin, it seemed; like he was hiding something maybe.

"Yeah." I kept my nose in the book.

"Is it fun?" It seemed like he was digging for a connection.

"Fun? It depends on what you call fun. It's a lot of work." This time I looked up from the book; he looked past me like making eye contact wasn't possible. Or comfortable.

"You staying here tonight?"

"Probably not." The longer he stayed, I reasoned, the more likely I wouldn't be staying.

"You should. Lots of people do."

"You a hiker?"

"No."

"What do you do?"

"Nothing."

"School?"

"No."

"Have a job?"

"No."

"What are you doing here?"

"Nothing. I live nearby."

"What are you reading?"

"A book by Mark Twain," I held it up for him to see the title and buried my nose further into the book.

An uncomfortable silence followed and then he was gone.

Just as I settled back into the book and the relative security of the place, he was back and standing uncomfortably close in front of me. "Can I ask you a personal question?" Now he looked right into my eyes, and my heart beat faster. The world came to a standstill. I wasn't sure things were as they should be.

"What?" I wasn't sure I'd heard him correctly.

"Can I ask you a personal question?"

I should have said, "No," but I didn't. Instead, against my better judgment, I politely nodded.

"Can I give you a blowjob?"

"What?" I wasn't sure I'd heard him right. No, I knew I'd heard him right, I just needed a few seconds to figure out if the situation posed any danger or if it was just hugely awkward. He repeated his question. Despite the complete unraveling of my composure internally, externally, and throughout, I remained poised mostly, "No, thank you," I said. "No, thank you," I thought? Not all situations call for such politeness.

He turned and left quickly, and I packed in a hurry. I wasn't convinced that he was an evil kid or that I was in danger, but luck favors the prepared. I looped a bandana through the top of my metal water bottle to improvise a makeshift medieval mace of sorts. I hurried to move on from there. His idea of that place as paradise was undoubtedly not the same as mine.

And then he was back, sheepish and stressed, paler than before, looking like he'd been smacked down hard, and my heart beat even faster. I was concerned, not scared exactly, but I picked up the half-full water bottle and gauged the arc of a swing that would catch him squarely on the side of the head. "Yes?"

" I just want you to know I'm not gay."

"What?"

"I'm not gay."

"I don't care." He turned toward the door, defeated, deflated and filled with sadness. I felt bad for him. No one should feel that way. "Then what are you doing?" I asked.

"I don't know. I'm bored, I guess." He didn't turn towards me. He just looked down.

That set me off. I tried not to lecture, but I couldn't stop myself completely. "Bored? Hell, if you're bored do something worthwhile. Get a job; go to school; build something; join the army. Hell, Go hike the Appalachian Trail. Doing stuff like this -- stuff that makes you feel like crap -- isn't going to get you anywhere. At least nowhere good." He listened intently, at least seemed to, and finally made eye contact. "You have to take charge if you want good things in your life. Pick a place to go and busy yourself getting where you want to go. That's what you need to do."

"Damn," I thought. "I wish someone had lectured me like that -- about making better choices for living a better life."

"I do want good things in my life," he said.

"Then you've got to make them happen."

It wasn't precisely a therapeutic exchange; mostly I just wanted out of there without getting my throat slit. I've sometimes thought about that young man and so many others that find themselves stuck in places they don't want to be. Maybe that's where I was thirty years ago in some ways – stuck. Taking risks associated with a thru-hike, especially the emotional ones and those related to fears of failing, were perhaps the perfect tonic for me in that situation. They freed me.

I've often heard people lament about never being able to or never having taken the opportunity to pursue their own epic adventure. They've admittedly struggled because of it. And that's too bad. Few among us, I believe, would not reap benefits from setting a target that seems too big, investing more than they can afford to lose in pursuit of that goal, and then setting off into the unknown to test themselves sensibly.

Want some advice from this book? That's it. Test yourself sensibly. That's one ticket to better days for a long time to come.

If there's a contribution I hope to make to the "science of living" it's the idea summed up in this line from a 1987 journal post: "Everyone should hike AN Appalachian Trail but not necessarily THE Appalachian Trail."

Adventuring is good for the soul, maybe even necessary for finding peace and balance in one's life. My Appalachian Trail happened to be the Appalachian Trail, and for that I'm thankful. Setting a goal, stretching boundaries, and committing to the process of reaching that goal despite hardships is an important, even essential, part of growing up well.

I hope that the boy grew up well. More than anything, I'm pleased I didn't hit him upside the head with my water bottle. That's not at all what he needed that day or what any of us need on any other day.

New York was hot as fire that summer and dry enough to burn. The thirteen-hundred miles ahead to Springer seemed longer than the original twenty-one-hundred miles I faced from Katahdin. I was alone and lonely. Something was wrong with my right foot; every step hurt. I wanted to cry out every with every three-foot of progress. I hadn't spoken to a soul for two-days, and it was hard to find anything uplifting in the New York forest. It was desolate and not so stunning as Maine or New Hampshire. Not even close. Everything was hot and brown and dry, and every step wore me down just a bit more. Finally, I gave in. I collapsed on a boulder and quit. I quit the whole God-damned thing. "I'm done," I screamed to the rocks and trees and burst into tears. "Dad, you were right," I shouted out loud, tears streaming down my face. "This was the stupidest damn thing ever."

Three days, I figured, and I'd be back in Missouri. I didn't care that I'd go home a quitter, tail between my legs, no prospects and nothing to brag about. I'd deal with that crap later, I told myself. I'd had enough. Sure, I'd seen some great things and hiked more than 800 miles, but there were thirteen-hundred more to go, and traveling alone wasn't much fun.

I wasn't cut out for this, I told myself. Not even thinking of those boys from Tenth Mountain Division and that plaque on Mount Washington inspired me in the slightest.

So, I sat on that rock a good long while. I waited for somebody to rescue me, but nobody ever came. Emotionally, I was wrecked; my water bottles were empty, and frankly, I was feeling pretty empty every other way, too. I didn't have many choices left. I pulled my sorry ass off that rock and limped towards the nearest water source, a spring some miles further on where the trail crossed the Orange Turnpike.

It took a while, but I made it to that spring. There was no bounce left in my step or in my spirit. And the spring didn't do much to help. It was almost disappointing, not much more than a metal pipe coming out of a rock and a trickle dripping into a shallow puddle. It was cold and clear, though. I sat there, pissed at the world, angry and heartsick, trying to figure things out. All I knew is that I was heading home. That morning I awakened as an AT thru-hiker. By late that afternoon, I would just be a guy who quit because his foot hurt and he was tired of being alone.

That's when she pulled up in the beat-up Ford. Neither car nor woman was much to look at. Even if they were, I didn't want to be bothered or cheered up. I did my best to let her know that I didn't care about her or anything else and that I wished she would leave. Her car had seen better days, and I told her so; I shared my surprise that it got her anywhere at all. I responded with one-word answers; no smiles; little eye contact. Honestly, I was a genuine ass.

She didn't seem to notice. She filled her jug and left, all the while smiling pleasantly and talking about the wild blueberries covering the hills. Apparently, it was a pretty good year for them, but a lousy one for me.

I was glad to see her go, but I felt pretty crappy about the way I'd treated her. I wasn't that sort of person, I reminded myself, but I knew I'd done her wrong, and she was just trying to be kind. I was sorry and bitter and feeling guilty, wishing I had a second chance to make amends. I was, at that point wishing I had a whole slew of second chances. Oh, well, I figured, seemed like I was going to be dealing with shitty feelings like those for quite some time.

I prayed out loud, spoke what I could remember of a verse from the gospel of Matthew I'd once committed to memory:

"Therefore I tell you, do not worry about your life, what you will eat or drink; or about your body, what you will wear. Is not life more than food, and the body more than clothes? Look at the birds of the air: They do not sow or reap or gather into barns — and yet your Heavenly Father feeds them. Are you not much more valuable than they? Who of you by worrying can add a single hour to his lifespan?" (Matthew 6:25-27).

Praying didn't help. I sat there feeling defeated and stupid. I didn't have the slightest clue which way to go -- where the nearest bus stop was or the nearest pay phone. Which way should I head? East, west, south, or north. Who knew? I certainly did not. None of my maps or trail guides or even the Philosopher's Guide said anything about how to run away from the trail.

And then she was back, the lady in the beat up Ford. She had to keep her foot on the accelerator to keep the motor running. She motioned me to the car. I approached cautiously. She had every reason to shoot me or splatter me with paint or spit on me for being a jerk earlier. I expected the worst. I approached cautiously, got within a few feet of her, and then she extended a six-pack of Coca-Cola out of the window. Hitting me with a sledgehammer might have achieved less of a reaction; I deserved nothing from her, and yet here she was. Feeding me with kindness. She smiled softly, kindly; told me she hoped my day got better, and said, "Who can add a single hour to his lifespan by worrying?"

Actually, I'm just kidding. I made up that last part. The woman didn't say that. As if she had, though, the words bounced around in my head. "Who can add a single hour to his lifespan by worrying?" I warmed to her, warmed to the world, took the gift, smiled at her, thanked her graciously, and settled back at the edge of the spring and watched her drive off.

I drank one, then chugged a second, slurped a third and tucked the other three in my pack for later. It was the woman's gesture, her smile, and her encouragement that gave me the strength to stand, forget my troubles -- at least for the moment -- turn South and keep going at least for a while.

That's all it took though to give me the strength to weather that crisis – a little kindness from a stranger. It was August. Without her, there would have been no September, October, or November on the Appalachian Trail for me. And no Springer Mountain. She, more than anyone, was my trail angel.

Make no mistake. It wasn't caffeine and sugar that changed my life; it was the simple kindness of a stranger. My journey would have ended there on the Orange Turnpike without her gifts – the smiles more than the six-pack. Without them, I would have stood on the Orange Turnpike, stuck my thumb out and beat a hasty retreat home. The 10,000 days after that, I wager, would not have been the same.

In 1987, I never heard anyone speak the specific words, "Trail Magic," though it was frequently encountered. It's now part of the language and culture of the Appalachian Trail. "Trail Angels" from Maine to Georgia stand poised to share food, drinks, and well-wishes with thru-hikers as they pass. I wonder if those angels understand their potential to change the world with their tiny gestures.

I've told the story of the angel I encountered along the Orange Turnpike a thousand times. It resonates with nearly most people. I wish I could thank her, that unsung hero of my life, but I know too little to find her. I know I'll never be able to thank her. To those reading this, I do have a favor to ask. Perhaps you can celebrate her by following her example and the example of so many other trail angels? Do something for someone in need. And it doesn't have to happen along the AT. It doesn't have to be much, maybe just enough to unseat their anger or to buy them the slightest peace that allows them to re-focus. Kindness, as small as it might be, could change the future for one or for many.

That was thirty years ago, and her gesture still matters. It changed the trajectory of my life.

Later that same day, I met a couple who drove me down the road and treated me to a burger, fries, and a big chocolate shake. Not long after that, I met 3 northbound hikers, one of whom treated me to Coke and ice cream. Later that evening, I stopped at a small fruit stand to buy several potatoes for dinner. The spirited lady behind the counter insisted I take two ears of corn, an onion, and a big, red-ripe tomato as well. Then she tossed me a ripe, red plum as I walked away. What a feast it was that night. Isn't it wonderful how the Lord answers our prayers! And that plum? Well, it might have been the sweetest I've ever tasted.

I went to bed strong that night and filled with energy that carried me the next 100 miles.

Unionville, New York, was a quaint little village then, the kind of place strangers didn't go unnoticed, especially bearded ones with backpacks who lounged in the park at the town's center.

On the way into town, I picked my way daintily through a field of chest-high poison ivy, when quite unexpectedly, I encountered a man hiking in nothing but boots and a backpack. Nothing. He was polite as could be, even

119

stepped to the side to allow me to pass on the narrow trail. He stepped directly into the poison ivy and stood patiently.

We shared a few words, I maintained eye contact as I've never maintained eye contact with anyone ever before. I chose to say nothing about the poison ivy. As we shared trailside pleasantries, I couldn't resist asking where his clothes were. I expected a simple response but instead heard a lengthy tale about an estranged wife, an ill-advised visit to her place of employment with a rifle that he used to shoot off the lock on the door, a few nights in jail, probation, and now having plenty of time on his hands for naked hiking. He was the most pleasant of fellows.

Later that night, I noted the encounter with an entry in my journal, "Ran into a naked guy in a field of poison ivy outside of Unionville. He was bat-shit crazy. What a long strange trip it's been."

A few yards beyond, I mumbled, "But for the grace of God go I," and made a mental note to tell Lori that she would never need to worry about me going off the deep end like the naked hiker.

I walked into Unionville, shaking my head, to wait for my parents who were navigating by roadmap from Missouri to this place. It was an essential skill in those days, reading maps. There was no GPS. Instead, there was an atlas under the front seat of every car, and every glovebox was stuffed with torn and tattered state maps that had been folded and refolded a thousand times. That's how you found your way from point to point back then -- with maps and by asking directions. Traveling so far, me on foot and them by car, and without cell phones or any other way to update connections, "We'll get there around 4 pm," really meant, "We'll see you when we see you."

I stopped in at the local inn to buy a Coke. In casual conversation with the older woman at the counter, I mentioned the young man in the poison ivy field outside of town. I didn't make mention that he was buck-naked.

"Tommy?" The woman asked with the patience of a devoted grandmother. "Was he wearing clothes? He is an interesting young man, isn't he? He was the nicest boy growing up. Still is, though, he's a little off since that woman he married done him wrong. He'll bend over backward, though, if you ever were to need his help."

Her last comment conjured the wrong image, and I chose not to continue the conversation. I took the Coke to the porch, sat in a rocker, and sipped it in the heat.

Mom and Dad were driving in from Missouri with my sister and brother-in-law. Ostensibly, it was a stop on their vacation route, but I knew better. They were there to lay eyes on me -- to be sure I was okay, and maybe even to wrestle me home if my condition didn't meet their expectations. They pulled in surprisingly close to 4 pm. There were hugs and comments about thinness and roughness, and Mom said, "Don't worry. We'll feed you well." And she did, but how could she have known what a thru-hiker eats? We drove to a campground, where I don't remember. Dinner that night was a favorite meal from our family camping trips as kids – a stew of green beans, and potatoes simmered with chunks of ham. What Mom made for the five of us, would nearly have been enough for a single thru-hiker. When no one was looking, I downed a couple of Snickers bars.

These were "my people," I knew, and they were beautiful, and for the first time in two-and-a-half months, I was home. Their visit gave me strength as it always had even before I ventured out on the AT

There's no need to wax philosophical about family and its importance, I know. It may not add to our physical strength, but it adds to our ability to push through tough encounters. That's something I'm sure of. I didn't hike the Appalachian Trail alone or mostly alone. I managed it as part of a family. Every moment of every day, I sensed that without their support, I wouldn't have weathered the challenges. I intentionally say, "I wouldn't have weathered the challenges," instead of saying, "I couldn't have weathered the challenges." Physical strength was never the deciding factor. Motivation was. There wasn't a hill I couldn't climb, but without their support, it's entirely likely I wouldn't have found a reason to keep climbing those hills.

We camped in their style for a few days – a big tent, big stove, dining fly, plates, cups, and tablecloth with clips to hold it in place during a still breeze.

It was the morning before they left that my father said, "Let's take a walk."

We walked for a while without talking about anything important -- how the baseball Cardinals were doing, whether the food boxes he mailed every week or so were ample, and about how the heat had scorched the grass back home. And then he changed his tone. "We could make room in the car for you and your pack." After a pause, he said, "You don't have to keep on if you don't want to. Nobody will judge you. Me least of all." At that moment, he was as fatherly and supportive as any human I'd ever known. Or even heard of. It caught me in the throat. "You didn't expect to do this on by yourself. Everybody understands that."

121

It took a minute to recover before I could speak, "I'm not ready to quit. I've got more miles in me. And I'm not afraid to come home."

"Okay," he said. "Just know you can come home without shame any time." There was not the slightest judgment or impatience or "I told you so" in his voice. There was just the love of a father.

God, how fortunate I am to have had that one moment with my father.

I nodded. It would have been unwise to try to speak. I would have broken down.

We walked a while more, not speaking; then he said, "Eight hundred miles is a long way. Lots of people are following your hike. People I've never even met before stop by my office to ask how you're doing and where you are. They're all keeping track. You've made me a bit of a celebrity at work." He stopped short of saying, "I'm proud of you," but I knew that's what he meant."

"If everything goes well," I told him, "I'll be home sometime in November." It was August 13th.

"You have enough money?"

I nodded. "I'll be okay."

He handed me a one-hundred dollar bill. "Just in case."

I doubt he told my mom about that conversation. Or the hundred dollars. He was that sort of man. He spoke what he had to say with an economy of words. He kept secrets. He was a good father.

I wanted to ask him if he still thought hiking the AT was "the stupidest thing he'd ever heard." I was pretty sure he didn't, but there was no need to make him say so.

NEW JERSEY

From my Journal:

August 14, 1987

"And yet to comprehend what the vague words, '800 miles of rugged mountains and dismal deserts' mean, one must go over the ground in person. Pain and descriptions cannot convey the dreary reality to the reader." -- Mark Twain

"As of today, I've traveled 900 miles or more. I won't attempt a feeble description of my trip. May it suffice to say that I've experienced a thousand emotions, felt a million sensations, and seen a billion shadows of beauty. That and more have made me a very different man."

Most everything I'd ever known about Jersey I learned through the lens of reality TV and exaggerated depictions of tough guys and in-your-face attitudes. I only remember meeting two human beings as I crossed the state. One of them reinforced those stereotypes; the other dispelled them.

I climbed into High Point State Park on a beautiful day and filled my water bottles at a fountain near the monument there dedicated to war dead. I took a seat on the water fountain. It was built from stone and stainless steel and basked all day in the sun. All the metal parts were hot enough to burn your skin if you touched them. The view was extraordinary and the breeze quite pleasant despite the heat.

The caretaker wore a uniform and carried himself as if he marched among the elite of law enforcement. He took his job seriously. His cleaning supplies were arranged in neatly in a plastic tote; he scrubbed and swept every last speck of dirt and dust and grime from the sidewalk as he made his way towards me. I quite enjoyed watching the pride he took in a task most might consider menial.

Then, he saw me perched on the fountain. His expression changed as if from day to night. He approached directly, almost aggressively, and spoke with a practically impossible-to-understand accent which I interpreted as American a style of speaking as any I'd ever heard. Only accents encountered in Maine's backcountry were as difficult for my southern-tuned ear to understand. It seemed to be an amalgamation of every dialect and regional accent from the last two-hundred years without the slightest influence of a southern drawl. There was a roughness about him and a bluntness that aligned with everything I'd ever heard about New Jersey. Don't mess with Texas? I got the message that messing with New Jersey might be an even worse idea.

"We don't put our butts on places where we drink." That was, I interpreted, his way of politely asking me to get off the water fountain. I knew, though, there was a veiled inference in his statement too; one that might suggest he'd smack me in the head with his broomstick if I didn't.

"That's how people get AIDS," he scolded. It was the middle 1980's, and some things were deeply steeped in myth and misinformation. I started to launch into a lecture about how HIV and AIDS and how neither was communicated by a man sitting on a water fountain, but looking into the man's eyes convinced me it would take too much effort. And likely be a waste of time. His and mine. I picked up my gear, bid him good day, and lumbered off without saying much. As I did, he squirted the fountain generously with pink liquid from a spray bottle and scrubbed the fountain vigorously.

"Damned hikers," I heard him mumble. "Think they own the place."

I smiled to myself, quite glad the man took his job so seriously and genuinely impressed by his convictions. I wondered for a short while what it might mean if I approached work and life with such commitment.

I'm sure I grumbled some, too, as I descended from there until I looked around and realized New Jersey was indeed a beautiful place. What a pleasant surprise! And then I came to Sunfish Pond. It was peaceful and unassuming, the kind of place created, it seemed, for lounging in the sunshine with family and friends or all alone. And picnicking. It conjured images of family gatherings when I was young and fishing from the bank of a pond back home with worms and a red and white bobber. What a treasure such places are.

Half-way around the pond, I quite unexpectedly came upon a rattlesnake, fat and happy in the center of the trail. Had he not politely warned me with an abrupt rattling of his tail, I'd have tread on him squarely, and he, motivated by a will to live and without animosity, would likely have bitten my ankle and changed the course of my trek.

The snake and I shared a few moments there in the sunshine. He was intensely ugly and beautiful all at once and entirely polite and unbothered by my presence. Eventually, he slithered off into the forest. Neither he nor I was the slightest bit impatient with the other. Had either of us been so, I imagine, either I would have wound up in the emergency room, or he'd have lost his head – literally.

"How gentlemanly," I thought of that snake. Such courteousness was not what I expected from New Jersey. In contrast to the caretaker at the monument, the snake represented the 9 million people of New Jersey quite well. He portrayed them as I believe they'd have wanted to be portrayed -- polite, unmoving, respectful, tough, measured, and not beyond leaving you howling in the trail if you didn't give them space.

I sidestepped the snake and kept heading south, aware that the trail was getting more rocky and treacherous by the mile. Pennsylvania was ahead. Eons before, retreating glaciers had abandoned so many rocks and boulders as to make smooth going nearly impossible for hikers for the next hundred miles or so.

I can't recall speaking to any other human as I trekked through New Jersey. There was a man who nodded at me as he headed with an old cane pole towards Sunfish Pond. I must have passed people others, but it wasn't a weekend, and if there were chance encounters on the trail, none have stuck in my brain thirty years later. Perhaps I should have done more to initiate meaningful conversations.

There were barely forty miles of trail through New Jersey, yet like everywhere else, nature flourished there.

Like a medicine cabinet packed with healing potions and properties, nature overflowed everywhere along the AT Every step, every breath, and every vista was like a dose from that storehouse of natural cures that improved health, strength, and well-being almost with every step. I've never been stronger (and hurt more). And seldom happier.

I walked away from the trail experience knowing something about Nature. It is the cure for most anything that ails you, and for me, five-million steps became a healthy addiction. Sure, there have been times when I've gotten stupid and careless and side-tracked; times when I've neglected to immerse myself in wild places; times when I've let stress and the crazy pace of everyday life get the best of me, but I've never forgotten where real peace is to be found -- outside. Even in New Jersey.

We forget how fortunate we are to live in this country with millions of acres of wide open spaces. There's a reason we sing, "This land is my land; this land is your land." Because the trees and forests and lakes belong to us. Public lands are bequeathed to all of us for recreation, enjoyment, and exploration. And they are protected from exploitation. They are the foundation of our collective health physically, mentally, emotionally, and spiritually.

It wouldn't be such a bad idea to get out and enjoy our open spaces even more. And protect them with more vigilance. There are few nations on earth which provide their populace with such access to remote and wild places.

Public lands are at the center of the most remarkable public health system in the world. Feeling blue? Go outside. Under the weather? Breathe fresh air – lots of it. Struggling with meaning? Take a journey. Want to avoid feeling crappy in general? Live right in a naturally beautiful place. Hike, run, paddle, climb. Pastimes like these surrounded by trees and hills and clear skies are the ticket to longer and more satisfying lives. If only more of us would embrace opportunities to get outside, we'd collectively enjoy life more and likely live longer, more productive lives.

Public lands are the foundation of our nation's health. And strength. In those terms, the value of resources like the Appalachian Trail is staggering. All we need to do is get off our collective butts and take advantage of what's available.

Every landscape and skyscape; every tree, bug and clear-running stream added to the wonder of the Appalachian Trail. And it does the same for every tentative day-hiker or sure-footed thru-hiker. What a resource it is; what a blessing! So many uplifting images, thirty years later, are still within easy reach. I just need to close my eyes to find a unique brand of peacefulness spawned in any one of fourteen states.

In Maine, there were moose and bear and a fascinating assortment of leeches in the ponds. My favorite was the slow and docile cow leech, a particularly entertaining plaything in the icy cold waters in June. From end-to-end, there was so much to discover and so much to contemplate. New Hampshire was filled with vistas and raspberries, huckleberries and maple syrup in little roadside stands. There were porcupines in Vermont, gentle slopes, and the grass was as green there as anywhere I'd ever been. The beaver that lived along iron-colored streams in Massachusetts sometimes shattered still night with warning slaps of tails in the holding ponds forced by their home-built dams. The cathedral pines in Connecticut were breathtaking and the sound of running streams so soothing. Throughout New York, there were blueberries thick as carpet and sweet as sugar. There was the gentlemanly rattlesnake and the serenity of Sunfish Pond in New Jersey, peaceful and embracing. There were magnificent views throughout Pennsylvania and Maryland of unending expanses of farmland and clear endless skies. There were spectacular sunsets, too, and an occasional buck, majestic as some ancient king. West Virginia rivers were gorgeous, and the approach to Harpers Ferry, looking down on the streams that converged there was a view second to none. Through Virginia, there was some of everything – bears and mountains, apple trees left from farms long-gone, and a million wildflowers or more. The way fall colors played among the Tennessee and North Carolina mountains was hypnotic and mystical and magical. And in Georgia, as leaves fell from the treetops and left a clear skyward view, the crystal clarity of the night-time sky was so star-filled, sharp and clear, that sometimes I was so overwhelmed I forgot to breathe.

Every state offered something different; each provided a soul-filling dose of nature guaranteed to heal not just for the moment but forever after. Thirty-thousand days later, I still reap the health benefits of time spent immersed in Nature.

I knew so little about New Jersey then; and I know so little now, too, except what I've gathered from tiny glimpses of reality TV. But I know a secret about New Jersey -- Parts are beautiful, and it deserves the moniker, "The Garden State." I've never been back there, but I find it funny that despite the stereotypes of the roughness and brashness of the place and the people, it's where nature's overwhelming healing power embraced me so thoroughly at the calming edge of a quiet little pond. And that a kindly rattlesnake played a significant role in shaping my positive regard for that part of the trail.

PENNSYLVANIA

<u>August 16, 1987</u>

From my Journal:

"Last night I stood on the Kittatinny Ridge, just north of Lehigh Gap, and watched a thunderstorm roll in. It was a beautiful night; clear, warm, and moist. The rising winds were cool and energized with the power of the approaching storm. I stood alone above the lights of Palmerton, Pennsylvania, amidst the quiet of cicadas and rustling leaves, amazed, enthralled, and involved in a great symphonic movement. I felt as if I belonged on that ridge as much as the rocks and trees and wind. As a charge gathered in the air and grew, the hair on my arms would rise to meet the flash of lightning. Then the whole world jumped to life as a million strangely silhouetted shapes, and the sky exploded in a thunderous crash that trailed far off into the distance. And then there was stillness, briefly, as the Heavens built to another glorious display."

"Around me, the violence of nature swirled and added to my peacefulness. Like a man from a million years ago, I stood alone on the ridge filled with wonder, filled with life, filled with celebration. 'God is near' I thought. 'How curious it is that I should find peace in a violent storm; that amid the chaos of a summer squall, I should sense order within."

"As the rains came, my excitement mounted to a near-frenzied state. I wanted to shout, to sing, to praise the glory of the Lord! Words don't matter at such a moment; only feelings and sensations and movements hold substance. I suppose I danced as droplets splashed and cooled my face. What refreshment! What glorious refreshment! Wind and water and lightning and thunder! At last, filled and satisfied, I breathed deeply and left the ridge to seek shelter and a night's rest."

Sixteen miles on a foot that may well have been fractured was Hell. I'd hoped to make Neys Shelter seven miles further on, but I wasn't moving like myself, and it was nearly dark. I limped into tiny Port Clinton, Pennsylvania, without ceremony, hoping others like me would be there, needing a hiking companion. But there was no one there, and no greetings, no acknowledgments, and no fanfare. Still, it had been a good day, sixteen plus miles; there was no news of anyone I knew in the trail register. That meant I'd gained half a day on hikers I called "friends" even though I could barely remember more than their trail names.

Three back-to-back twenty mile days and I'd likely catch them. Unfortunately, success mostly depended on being able to push through the pain of an injured foot. A handful of ibuprofen tablets now and then, clear weather and early starts would go a long way towards catching them. A half-assed day of hiking or two or a full day of rest and any chance of catching them might be gone completely.

Maine through New York, and especially in New Hampshire, I met an abundance of Northbounders. Whether sharing a shelter or just a few minutes trailside, when North- and Southbounders crossed paths, lively discussions were the result. There were stories and insights to share about what lay ahead – the best places to eat, where to find water, places to avoid, great swimming holes, shelters worth visiting, people to avoid and people who were particularly fun to hang out with. The exchanges made it possible to keep up with people and to plan one's route in advance. By mid-August, there were almost no Northbound hikers still south of where I was in Pennsylvania.

For Northbounders, summiting Katahdin gets exponentially more difficult after October 15. Snow and ice and restricted park access complicate things immensely, make it more dangerous, and a whole less predictable. If they're not off the mountain by October 15, they might not complete their thru-hike until the following spring. For Southbounders, a lack of water in trailside springs and streams and cold temperatures become the chief villains.

After mid-August, once the field of Northbounders had passed, information about who was ahead and by how far and where the nearest water sources and amenities were was getting tougher to find. It's not that traveling alone was a bad thing, I just missed the camaraderie.

Port Clinton was a ghost town that night, almost completely still. It was a tiny blue-collar burg; peaceful enough. At the town's center was a wooden pavilion where hikers were welcome to sleep. The floor was concrete. Sleeping in the center of town seemed exposed but safe. There was a laminated sheet tacked to the wall with directions to the nearest water, restrooms, telephone, and food. Around the corner, a half-mile or so was the CCC diner, closed then, but opening at 7 am. The CCC Diner had a reputation. Good food, simplicity, and friendly to hikers.

Loneliness is a pretty strong motivator to get your ass out of bed early and to get an early start. I got up before the sun and was waiting at the door to the

CCC Diner when it opened. It was just around the corner and down the road. Their pancakes and coffee were legendary among hikers.

It was 7:00 am, the weather was clear, and I sat in the diner waiting, hot coffee in hand, for a steaming plate of pancakes, ham, eggs, toast, grits, sausage, French toast, and biscuits. The waitress smiled, "You expecting somebody else?"

"Nope." It was an excellent start to what I expected to be an excellent day.

The waitress's smile was the sweet sort that had she been twenty years younger or me twenty years older might have given me a reason to stay in Port Clinton. She was another of the pleasant people along the trail who left me with a sense of well-being and pride in the hardworking and unheralded sorts who are the backbone of out-of-the-way and off-the-beaten-path America.

I was glad to see there wasn't another soul in the place. I wasn't particularly sociable or jolly that morning even though she made me want to be. I was intent on getting an early start; I wanted to catch my hiking band, and I wanted desperately to move past traveling alone. I was feeling good, starving and thankful for something other than instant oatmeal and cocoa this morning, ready to eat like a horse and cruise like a madman 20 miles or more.

That's when the silence shattered. The stillness was wrecked by the roar engines, ten or maybe twenty, all revving as one, screaming like banshees, and then, all at once, coming to a simultaneous stop. "What the hell was that?" I said out loud, looking over my shoulder at the door. Everything was still inside, but I could see figures, a lot of them, moving outside the windows. And then there the voices outside grew louder, the shadows through the windows got closer, and the door banged open.

They stomped in like a band of stormtroopers, a dozen of them, at least, dressed for the road almost entirely in leather. Collectively, they jingled as they moved. They were decked out in so many buckles and dangling chains. They were boisterous and loud, they filled the place with voices and helmets, scrubby beards, bandanas, and creaking leather. They looked more like seasoned warriors ready for battle than men looking for pancakes. They crowded around the tables in front of me, behind me, and sat damned-near next to me.

There was nowhere to run. I was pretty sure I was dead.

I stared straight-on at my pancakes, afraid I might otherwise make eye contact with one and wind up without a trachea as a result. I tried to be small and inconspicuous. Suddenly, I was less hungry than before. It seemed, as the food arrived, I'd ordered a ridiculously huge amount. I wanted to tell the waitress to quit bringing stuff; that she was attracting too much attention my way; but the food was too fantastic, and the coffee, well, I'd never been one to turn down a third or even fourth cup even at risk of bodily harm. "God," I prayed, "get me out of this."

Fifteen minutes, I guessed, and it would all be over – my brief time on earth. National news, yep, I could just imagine the headlines, "Bikers Devour Hiker, Skip Pancakes" "Hiker Should have Listened to Dad, Stayed Home." Me and my pack, I figured, were destined to be their morning's entertainment, both to be dragged out back and the contents of both of us to be spilled by a switchblade knife and scattered unceremoniously through the woods in back in a frenetic feeding frenzy.

Crap, I thought. Dad was right. Stupidest thing ever. I could be in my office at the university eating an Egg McMuffin and drinking a large coffee with three shots of cream, I thought. Instead, I was in the CCC Diner eating the best pancakes in the history of Earth, sipping excellent coffee, about to be torn to shreds by a pack of marauding bikers.

I wore a banana on my head; the tail trailed down my neck and back pirate-style. My hair was long, and my beard thick enough. If not for the short nylon shorts and gaiters, I wore I might have almost blended in with them. I expected a big beefy hand to encircle my neck and yank me out of my chair at any second. I braced myself. Instead, it was a warm breath in my ear, and a voice, thick with an exaggerated pirate's accent asked, "Arrrrgh, Matey, can you pass me the salt?"

I froze. I was pretty sure I was dead. Or about to be. It was the beginning of my last 15 minutes on earth. What would Clint Eastwood do? Or Stallone? Or Jackie Chan? There was no option, I decided, but to face them. I turned towards the voice and passed the salt.

"Thanks," the man with the biggest beard said politely. His tone was gruff, but not what I expected. "Where you headed?"

"Georgia."

"Long way to walk," he seemed unimpressed. "Where'd you come from?"

"Maine."

"Maine? That's a thousand miles!" Now, he was genuinely impressed. "You walked a thousand miles? Dang." He turned to the stormtroopers at his table, "This guy hiked a thousand miles from Maine. Ain't that cool?"

He turned back to me. "I bet you got stories to spare."

His buddies thought it was pretty cool, too. They pulled in close, two joined me at my table, brought their coffee mugs with them. They fired questions my way, one after another.

"What do you do for food? Kill things along the way?"

"What's your old lady think of this?"

"You carrying?"

"Had any trouble with the law?"

"Could a guy do that trail on a bike?"

Stupid me, I asked, "On a bicycle?"

They laughed and shook their heads. "No man, on a MOTOR-cycle."

It was a spirited conversation for the next half-hour. And fun. And innocent. We downed plenty of coffee; told lots of stories, laughed a lot. I had people to catch further up the trail, though, and told them so. I stood to say goodbye. The meanest-looking among my new friends, Joe, spoke up in a gravelly voice. "We're heading to a rendezvous next county over. Music. Free grub. Women. You can ride on the back of my bike. Spike, there, can strap your pack to his bike."

No kidding. One of the guys was named Spike. He looked like he might eat you for breakfast if you crossed him in the slightest. He was more than willing to accommodate my pack, though.

I politely refused. "I got places to be." They understood.

Spike offered to run me a few miles down the road if I wanted. "No, thanks. I've walked every step so far. I don't want to get to the end and remember the one stretch I skipped."

They all nodded in agreement and grunted small words of approval if I'd just preached an inspiring sermon.

So, I went to the bathroom, left my pack leaning against the table, something I wouldn't likely do anywhere else. These men weren't thieves, though, I gathered. They were adventurers like me, and not in the least ways hard to trust. We said our goodbyes as kindred spirits, both a little in awe and envious of the other's freedom. I made my way to the restroom, where I more or less bathed in the sink. When I got back, they'd gone. Not surprisingly, my backpack leaned against the table still.

Unmolested. I walked to the waitress, cash in hand, "How much do I owe you?"

Gosh, she was pretty.

"Nothing," she smiled. "They settled your bill. Wanted me to wish you well." Hers was an amazing smile, a little seductive, a bit mysterious, and a whole lot friendly. "Good luck," she said softly and squeezed my hand. Maybe she knew I was a little smitten. Or she was glad I had survived breakfast.

I tossed five bucks on the table, stepped out the door and turned south.

Not too far outside of Port Clinton, I stopped to fill my water bottles and brush my teeth at a small trailside spigot. While brushing and flossing, an older, rather unhealthy woman walked-up and began asking about the trail. In the course of our conversation, I mentioned that one of my favorite parts of the day was brushing my teeth. "If I can't keep the rest of me clean," I told her, "at least I can keep my teeth clean."

"Ooooh, that's so important, she said. "I feel the same way!" She repeated that over and over as we talked -- mostly about dental hygiene -- for the next fifteen minutes. It's funny how when you're a thru-hiking, brushing and flossing in front of a total stranger doesn't feel the slightest bit unnatural.

"Now don't you leave just yet," she said. "I've got something for you. I'll be back in a jiffy. Just stay put 5 minutes." She hurried away with a purpose to her step.

As promised, she was back in a few minutes. She handed me a small, unopened tube of toothpaste. "Now you can think of me every time you brush," she said.

I thanked her, saddled my pack, and smiled at her one last time. As I did, she flashed an amazingly wide grin, one filled with four brown, broken, and crooked teeth. I walked away laughing some, shaking my head, and humming, "What a long strange trip it's been." As for her gift of the toothpaste, I guess she didn't have plans for it anyway.

Pennsylvania, despite the rocks, was beautiful.

MARYLAND

From my Journal:

   "I have never worked so hard for one thing in my life as I have to fill myself
with this sense of security, confidence, and achievement. I am strong; I feel it. I'm
excited not only about the trail but also about life and God and the future. 1150
miles has made that possible. I have truly never been alone on this journey. I've
always felt spiritual strength and support for my parents, brothers, and sisters."

God walks with you when you walk alone. That was the clear lesson,
Massachusetts through West Virginia. I had always hiked alone, even when
traveling with Rusty and Joe. Through those states, though, I was mostly
alone at night, too. Early on, I worried some about the sounds I heard
deep in the night. I wrestled with fears of unwanted marauders like the
monster who in 1981 had brutally killed two hikers in Southeastern
Virginia. Such fears left me eventually, and the darkness felt like a security
blanket.
   And then I crossed into Maryland.
   Maryland, folks said, felt different than other states. Unsettled energy
hung in the air, they said, especially near South Mountain where, in 1862,
battles for three mountain passes -- Crampton, Turner, and Fox Gaps --
cost a thousand men their lives. Thousands more were wounded there,
many of whom lost limbs in makeshift hospitals where amputated arms
and legs were piled in holes and buried unceremoniously and without so
much as a marker.
   A hundred and twenty-five years later, some told tales of hearing
muffled cannon fire still and saw phantom campfires deep in the woods or
talked of encountering ghost soldiers near South Mountain. I didn't see
anything odd, though, I slept, I'm sure, where panicked men likely crawled
to the creek near Turners Gap for a last cool drink before succumbing to
ghastly wounds. I lay there alone, in the pitch black night, uneasy, listening
for strange sounds, half-expecting gray and blue soldiers to come tramping

out of the forest or to hear the mournful cry of a specter rooting through the woods, "Who has my other arm?"

There were those who claimed encounters of supernatural sorts along the A.T., but I'm not one of them. Neither ghosts, goblins, nor aliens molested me along my hike. Mice were more of a problem.

I do recall a disturbing series of trail journal entries chronicling the gradual deterioration of the mental well-being of a southbound woman. It was in the thick of the Hundred-mile Wilderness in Maine. She was ahead of us by several days and wrote long rambling entries each night in trail journals at each shelter. She wrote about the adventures she shared with her traveling companion, a .38 caliber pistol named "Wilkes Booth" or some such name. Her entries personified the pistol as if "he" were more than cold steel. It was eerie but entertaining in a sickening sort of way to read her posts each night. The woman was beyond where we could have reached out to her easily, ten or fifteen miles ahead. And besides, none of us relished the idea of meeting a crazy woman toting a steely friend with a name like "Wilkes Booth."

Every evening for the first six or eight nights on the trail, Joe, Rusty and I would pull out the trail journal and read her posts aloud. That she was spiraling deeper and deeper into a hole was plain to see. And disturbing. Still, we read her posts like years later we might watch the latest reality TV episode. She was pure entertainment for those few evenings.

We kept expecting to meet her along the trail as we picked our way through the Wilderness.

Admittedly, there were just twinges of guilt as we profited from her misfortunes. Then, we came upon her final entry. Her last words left us off-balance and wondering, "Should or could have done more to help her?"

The woman was a few days from Monson still when unexplained lights in the forest teased and tormented her throughout the night. She wrote about an all-night buzzing and shadowy figures moving among the trees. She wrote she was sure "they" -- whatever "they" might be -- were coming for her. She fired warning shots at the lights throughout the night and shouted for them to leave her alone. Apparently, they didn't. The lights continued to pester her until daybreak. After a sleepless night, convinced that evil of the most disturbing sort inhabited the woods there and all around, she wrote that she'd be leaving the trail at the earliest opportunity.

Leaving the trail may not have been the greatest misfortune to befall the woman, however.

After that, her journal entries stopped. Hiking out from where we were then would have taken several days. There should have been at least another journal entry or two before she exited the trail conveniently. There were none. She'd simply vanished.

At Shaw's Boarding House a few days later and at the grocery in Monson, we inquired after the woman. No one recalled having seen any such person.

There was an episode in Delaware Water Gap, too. The woman wasn't a ghost, for sure, and I have never called it a supernatural occurrence. Parts of the encounter, though, made little sense and left me wondering.

She was too beautiful not to notice, sitting on a park bench, a well-loved guitar leaning next to her. She was a gypsy with sleek black hair and deep dark eyes. Her feet were bare, nails unpainted; she was earthy and tan with feathers in her hair and dangling jewelry, bracelets and earrings and long chains. She wore a flowing skirt. Her shoulders were bare and smooth like silk.

She was as beautiful as any mountain vista.

"Do you play?" I asked, nodding towards the guitar.

She picked it up and smiled sweetly. My heart skipped a beat, and a warm flush flowed through me. She gently strummed a few chords thoughtfully, then sang in a soulful voice, "Sometimes the light's all shinin' on me; other times I can barely see; lately it occurs to me; what a long, strange trip it's been."

She laughed at the shock on my face. "That's been my theme song lately," I told her.

"I figured," she said and invited me to sit next to her.

God, she was young, I thought; and she strained the bounds of beauty. "Lori who?" went through my brain, and then it was just her.

She played more. All were among my favorite songs; each more familiar than the last. She sang songs by the Grateful Dead, Marshall Tucker, and Poco. I didn't have to request a thing; she just knew.

She was fantastic. Her spirit was free and happy and nonchalant. The tone of her voice was deep and hypnotic and fun and meaningful. I sang some when I could; our voices blended well enough. Mostly, though, I listened to her and watched, certain I stared as much as anything. She could have played forever, and I would have stayed for every minute.

After a while, she set her guitar aside. "Let me see your hand." She took my hand in both of hers; pressed it to her cheek; studied it; kissed it once or twice unexpectedly and in a way that made me weak. Her hands were small and soft, warm and strong. Her touch made me squirm.

What's this all about? I wondered. I wanted to ask her, but instead thought, "Who cares? Whatever this is about, that's what I'm about, too."

"Your hands are beautiful." She said. "Strong and just weathered enough."

"They're yours," I wanted to tell her. She could have asked for anything, and I'd have given it. "If I'm being swindled," I thought, "Go ahead and swindle me."

"Can I read your palm?"

"Okay." What else might I have said?

"I learned from my mother. She was Cajun. She grew up in the swamp outside New Orleans. Never traveled far from the French Quarter. Now that was a woman with stories. My father was a grifter – a con artist. He disappeared when I was young. Mother said he might be up here but that he was more likely dead than alive. I'm looking for him. I have been for quite some time."

She took my hand in hers. My heart beat faster. Her hands were small and soft and without callouses. They were so unlike mine which were darker than hers -- but only because of months in the sun. She traced lines in my palm. Studied them intently; searched for something written there in some ancient, unknown language. I could only watch her, wholly fascinated. Her eyes, her lips, her bare shoulders were as alluring as anything; like a fairy tale come alive. She was gorgeous – heart-stoppingly so; everything about her was hypnotic and appealing. I would have surrendered anything, even everything at that moment. And then, as if she'd glimpsed something terrible, her expression changed all of a sudden. She looked up at me, sadness in her face, the most profound sort, almost in tears. She was close enough to kiss. I wanted to, I started to; something was unquestionably unfolding between us, and then she said, "I need to go."

"What?" There was a lump in my throat. "Did you see something? Am I going to die?"

"No, nothing like that." Her smile was back, but different than before, fainter and far more subtle.

Lori, I thought, she knows about Lori. Damn! I was sure she'd seen her in my palm, and she wasn't interested in being third. Before I could say anything

137

– that I'd leave all memories of Lori behind and surrender to this beautiful gypsy, she spoke softly. "No, not that either. I don't care about that." She spoke as if she'd heard my thoughts. "You and I," she said, "Are on different paths. We're from different worlds; different times, too. You'll live long and happy; I won't. My time is short."

She stood and slung her guitar over her shoulder; her sadness was deep. She bent to kiss my cheek softly, lingered there a while; maybe even wiped a tear from her cheek against mine. She didn't ask for anything more, just whispered, "I wish things were different," and pulled away.

"Yeah, me, too," I muttered.

"There are good things ahead for you," she said softly over her shoulder as she turned down the sidewalk. I watched her go, her hips swaying so perfectly as she did.

"What the hell happened?" I said aloud. She'd been so close. So close. I looked down at my pack for the briefest of seconds, looked up ready to beg her not to go, prepared to plead with her to spend her life with me, but she was nowhere. As if into thin air, she'd disappeared so completely that I was left wondering if she'd ever been there at all. I ran in my awkward thru-hiker pained sort of way to where she'd stood seconds before -- looking for something, anything -- a glass slipper maybe or a feather from her hair, but there was nothing, not the slightest trace that she'd ever been there at all.

Was she a ghost? I don't think so. Was I hallucinating? Probably not. Maybe I just needed a day off. I spent the next day and night in the Presbyterian hostel in Delaware Water Gap reading and resting and writing. I walked through town looking for her, but she was nowhere, and no one knew a thing about her.

Maryland's nice in September, gorgeous year-round, I bet, but there were no ghosts there even though other hikers said there were. Sometime before, I'd met a pair of Northbounders who'd hiked the 42-miles across Maryland without stopping. Impressive, I thought, but not something I envied them for. There was too much to enjoy and too much scenery to miss.

Something else happened in Maryland. Something important and life-defining. It happened at the Pennsylvania–Maryland border.

The shelter at Pen-Mar Park sits on the edge of an overlook. I don't recall what direction it faces; I do remember beautiful colors across the horizon at sunset. The view is expansive and embracing, and it's an altogether peaceful place. I sat in the shelter alone, thinking about Lori and the Gypsy woman. My heart was unsettled as was my sense of where I might head after the Appalachian Trail. It was early evening, and I watched a young family playing among the grass and trees nearby. They laughed and wrestled, hugged and chased each other until the young ones were exhausted. They came to sit in the shelter to watch the sky turn from blue to a mix of too many colors to name. The smallest was asleep in his father's arms before the sunset; the other two cuddled next to their mother and dreamily looked out over the gorgeous view. Mom and dad were tired but satisfied, the stress and strain and joys of raising three boys were apparent on their faces.

The father said something to me about "what a great thing I was doing.

I just laughed. "Me? You're the one doing something great. I'm just taking a long walk."

"I wish I had time to do that," he started to say, but I interrupted.

"You're doing something much greater. You're building something permanent. Something likely to change the world. Watching you play and wrestle with your kids, I'm pretty certain you'll change the world for the better. It looks like a tough job, and you do it well. I'm not doing much for anybody these days. But, you, you're doing something that matters."

"Yeah," he said, "It's tough." He bent to kiss the child in his arms, "but worth it." He smiled in a far off, satisfied, and exhausted sort of way. I envied him more perhaps than I'd ever envied another human being.

That night, I lay awake and thought about the young family -- mother, father, and three kids, none more than waist-high. I thought about how raising a family was one of the hardest and most crucial life journeys any of us ever takes. I thought of my father's reaction to my announcement that I was quitting my job and grad school to hike the A. T. He was a wise man who cared a lot about his children. I'd shared my plans to hike the AT with him in the wrong way, I realized. I let him think I was setting off on another hare-brained, half-hatched adventure. If I had connected it to something more significant and essential like raising a family, he'd have been on board all the way.

In Maryland, it occurred to me that no matter what I did after the Appalachian Trail, raising a family would have to be one of them if I was ever to feel true fulfillment. Thanks, Maryland. That realization has made all the difference.

It was easy enough to inject myself into the scene with three kids frolicking in a playground but raising a family required more than just willingness. I had a long way to go before I'd be ready, I knew, and I knew the AT could be no more than a stepping stone to bigger things.

I couldn't find Lori in that picture, though. That was something I came to accept that I always knew. Our paths were as different as if I were traveling south and she was heading north. Our paths would intersect once and for a very brief time.

WEST VIRGINIA

From my Journal:

"Today I am thinking about freedom and not much else; ruminating on the men and women who lived and died to make so much possible for the rest of us. You can't wander places like Harpers Ferry and Washington D.C. without reminders that we stand on the shoulders of giants. That so many steps and experiences and vistas and possibilities are within reach only because of those with vision and those who sometimes gave more than any would want to lose. Walking into Harpers Ferry, I could feel the spirits of many past and present who cared about and understood the importance of freedom for all. Included among them are those who conceived of and built the Appalachian Trail. "

"Where can a guy get a haircut around here?"

"Oh, there's a place up on the road leading out of town. I've never been there, of course, but the men say it's nice. I've known Scotty since he was a boy. I'd let him cut my hair if I were a man." She never broke stride as she put two more gooseberry pancakes on my plate, pushed a pitcher of homemade elderberry syrup my way, refilled my coffee and described how to get there. "It's two miles out the road that runs above town. Look for a white house. He cuts hair in his front room."

She was kind and gray, full of stories and smiles and an abundance of energy. Had she told me she'd churned the butter and milked the cow for the cream, I'd have believed her. She'd already introduced me to soldier berries, asparagus beans, and heirloom tomatoes that neither looked nor tasted like the ones at the grocery store but outpaced them for flavor by a hundred miles hands down.

The four of us met there as we'd planned some weeks before: Kenny Bob, a petroleum engineer from Louisiana; the White Rabbit, a barrister from Manchester, England; the Fireman, a civil engineer from Atlanta, and me, still Mac and the Boys – a grad. school dropout seeking a story. It was the first time in a long stretch I found myself part of a hiking group. I didn't really know these guys. I'd met them before and spent a night perhaps in hostels or shelter with each, but we'd never been together at once. And that had been long before, back in Maine, when we wondered, each of us, if we were likely to reach Springer. Or even Harpers Ferry. They'd met Joe and Rusty and perhaps Jim, too, but only in passing. Those guys were long gone, though, and so was Ken's hiking partner, a young woman named Fritz. There were others who'd left the trail for various reasons, too. Thirty years later, I don't remember their names.

Connecting with Hugh, Brett, and Ken was the start of a new chapter of my hike. Each had come more than a thousand miles since Katahdin and each was doggedly independent and unwilling to surrender their identity. Each was intent on completing the rest of the Appalachian Trail on our own and for our reasons which I can't recall ever being a topic of conversation. All of us were content to hike our own hikes and let others hike theirs.

From that point, though, we'd proceed as solo hikers still, but we'd do so in proximity to one another. Being lonely and not part of something else had grown tiresome. The fellowship shared with this group was instrumental in each individual's success. And enjoyment.

For a few bucks, Cass Cassidy opened the shed behind her house to hikers. She'd outfitted it with four wooden bunks and a spigot for washing. Immediately adjacent was her garden, a pleasing tangle of vegetables and flowers -- bachelor buttons, cornflowers, zinnias and the like. It was the kind of place worth spending time, especially if you were searching for peace. It was a tiny slice of heaven that quieted troubled minds and granted further peach to those already contented. For a few dollars more, Cass would feed you at her kitchen table. The meals were incomparable and included ingredients harvested from the garden or picked from the surrounding hills.

Along the whole of the A.T., only the pancakes at the CCC Diner -- shared that morning with my biker buddies back in Port Clinton -- compared with Cass Cassidy's gooseberry pancakes topped with elderberry syrup. After too many pancakes at her table and one cup of coffee passed my limit, I set out in search of a guy named Scotty who cut hair in his living room along a road that felt like it stretched to nowhere.

The road above Harpers Ferry was gorgeous. I walked the couple miles effortlessly, immersed in long-views and wildflowers. I found the house as Cass described it, there was a striped barber pole on the outside of a simple clapboard house and a rather modest sign that read "Scotty's." Nothing more. I climbed the porch stairs and pushed open the door into another world, not at all unpleasant, but nowhere like I'd been before or have been since. It was another dimension, not like one from a Twilight Zone episode. It was another time. The place was immaculate; there was no mistaking it as a place intended for men. It was bedecked with sports heroes; models of cars; pictures of military hardware on the walls; ashtrays on the tables and cigars for sale on the counter. There was an array of magazines neatly spread on the coffee table – Playboy, GQ, Popular Mechanics. That month's centerfold hung unabashedly behind the single, shiny barber chair.

I don't think we're in Kansas anymore, Toto, I thought. Or on the Appalachian Trail.

Scotty leaned in the corner, an unlit cigarette hanging from his lips. I knew he was Scotty because his name was embroidered on his pink, untucked starched barber-shirt. I'd only seen such a character on TV. He was beautiful and worth a chapter of his own in some other book. Everything about him was crisp and polished and manly, even the white towel over his shoulder. His short sleeves were cuffed slightly and ironed flat; his pointy black shoes shined like glass; his black straight-leg black jeans were so tight I was sure he'd never father a child. And then there was the gold. He wore a gold chain around his neck, a gold ring on his finger, and a gold bracelet. His watch was gold, and so was his belt-buckle and one tooth. But the best part about Scotty was his hair – black as pitch and slicked back with something akin to motor oil, maybe. Every piece was perfect. He sported a spectacular pompadour with one errant twist of trailing down his forehead nearly to his eyebrows. I'm sure there was a leather jacket within reach with a switchblade tucked in a pocket.

He greeted me like we were old friends and offered me a 10 a.m. beer.

"You having one?" I asked.

His tone grew serious. "I never drink when I'm cutting hair." I came close to offending him, I gathered, by even asking. I passed on the beer.

He stopped me when I started to apologize, slapped a razor across a strap and adjusted the towel on his shoulder. When everything was just right, he motioned towards the chair, "What'll it be, young man?" I took a last long look at Miss July hanging on the wall. He smiled and waited patiently. I suspected he and I were the same age, but there was no need to correct him.

"Great place," I told him.

He took a long look around and nodded with a satisfied smile. "It's home."

It really was, I gathered.

Somewhere along the Appalachian Trail, amidst long stretches without showers, plenty of sweat, and few opportunities to look at myself in a mirror, I'd stopped worrying about hair and most anything else related to fashion.   A quick dip in a clear pool was usually the best I could do to stay clean. Most mornings I pulled my fingers through the tangle on my head and tied it back with a wet bandana.

I caught sight of myself in Scotty's mirror that morning. I was rough and wild and a complete contrast to the perfectly groomed barber who waited expectantly.   In the spirit of the moment, I sat back in the chair and surrendered with an exuberant, "Clean me up, Scotty!" Unfortunately, the Star Trek reference -- a pretty clever pun, I thought, of which I was quite proud -- was lost on Scotty. He went to work on my head and ears with gusto. Like a true craftsman and maybe even a true artist.

Scotty had been blessed with a gift. That man could talk. While he trimmed and snipped, brushed and slathered potions on my head, he bounced from politics to sports to weather and then on to that month's centerfold on the wall, back again to politics, and then on to women and the woes and wonders they add to our lives. It was the greatest haircut experience ever.   He trimmed my beard and eyebrows and applied a little wax to each.

At what seemed the exact right moment, he yanked off the cape with a dramatic flair, swept the stray hairs from my neck with a miniature broom, and spun me around to have a look in the mirror.   I was flabbergasted! The transformation was remarkable! In the mirror before me was anything but the ragged wooly man who'd walked into the place.   Staring back from the mirror instead was a man I didn't recognize. My hair was the spitting image of Scotty's except that mine was blonde and sun-bleached, rather than coal-black like his. I even sported the pompadour and errant twist of hair trailing down my forehead nearly to my neatly-trimmed eyebrows. I burst into a wide grin and laughed out loud. "Best haircut ever," I told Scotty.

"I aim to please," he said.

I knew I'd likely be the first AT hiker to cross West Virginia looking like Bowser from the rock group, Sha-Na-Na.

A few months later, I might take exception to any stylist who took such liberties with my head. That day, though, it was refreshing and more than a little fun. As I wandered through Harpers Ferry, later, I noticed more than a handful of men with haircuts remarkably similar to mine and Scotty's.

Kenny Bob, the White Rabbit, and the Fireman or Ken, Hugh, and Brett as I'd come to know them, laughed when I cruised into the shed behind Cass's house. I chose to believe they were just jealous.

I slapped a wet bandana on my head to tame the nonsense; Hugh and I set off on a new adventure to Washington, D.C. Ken headed to meet friends in Rhode Island for the weekend, and Brett headed home to a wedding. The four of us committed to a plan, though. We'd meet on Springer Mountain on November 7th and walk the last mile together.

Hugh and I rode the train to Washington DC. We had little choice but to carry our packs into D. C. and with us to the Smithsonian, the Lincoln Memorial, and the Vietnam War Memorial. It was a day of conflicting emotions, fascination, pride, and profound sadness.

Having traveled twelve hundred miles by then, the last four-hundred mostly alone with my thoughts, I was prone to reflection. It had become my brain's default mode by that point. I thought much about the whys and wherefores of living and history. Often I wondered where I might have fit long before. Along the A.T., distractions of everyday life were few and rather mundane. That left room for introspection. And daydreaming. Walking through Washington D.C. with such a mindset was remarkable. Its' power was amplified well-beyond what I ever could have anticipated.

The guard at the Smithsonian American History museum wanted to know what we had in our backpacks. "Stoves," I said. "Fuel," I added. "And matches. "

"I have a knife," Hugh added in his unmistakably non-American accent.

"Oh, yeah, I have a knife, too. But it's only a couple inches long."

"Well, you can't carry those things in here," the guard said. "But I guess I can keep them behind the desk for you." He was polite as could be. There were no metal detectors, no pat downs, and no one seemed hardly worried about bombs or even vandalism. The guard was more concerned with being friendly and accommodating. Oh, how times have changed.

We entered the museum, and there was George Washington's army uniform. I doubt it was the one he wore tramping around Valley Forge or on the raid to Trenton or on Long Island as the Continental Army fled for its' life from British regulars. It was too clean, stain-free, and unwrinkled. I'd trekked a few months from Maine, and most everything I owned was worn and nearly played out. The impracticality of George's uniform struck me, especially his boots. Versus my nylon gaiters, running shorts, hiking shirt and rain jacket I wore, his was heavy and bulky. There was nothing high-tech about it. I was further struck by the enduring impact that uniform and the man who wore it had on history. Now, I still have my gaiters, shorts, a favorite MATC t-shirt, and the bandana I wore tied on my head most days. They're in a box in my closet. None of it is museum-worthy like George's uniform. 243 years later, his is museum-worthy and priceless; mine wouldn't fetch five bucks at Goodwill.

I guess that says some about the magnitude of a simple hike compared with a life that changed humankind's trajectory for the better.

George Washington inspired thousands of free-thinking souls to pursue a dream of freedom and independence and to build something substantial and enduring and far more significant than one person. His is a remarkable legacy. I remember thinking how those who followed George and others like Tom Jefferson and Ben Franklin were likely the sort of dreamers who hundreds of years later might have responded to the lure of the Appalachian Trail. If ever lured to start a thru-hike, George and Tom and Ben and those who weathered a winter at Valley Forge are the exact sorts who not only would have finished what they started but used their accomplishment as a springboard to 10,000 better days beyond that. For themselves and for others.

Hiking the AT was a good thing. For me personally, as someone seeking to know more about myself and the world, it was a great thing. It would have been easy to overvalue what the accomplishment meant, though. It would have been natural to embrace it as something great and then to rest for a good long time or even to stop adventuring. Doing so, I think, would have meant squandering the opportunity that comes with completing a thru-hike. Remember summiting on Katahdin or Springer is best considered arriving at the beginning of something better rather than the end of something good. It's best to embrace a thru-hike as a stepping stone and then to move on to bigger and better things armed with new understanding and valuable perspectives. Hikers who live what they learned along the Appalachian Trail long after their return to what must of us incorrectly refer to as the real world" tend to benefit the most from their experiences.

Those who stuck with George Washington through some of history's more harrowing and meaningful adventures changed the world in a big way. Thru-hiking, while significant for this one man, was not great on the scale of what was endured by those at Valley Forge or those who crossed the ice-choked Delaware in tiny boats to defeat the Hessians on Christmas night in 1776. Hiking the AT suggested how I might have fared under similar circumstances like those endured by great men and women thru history. It challenged me after that to raise expectations for myself each day that followed. It was not by itself, a particularly great thing.

Walking through Washington D.C. as part of the Appalachian Trail was about history, not politics. And that was refreshing. 10,000 days later, it's almost impossible to avoid heated conversations about democrats and republicans and what it means to be American. Lately, such conversations have become nauseatingly divisive and not altogether productive.

When someone asks me if I am one or the other, I usually keep silent, but I in my head I think, I'm neither. I'm a thru-hiker." What does that mean? For me, it means I have through the years thought considerably about a lot of things in the context of thru-hiking the Appalachian Trail. I believe that the path to a greater world winds through the compelling personal adventures done well. Want my vote? Encourage meaningful adventures as a component of education, health and healing, and growing up in general.

Through the lens of a successful thru-hike, a lot happening in our communities these days makes little sense.

How might things be different if collectively we embraced the core values of a successful thru-hike? What if we adopted ideals like "Hike your hike, let others hike theirs"? Or cares for our stuff like a thru-hiker must? Or lived simply, had a vision, and planned most days well? What if we each had a destination in mind each day and took care of our feet and fed our spirit well? And what if we laughed with others more often and never at them, immersed ourselves in nature, and made it a point to log a little progress towards the end goal most days? What if we appreciated those around us and never took ourselves too seriously?

I did those things along the Appalachian Trail, and it made for better days then and long after. I still do those things more than I otherwise might have.

I don't, however, do them as often as I should. Imagine what it might mean to an entire nation to live that way?

I am moved to follow people with a vision and those steeped in the quiet confidence that comes with knowing because they have -- figuratively speaking -- been to the mountain top and back.

What would the outcome be if we encouraged more people -- especially young ones -- to set off on epic adventures, to push boundaries, and to pursue big, audacious goals at least once in their life?   I tend to believe doing so would result in 10,000 better days for most of those who adventured and that would have a snowball effect for the rest of us.

A lot of people take stands for and against things they haven't thought about. Hiking the AT changed me. It encouraged me to be comfortable with who I am, what I am capable of, and what I stand for. Hiking alone eight hours a day left little choice but to either tune in or tune out. Tuning out meant you walked along with an empty head; tuning in meant you wrestled with some of the more profound things that surfaced from deep within. Remember Socrates? An unexamined-life-is-not-worth-living Socrates? Examining the thoughts bouncing around in your head at a more profound level makes us better men and women, That's especially so when we can be honest with ourselves and simplify perspectives.

Many of us would do well to think about things a little more before opening our mouths and letting half-baked ideas and unfounded beliefs slip out. "Hike your hike, let others hike theirs" was the near-universal code among AT hikers. It was refreshing. And it made a difference. Rarely did I encounter many who were judgmental, overly critical, or excessively insistent that theirs was the better way. What if more of us understood and embraced the sorts of values that come with accomplishing something epic and personally significant? What if more of us lived more-examined lives with a bit more passion and practiced such values regularly?

The Lincoln Memorial was among the most humbling place I've been. I found inspiration there. I remember thinking then that Lincoln was perhaps the ultimate thru-hiker. He stayed the most difficult of courses ever traveled and endured the journey through to its painful, and ultimately future-defining conclusion despite near constant doubts.

I imagine Lincoln wrestled with temptations to quit or at least to do a little yellow blazing. Thank, God, though, he didn't. Lincoln was anything but a quitter. Or a blue blazer or a section skipper. He was a man of vision.

This partial and "doctored" quote is inscribed within the Lincoln Memorial:

"With malice toward none; with charity for all … let us strive on to finish the work we are in … to do all which may achieve and cherish a just and lasting peace, among ourselves, and with all …"

Doesn't that mean about the same as "Hike your hike, and let others hike theirs?" If Lincoln were a thru-hiker, he'd have been a purist. And would have without a doubt made it to the opposite terminus, Katahdin or Springer. As long as his knees held out.

The AT brings out the best in most of us. It's about celebrating life and squeezing the most from it -- joy, understanding, perspective, peace, and the ability to appreciate life. The 58,272 names on the Vietnam War Memorial are overwhelming to look at. The monument is about death and lives cut short. In the middle of a thru-hike, it was hard to be there without emotions overflowing. Hiking the AT pushed me to embrace challenges and possibilities and to live more than I otherwise might have. The Wall, on the other hand, chronicled wasted potential. It was hard not to cry.

I stood at the Wall for a long while and watched a man lightly stroke a name on the wall. William C. Powell. His stare was far away as if he was remembering the young man who'd been a boyhood friend. Or perhaps he'd been with William Powell when he died. It was a heartbreaking scene. Impossible to reconcile. At that moment, I think, I was more capable of understanding the scope of pain and heartbreak represented by that memorial. I knelt and gave thanks for my opportunity to thru-hike. And to live. And to be young and healthy. I'm not sure I've ever been as humbled as I was that day.

Hugh and I walked away in silence, rode the train back to Harpers Ferry, shouldered our packs and turned south later that evening, more somber than we'd been any day before.

West Virginia, including Washington D.C., was beautiful and hard.

VIRGINIA

From my Journal:

I'm shivering beneath a sunny sky, lying in a dirt road somewhere in the backwoods of Virginia. The sun is hot, but the breeze is cool, almost cold, and my shirt is soaked with sweat. I don't know where I am; I don't know where the nearest paved road is; I don't know where the nearest phone is or how far I am from the closest person, but I neither care nor does it matter. I feel a sense of "home" exactly where I am. Life is good, the world is good, and I sense that I'm good. I am in the middle of nowhere, but I feel neither fear nor loneliness. Times have changed. Once in a while, I'm filled with a dreamy wistfulness, but I'm never burdened with an urgency that I need to be somewhere else. I'm happy where I am, and I don't wish for much. This is where I belong. Joe calls me "Mad Max of the East." In his last letter, he compared me to an animal – the best kind -- and called me a mystic, of sorts. I'm neither. In truth, I've never been more human than I am now. I've never been so focused, so directed or so sure."

People define the AT experience as much as any one thing. There are those you hike with, those you encounter for brief moments along the way, and those back home who without their support it might be easy to lose heart. There are good ones and bad, weird ones and fun ones, and those you can never forget no matter how hard you try. And in every person, there is an opportunity to learn something about love or life or glimpse what you never want to become.

It was September in Shenandoah National Park. The leaves had not yet started to change, and the weather was soft and the nights were cool. The region was gorgeous and pleasant and perfect. In Gravel Springs Hut, we encountered Jerry sitting quietly with his legs crossed and his folded hands in his lap. Hugh & I cruised in rather abruptly as if we owned the place. Jerry was neither offended nor startled. He was pleasant and patient and smiled the whole time, completely unflappable and wholly content.

Jerry was considerably older than we were -- in his sixties, maybe, and well-seasoned by many months on the trail. Or more. He was not a typical thru-hiker.

Jerry traveled with a bicycle from which hung an assortment of interesting items: a lawn chair, a violin case, an umbrella, and a briefcase. He didn't ride the bike but pushed it as he hiked. "Hike your hike," went through my mind. "Let him hike his."

He wore an aviator-style cap, earflaps up and chin straps dangling loose. His gloves were fingerless. Though he wasn't bedecked in the latest hiking gear, neither was he the out-of-place sort who might give you the creeps. His gentleness and humility were palpable and almost inspiring. He welcomed us cordially and watched with interest as we set up for the night. Often, he nodded approval. He was quick to extend a compliment when the opportunity was presented, but I don't think he once spoke without being spoken to.

There was extreme patience about him; and though quite likable, he seemed steeped in a palpable sadness as if he wanted nothing more than to be part of things.

He was hard to figure. Most of his gear was good stuff though somewhat worn and dirty. His pack and sleeping bag were of the same quality as ours. He just carried lots more of it. "I like a few luxuries," he told us, nodding towards his bike and the sundry items suspended there. It was a plausible enough explanation.

"Do not judge lest ye be judged," I thought. "Enjoy your way. Let him enjoy his."

From the day we started planning this trip, "Hike your own hike" was an important mantra.

The first time I encountered that wisdom, it came from an unnamed thru-hiker who'd scrawled the phrased at the bottom of a survey I'd sent to a handful of thru-hikers while planning my trip. The ATC had provided names and addresses of some who'd expressed willingness to help others prepare. I'd sent them questions and self-addressed envelopes. The response rate was high, and I came away with quite a bit of trail wisdom. There was no name signed to the comment about "Hike your hike, Let others hike theirs. I took the wisdom to heart, though. And so did Rusty. The phrase has been part of my language since.

Brett and Ken cruised in a later. They regarded Jerry with interest.

Hugh and I fixed dinner. Two stoves, coordinated output; ours was machine-like efficiency after a hundred nights. He was British so there was always tea first on his stove and instant soup on mine. Then, while we shared those, we'd each prep rice or noodles on our own stoves fortified with a can of tuna or chicken or mashed potatoes and gravy. There'd be a slab of cheese with that, too, and everything would be drenched in squeeze margarine. And then there was dessert. Instant cheesecake or pudding. And coffee. The instant international flavored kind with plenty of caffeine and sugar and trans-fats likely. And then there'd be Snickers bars and handfuls of granola.

Such a feast would round out our need for at least 6,000 calories per day.

Jerry just watched.

I asked him the same questions I'd been asked a hundred times in the last thousand miles, "Where you headed?", "Where'd you come from?", and "Where's home?"

His answers weren't like mine, though. Gradually, I understood Jerry's purpose along the AT was vastly different from mine. I was there to grow some. Or as I told so many so often, I was there because I was looking for a story to tell. Jerry, on the other hand, was there because he needed a place to live.

There was no telling how many nights he'd spent along the AT or in places like it, and no telling how many days he'd spend along the trail in the future.

How would my experience have been different if there was no finish line? Outcomes would have been very different, I knew. Jerry was happy to share his story. By his report, he'd grown up in an "orphanage." He'd never belonged to a proper family. The boys at the Home and the nuns who cared for them were the closest to a family he'd known.

"But for the grace of God go I," I thought. "And the love of a family. And the devotion of a father who cared." It was my dad who months before had said of hiking the A.T., " That's the stupidest thing I've ever heard." I'd come to understand he'd said such things not because he lacked vision or didn't care. He said those things because he wanted the best for his son and nothing more.

"Where are my manners," I said. "We have more than enough. Will you join us for dinner?" Jerry graciously accepted and produced a battered tin dish and spoon. I was quick to re-fill his bowl before he asked. The last thing I wanted was to make this man say, "Please sir, I want some more."

Along the trail, so many extended so much kindness. There'd been cookies and Cokes; rides and invites to showers and to do laundry; there'd been sandwiches and places to sleep; well-wishes and words of encouragement from people I'd known a few minutes. It was easy to take such gifts for granted and to come almost to expect them from those who took an interest in my hike.

By Shenandoah National Park, twelve-hundred miles from Katahdin, I'd become rather adept at an innocent form of panhandling, called "Yogi-ing". It's still a time-honored Appalachian Trail tradition – to pursue handouts from people you meet along the trail. The most important "rule" is that one must seek without asking. Success relied on subtleties and theatrics. Walking into a picnic ground, for example, it never hurt to pour out all but the last inch of water from your bottle. Then, in mid-conversation with an unsuspecting picnicker, pull out your bottle, toss down the last swallow, and ask "Any idea where I can find some water?" More often than not, that person would point you to the nearest water fountain, think better of things, reach into their cooler, and pull out a Coke or offer homemade lemonade or an apple. That was the anatomy of a successful "yogi". Procure a handout without asking.

Now, historically, I may be absolutely wrong about this, and I would like someone to set me straight on this if anyone knows the truth about the origin of the verb, "To yogi." I wonder if perhaps Rusty and Joe and Brett (a.k.a. the Fireman) had a hand in coining the term. They were the first I know of who likened our antics to those of the great Yogi Bear. As far north as Maine that summer, they came to call this not-quite-aggressive pursuit of freebies, "Yogi-ing." Maybe they picked up the term from another hiker. I can't be sure. Procuring a hand-out without asking or stealing became known as a successful "Yogi".

For thru-hikers, it's part of the fun. For Jerry, though, it was life. After my encounter with him, "Yogi-ing" wasn't quite so appealing. Giving up the habit, though, was hard.

"Do you play the violin?" I nodded towards the case dangling from Jerry's bike.

"Some," he said, smiling shyly, with seriousness and humility. I couldn't tell if it was just his way or a measure of the sanctity of his violin.

"I'd love to hear you play," I said. My request clearly touched him.

The idea of a concert surrounded by trees and mountains and peacefulness carried my imagination away. By then, I'd grown certain, Jerry was a master musician, a child prodigy all grown-up. Though not treated kindly by life, I suspected, he'd found living in the forest with his music satisfying and meaningful. At least that's what I assumed.

I braced myself for something beautiful. Others gathered too, four of us, captivated by the way he removed the violin from its case, every movement steeped in reverence and slightly dramatic – the way he gently wiped a bit of dust from the surface, inspected a minor scratch as if it the instrument were a living thing, and softly stroked strings and bow. It wasn't hard to picture him on stage wearing a tuxedo and surrounded by an entire orchestra.

Jerry did not disappoint in the way he stretched, cradled the instrument under his chin, re-positioned it, closed his eyes and leaned in as if trying to find oneness with his instrument. My heart beat faster. Jerry, the master showman, had zeroed in on my hopes and anticipation. He started to draw the bow across the strings, paused slightly, re-positioned, then started again. My palms were wet with sweat; my knees week with anticipation. Would he choose a Mozart Concerto or a little Charlie Daniels to start the show? Or something from steeped in the history of the West Virginia Appalachians? Maybe he'd begin with something unique or even an original piece.

And then it started, the concert to end all others. He pulled the bow across the strings, and it made -- unfortunately -- an evil hiss. It wasn't Charlie Daniels, though, that electrified the air or anything classical. It was Twinkle, Twinkle, Little Star, and it wasn't very good. In fact, it was terrible. But Jerry kept playing. For what seemed forever. The four of us stood biting lips and suppressing laughter that screamed for release. My comrades sidestepped Jerry's field of vision, stood slightly behind him, but I couldn't escape. I was trapped.

Their eyes were on me now. Between them, they wagered how long my composure would last. I was about to bust. They didn't help.

Fortunately, my composure held, barely, and only after I wiped tears from my cheeks. How long can one man play Twinkle, Twinkle, Little Star? That's something I know. That day, it seemed, that man could play damned-near forever!

Thru-hiking was a spiritual experience for me, but not exactly a religious one. I spent a lot of time with God and thinking about God, but I only went to church a few times. One of those times, was an exceptional experience, though. It started with the Happy Feet.

In Vermont, as we turned south to Springer and the Happy Feet went north to Katahdin, Bill and Laurie invited us to stop at their house in Lynchburg for hamburgers on the grill, a bed for the night, showers, and laundry. They'd have completed their thru-hike by then and would be happy to pick us up trailside. Two months later, they were unfazed when I called and asked if there was room for Hugh, Brett, and Ken, all of whom they'd probably met in Vermont and likely added song verses about each one, too.

"The more, the merrier," they said predictably.

It was a lovely visit, especially the time spent around the table sharing stories and the performance of their song in the living room.

Thirty years later, my favorite people are thru-hikers. They speak my language and have a more profound understanding of how the world should work. I find it easy to laugh with them, and if even for a little while, a conversation can transport me back to a simpler, less complicated time. Revisiting times like those are as good as any dose of medicine I've ever been given, except for the morphine the doctors gave me when the copperhead bit me. That stuff was pretty amazing. That's another story and not one in any way related to the Appalachian Trail, though.

I think I'd likely vote for most any candidate, Democrat or Republican, who'd completed a thru-hike and continued to live and preach the lessons learned in the process.

The next morning was Sunday. Hugh and I hiked the few miles to the nearest Catholic Church. Bill and Laurie didn't offer to drive us; they understood the absurdity. It would have been like loading up the family roadster to drive next door. It was completely unnecessary. Three miles was nothing.

We took our place among the congregation, Our efforts to dress like regulars didn't fool anyone. Bill loaned me a bright yellow polo shirt, crisp and new. Nothing else about me was fresh or modern, especially my haircut. The unfortunate aftermath of the scalping at Scotty's hand back in West Virginia was pretty obvious. At least no one laughed. At least not out loud.

It's hard to blend into a Catholic Church unless you grew up worshipping in one. Hugh and I'd both been schooled in the "Catholic Arts" as kids. We knew what to say and when to say it; when to stand and exactly when to kneel. We pulled hymnals out and sang familiar songs with the enthusiasm of thru-hikers, something that did not go unnoticed. Likely we sang a little too loud. More like drunken sailors, I'm afraid. We earned smiles and stares from those glad to see us and glares from those who wondered what the Hell we were doing in their world. Some seemed concerned we might be there to cook and eat them.

I'm sure we tested the faith of some.

On the way out the door, the Priest stopped us, "Who are you guys?" We tried to explain, but he had a long line of hands to shake as people filed out the door. Almost forcefully, he pushed us against the wall behind him and told us, as if we were school kids, "I want to talk to you boys."

After the last of his flock passed, he turned, "Now," he said, "Who are you, and what are you doing in my church?" I couldn't tell if he was amused or trying to figure out whether we posed a threat to his flock. He listened intently as we told him our story. He nodded a lot. When he'd heard enough, he reached up and traced a cross with his thumb on each of our foreheads. He said a few words as he did ending with, "Go in peace to love and serve." And then he pushed us out the door with a smile.

It's been a long while since then. Sometimes I can still feel that cross he traced on my forehead. I recall those words frequently, too, "Go in peace to love and serve." That's a pretty tall order. Hugh and I embraced those words differently. He's a Catholic priest in the UK now; I raised three children. Both of us, I'm sure, have "served" more than we might have imagined in our roles since then. And both of us have loved a good bit, too.

The whole of the AT experience was filled with intensities and nuances that I can remember like they were yesterday. Conversations or encounters that seemed insignificant then, thirty years later, may stand out as pivotal. I wished I'd written more.

How am I different thirty years later because of the one-hundred and sixty days invested in 1987? I know a lot of things today that I might not know otherwise. I know what wind and rain whipping against my face feels like; I know what it's like to be satisfied at the end of a hard day; I understand what a letter from a loved one is worth on a day when you're lonely and in the middle of nowhere; and I know that people are, generally speaking, kind and giving. Those are important things. They make a difference.

Folklore has it that more than five-thousand applicants responded to this 1913 ad that appeared in the London Times:

"Men wanted for hazardous journey. Low wages, bitter cold, long hours of complete darkness. Safe return doubtful. Honour and recognition in event of success."

While it's unlikely this exact ad appeared in any London papers at that time, it is documented that Ernest Shackleton was overwhelmed with thousands of applicants after an article was published announcing his intent to lead an expedition to Antarctica. At the time, he was widely known and those who were inclined to apply would have understood the nature of the journey.

I met so many along the way who would have jumped at the opportunity to live more simply if they just knew how. Many of them would have chucked it all and set out to encounter themselves in some wild and faraway place if they could have just figured out how. Most of us would embrace something more if we could just find room in our lives to do so. We thirst for a little bit of daring, but giving things up is hard, and most feel a little stuck when they think about walking away from the comfort of couches, homes, relationships, and secure jobs. Even when they know to do so might be a game-changer.

Letting go is hard. Sometimes, though, it's the first and best step towards something bigger, better, and more worthwhile. Letting go of unrealistic dreams and fears and insignificant but familiar things that tether us to a limited existence can yield immeasurable payoffs. That's a benefit of five-million steps along the Appalachian Trail for so many thru-hikers. So is coming the understanding that a simple existence might be the most satisfying kind.

It's too bad more of us don't chuck the trappings and complexities of modern life, at least for a while, and pursue something more profound and meaningful. Or do it more than once every ten-thousand days. If more of us did, the world might be filled with more wise men and women, and we'd all be better for it.

Hugh & I sang church hymns as we trekked through Lynchburg back to the Foote's home. Bill and Laurie drove us back to the AT Though we'd known them only briefly, the goodbyes were heartfelt, and we continued south.

Big Island near Troutville was an easy fifty-four miles. Don hung out at a crossroads there, smoking a cigar, maybe, or walking his dog, or both. He'd been retired a few days and was trying to figure what was next. He didn't seem to be the sort of man for whom early retirement or even retirement at any age was a good idea. He seemed to be the type who needed something to do. He was killing time when I emerged from the woods. He didn't know a thing about the AT even though he sat mere feet from it.

I wasn't in the mood for yogi-ing, and my water bottle was too full for theatrics. It didn't matter, though, Don was a pleasant character and happy to have someone to talk to. He invited me to sit on the tailgate of his truck; we talked about the AT and about life in general. He shared his lunch.

"Want a beer or a Coke?" He had a cooler filled with both.

I took the Coke.

"I have an extra sandwich. Want it?"

"Sure."

"Can I drive you a little further down the road? Save you some effort?"

"Thanks, no," I told him. "I'm committed to every step; not just to finishing. I have 6 miles more to make today."

"I could pick you up later if you'd like to come to my house and do laundry. Or shower, if you want."

"Generous offer," I said, and told him about Hugh, Ken, and Brett.

He thought about things for a moment. "Sure, why not."

We planned to meet at a crossroads some miles ahead at 4 pm.

"Dinner and a shower at some guy's house who just happened to be hanging around a trail crossing? Didn't you learn from that chick in Connecticut?" They'd all had similar "interesting" experiences while hiking. Brett spoke on behalf of Hugh and Ken. "Count us in."

Don was at the trail crossroads with his truck and a cooler of Cokes in the back. We piled in and drove to his home. It was a lovely place. Not ostentatious but large and clean and well-kept. How overwhelming it must have been for his wife and ninety-five-year-old mother to have four smelly twenty-something hikers invade their kitchen.

Don refilled bowls with chips and sliced watermelon as fast as we downed them. We showered and did our best to dress for supper, crowded around the table, and ate burgers topped with the reddest tomatoes of the summer. Miraculously, our laundry got done on its own, folded even, and dinner ended with an invitation to camp in the backyard which quickly became an invitation to sleep in the finished basement.

The seven of us sat in the living room that evening and told stories and laughed, even 95-year old "Gammy" who said, "Eh," a lot and used an antique horn pressed to one ear to hear the conversation. Don had to repeat everything to her in a loud voice shouted directly into the horn. She smiled and nodded a lot. I'm not sure she understood a bit of what was going on.

We were bedded down in the basement watching "Gilligan's Island" re-runs when Don came down with a tray of freshly-baked cookies and milk. The next morning, he greeted us with a tray of coffee and a five-star breakfast of eggs, bacon, grits, toast, and tomatoes. Then, he delivered us back to the trail.

I often wondered as I hiked south from Troutville what his motivations were. In the end, I figured he was just a nice man who wasn't afraid to extend kindness. I was glad to know such people existed.

By many standards and in some crowds, it's a story hardly worth re-telling -- how Don and his wife opened their home to us. Nothing about it was movie-script worthy. There were no drugs, no deception, no booze, no sex, no serial killers, false imprisonment or close calls with an escaped mental patient or worse. There were no gunfights or international espionage either. Or thievery of any kind. Hell, there wasn't unwanted evangelizing or attempted evangelizing after dinner. A man and his wife took four boys in for the night, fed them and treated them with respectfully and with kindness. And the boys were appropriately polite and gracious, thankful for their gifts. It's sad that it's the sort of story that gets so little airplay, even though it's entirely rare and unusual. Maybe even more so than the less than comfortable tragic encounters we so often hear about.

There was no way to thank the couple for their kindness except to send them a poster of the Appalachian Trail – and to re-count that evening in this book, the evening we'd stumbled upon southern hospitality in its most pure form.

A hundred miles on, I hitched a ride into Pearisburg with a woman in a tall truck. It smelled of diesel and seemed more machine than anyone might need for picking up groceries or dropping off kids at school. Hers was a thick southern drawl. Almost impossible to understand sometimes. She studied me; trying to figure out what manner of man I was. Whether I was on her side or on another one. That's the way, I figured, she experienced the world.

I explained where I'd been and where I was going. She was interested. "You pass through Gettysburg?"

"Close," I told her, "but not quite. I was closer to Antietam and South Mountain."

"We lost a lot of boys up there at Gettysburg," she said. "Five from my family alone."

The intensity of her emotions was unexpected and unsettling.

She wasn't just giving me a history lesson, it seemed. She was recounting a personal tragedy as if it had happened weeks before rather than one-hundred twenty-four years prior. "Each year, I take my kids up there to see where their kin fell. It's important not to forget, I tell them." Her stare was far-off and a little creepy.

"Yes, ma'am," I said, my voice sliding into the most southern drawl I could find within.

She looked at me more intently. "Where you from?" I got the sense that how I answered that question mattered much to her.

"Arkansas," I lied. "We lost men at Shiloh," I lied even more. "And Vicksburg." It was a complete fabrication of the truth. My family was mostly from Illinois in those days.

She smiled a satisfied smile. "And you ain't forgotten about that have you?"

"No, ma'am," I said. "There's no forgetting," It made me a little sick to say such a thing. I kept up with the lies until we rolled into Pearisburg.

She bid me goodbye like we were kindred spirits. I felt crappy for having lied through my teeth but entirely relieved she hadn't invited me to attend any middle-of-the-night meetings later that evening. Or measured me for my white sheet. "God bless you," she said. "And God bless this country," she said.

I wasn't honestly sure which country she meant – the one we live in today or the one that never quite got recognized a hundred-twenty-some years before.

TENNESSEE

October 10, 2018

From my Journal:

"Hiking the Appalachian Trail has been powerful. While it remains to be seen what impact it will have on my life, I suspect it might be great. The demands of this lifestyle have been more than I expected. Sometimes when I'm giving 100%, the Trail seems to ask for 110%. I feel weak and small sometimes and the urge to quit still wells up in longer and duller moments. At these times, though, I'm forced to look within and forced to face what it would mean to give in and take the easy way out. That's not what I want. That's not why I'm here, I know, and from somewhere deep within, I find the urge to get on my feet and push on. Where does the strength to continue come from? There's a lot of time to think along the AT I think that strength comes mostly from having watched you all my life, Dad, and the way you've lived. One foot ahead of the other, step after step after step. That's what'll get you where you want to go. There are no shortcuts."

Tennessee and North Carolina share a seventy-mile border through the Smoky Mountains. For Southbounders, the ground to the right of the trail is Tennessee; to the left is North Carolina. It doesn't much matter which state you're in, both are beautiful. And easy to enjoy, too. With so many miles already logged, mind and body were well-adapted for physical and even mental challenges, and exhaustion of either kind wasn't the threat it had once been.

By Tennessee, my brain worked differently than it did the day I climbed Katahdin. With so many hours already spent wandering its recesses, it became almost effortless to slip into a near trance-like state connecting me with long-forgotten memories and people no longer part of my life. People, living or dead, were easily conjured in such a life-like fashion that conversations with them were convincingly real – Grandmas, old girlfriends, childhood friends, my father. I found I could remember things I'd learned in school years and years before and recite the names of all but a very few of the twenty-six kids who'd been in my kindergarten class.

So much alone time, I sensed, pushed me across the border between normalcy and weirdness, but not too far to ever get back. The way my

161

uncluttered brain worked on the Appalachian Trail was what I assumed "normal" was meant to be before we cluttered existences with silly crap like sports scores, Peewee Herman, Judge Wapner from the People's Court, the Simpsons and debates about which laundry detergent gets whites whiter. When hiking I felt aware of nuances like the gradual changing of sunrises and sunsets or the path of the moon or changing sounds of birds and breezes. A brain not used well is not at its best. Neglecting memories and ideas and critical thought take their toll over time. The benefits of deep-thought are far more potent than typically acknowledged. And good for the spirit. I thought about a lot of things as I hiked, most with more clarity than ever before or after.

Lori and I didn't stand a chance. I knew that. Maybe she did, too. We were too much alike in too many ways and not even close to being alike in so many others. I was half-baked and a little broken still, starting to wrestle with daydreams of maybe turning back north after Springer Mountain or heading to Montana with a canoe and paddling the Missouri River back home to St. Louis. Or perhaps even going back to school to be an accountant and live life from then on between the lines. She was on a path to somewhere I wasn't likely to follow, at least not anytime soon. One thing was clear, things were changing. Not only that, I was changing, too, and that didn't bode well for our future.

She'd been a good friend for a long while before the A.T., and now she was my connection to the world I'd left behind in Columbia. She was my connection to anything that remotely resembled romance. Sometimes I missed her, but not always. Sometimes I didn't even think about her. It turns out I liked myself better with her at arm's length than when she was snuggled next to me. Still, she was something to hold onto mentally along those long stretches when there were few people and the miles got long. I daydreamed about her now and then, but those daydreams never seemed to go anywhere.

She faithfully wrote long rambling letters about life on a college campus. I sent back postcards and occasional letters, deep and reflective, about my experiences. I could never bring myself to sign those letters, "Love, Dave," and she noticed. Once in a while, though, when certain stars aligned just right, I found myself missing her and went in search of a telephone.

Collect calls in 1987 were expensive. It cost two to three dollars per minute to reach out and connect with folks at home. That meant that at minimum wage, a two-minute phone conversation cost the equivalent of one hour worth of flipping burgers or washing dishes. It was easy to rack up outlandish phone bills without discipline. I can remember some that likely cost thirty bucks or more.

Since long distance rates were far cheaper after 11 pm -- some 60% cheaper, when convenient, it made sense to take a late-night trek to a lonely crossroads to find a pay phone on the outside wall of a closed grocery or gas station. Nothing was open round-the-clock then.

It was somewhere in Tennessee or North Carolina, south of Damascus, anyway that I collected a few essentials -- the things I should have taken with me that night I went looking for water in Maine -- and headed down the mountain. I carried a rain jacket, headlamp, map, compass, lighter, fleece, wallet, and two Snickers bars, and backtracked several miles to the phone we'd passed earlier at a road crossing. Hugh, Brett, and Ken thought I was crazy.

It was 10 pm on a night that was getting colder by the minute. Even in the dark, three miles wasn't far. Without a full pack, it was an easy forty-minute stroll. Or less. I clicked them off in less time than I expected and got to the phone thirty minutes before the rates would drop. There was nothing to do but sit and wait.

It was in the middle of nowhere. The black silhouette of a distant mountain was visible down the road and bats zigged and zagged through the light of a single street lamp silently eating moths and mosquitos by the thousands. Even so, they flew in my face and gnawed on my neck. It was to be a long thirty minutes.

The phone hung on a utility pole outside a closed gas station. The single street lamp cast only enough light so I wouldn't need a headlamp when the time came to dial. It was a rotary dial. Nearby was an overflowing trash barrel with "No Dumping" painted on the side in big sloppy white letters. There was a similar sign nailed to the utility pole only the lettering was black.

The pickup truck that pulled in was nondescript except for the sounds of unseen crap rolling around in the bed, mostly beer cans, I figured. And the duct tape keeping the front quarter-panel from rattling. The driver was in his forties and equally non-descript except for the huge silver belt buckle at his waist and the air of crispness about him. It was as if this was his morning, not his night. His neatness was directly opposite to the roughness of his truck. His hair was combed, his boots shiny, and his shirt, ironed and starched, was tucked in. It seemed odd that a man should look so crisp and clean at such an hour and in such a place. He pulled a bag of trash from the back of the truck and stuffed it in the barrel.

"You waiting for the phone?" He didn't stop moving and barely looked at me. The belt buckle was huge and gaudy and impractical. It said something about being a bull riding champ from Texas. I wanted to ask about it but never got the chance.

"Yes, sir."

"Me, too."

He retrieved another bag from the truck and balanced it on top of the first. He looked across the lot, looking for a car, I guessed. My car. It made me uneasy. "Where'd you come from?"

"Maine."

"How'd you get here?"

"Walked."

He let out a long, low whistle. "Long way." He didn't seem much impressed after that. He got another trash bag from the truck and set it next to the barrel. "In case you were wondering," he said, "that sign's not for me." He nodded towards the "No Dumping" sign and grinned. "It's for everybody else." He laughed a mischievous laugh.

"I wasn't wondering," I said. I was wondering, however, why his truck didn't have license plates. That was a bit unnerving.

He opened the tailgate and pulled out the few items that blocked his pursuit of the last escapee beer cans rolling around in the truck bed. He leaned a shovel and a pickaxe against the truck and set an old milk crate stuffed with rope and a crumpled tarp on the ground next to them. Then he wrestled an overstuffed trash bag to the edge of the tailgate, let it drop roughly to the ground. It landed with a significant thud. When he dragged it to the barrel, it left a suspicious wet trail behind it that showed up black in the dirt.

"Want a beer?"

"No, thanks."

"Need a ride anywhere?"

"Nope, I'm good."

Things were beginning to not feel so right. "Crap," I thought, looking at the stuff spread next to the truck, "All the right things for a murder -- innocent enough looking guy, beers to ease inhibitions, pickup truck, rope, shovel, and a tarp. What more did a serial killer need? Duct tape, I

164

figured. When he dropped a hammer on the ground, I knew I was a dead man. But then he tossed everything back in the truck, slammed the tailgate, tossed the hammer into the cab, got in and fired up the engine.

He leaned out the window and yelled over the roar, "If the phone rings, and I'm not back, answer it. It'll be my wife. Take a message, and tell her things are fine. Be sure she knows the Sheriff's been up at the house a few times and Little Joe's doing better. He's our boy. He's been sick. Tell her they ain't found Petey yet. I don't reckon they ever will." Then the man drove off with a wave like we were old friends. It was 10:45 pm. I figured he was heading home for duct tape, and I was not likely to see another day of sunshine if I stayed there too long.

"'Ain't found Petey, yet?' What did that mean? Who the hell was Petey? Was he somebody they iced and buried in the lower forty? Was she in on killing him? And how long before the man would be telling another thru-hiker, "They ain't found old Mack and the Boys yet either."

I thought hard about spending the couple extra bucks to call Lori before the rates changed at eleven. It seemed like a low price to pay for a chance to keep on hiking and not to wind up a national headline or the subject of some trashy novel. I figured I could talk to Lori for five-minutes and high-tail it back to the shelter before he could waylay me with a shovel to the head and bury me in some out-of-the-way hollow. I was short on funds, though, and there was something about hiking three miles in the dark to use a pay phone that made a man stubborn. Giving in and running didn't feel right. I decided to stand my ground.

Just before eleven, he pulled back into the lot, got out of the truck and headed my way. There was something in his hand; I couldn't make out what it was, but it was neither duct tape nor the hammer. My water bottle with the bandana looped through the top hung from my hand like an improvised mace. I was ready to smash him upside the head if he pushed to that point. Then, from out of nowhere, he handed me a cup of steaming hot coffee, "You look like a cream and sugar guy," he said. "And it's getting cold up here." I took a few cautious sips, trying to figure out if it was laced with antifreeze or a little cyanide, but it wasn't. It was perfect; warm and sweet and so welcomed on such a cold night. Except for the coffee in the CCC Diner back in Port Clinton, Pennsylvania, it proved to be the most memorable of the many cups of coffee along the entire two-thousand miles.

I thanked him graciously for the coffee. He slugged down another beer and smiled. "You need a place to stay? I got an extra bed if you don't mind kids and dogs."

"No, thanks, I got buddies up in the mountains waiting." I tried to sound tougher than I was. Buddies in the mountains, hell! They were AT hikers wasted by 2,000 miles of walking. They were sound asleep most likely and oblivious to my comings and goings. They were men who could fly endlessly along a trail with fifty pounds on their backs who limped like stiff old men any other time. They were hardly tough in anybody's estimation. They were certainly not the kind of cavalry that might rush in and save me from the clutches of a killer.

That's when the phone rang. It was a strange sound in the middle of nowhere, an old antique-sounding ring. "You mind if I get that?" He asked. "I won't be but a few minutes. She only gets five."

I nodded and walked a respectful distance away wondering why she only got five minutes of phone time. I could only guess.

I couldn't overhear what he said, but he spoke in a soft, almost sweet tone touched with a bit of sadness. Five minutes wasn't long, I thought. "I love you, too," he said. "Hang in there." After a long pause, he said, "They miss you, too," and "Not too much longer."

He hung up and stood there for a moment staring at nothing. He wiped his eyes with his sleeve, then walked to the truck, his head hung low. He snorted and spit. I could feel his heart breaking. As he passed, he whispered, "Never should have gotten mixed up with that bitch."

Then he was back in the truck and whipping out of the parking lot. As he drove off, he leaned his head out of the window and hollered, "Petey's my dog. Ain't seen him fer two weeks. Guess the coyotes him. Boy's pretty broke up about it. Sheriff's been helping us look. Funny, I miss that dog more than I miss that woman."

Then he was gone, and my coffee was still hot.

I called Lori thinking I could do far, far worse and missing her more than at any other moment while out there. She wasn't destined to be my soulmate, I knew, but she'd be someone's someday.

"Where are you?"

"Tennessee."

"How much longer?"

"Three weeks."

"Do you miss me?"

"More than ever," I lied and told her about my evening. I left out the part about my deciding she needed to find a soulmate and that I wasn't destined to be that man.

What's going to happen when you get back?"

"Don't know. I'll need to find a job. I've been wrestling with a few options."

"Any of those include me?"

"I'll come to see you in the first week when I get back."

"You didn't answer my question."

"Twenty-one hundred miles is a long way. I have lots to figure out."

"Yeah, well, don't expect me to wait forever."

"I wouldn't ask you to."

"Don't slip into town unannounced," She said. Her tone was almost indignant. "I know you. You'll drift in and do things on your terms. Don't do that. People need time to get ready. God, people are crazy around here. 'When's he getting back?' 'When's he going to be in town?" People keep asking, even those who hardly know you. Jesus, you're still just a man. Don't expect a hero's welcome either. You're not that special."

She was right. She knew me well and slipping in unannounced was precisely what I planned. I didn't need any attention Or want any. She was wrong about me thinking I was a hero. I was less of a hero than I ever expected I might be. I was sure I'd not accomplished anything extraordinary. And that understanding was a good thing -- an excellent thing, indeed.

For five months, I'd gotten up each morning, strapped a pack on my back and did what I had to do for eight or twelve hours to get where I needed to go. What's so great about that? I went to bed each night exhausted and got up the next morning and did it all over again. I hadn't done anything more than anybody else does when they focus on a goal and work hard to accomplish it. Nothing more. In fact, far, I realized I'd done far less than what I watched my father do every day of his life. He got up, went to work, came home, slept, got up the next morning and did it again. Doing that day after day, year after year, built the rock-solid foundation upon which his life and the life of his family rested. He'd have been a successful thru-hiker. Hell, he was a pretty successful thru-hiker already, only his Appalachian Trail was something far more significant than the actual Appalachian Trail.

There was nothing glamorous about what I'd done and certainly nothing heroic about it.   I'd merely gained some perspective.

I tried to explain those things -- about being humbled by people like my father who worked hard every day of their lives and who built things like families and foundations for the lives of others. I tried to explain about appreciating simple things especially love and relationships. I tried to explain my need to get focused and get on with building a life rich in meaning. It was hard, though, to help someone who thought hiking the AT was a great accomplishment to understand that it was really just a long walk in the woods with almost too much time to think.

I hung up the phone and ambled back to the shelter, my head swirling with thoughts about my future and how different I was from the version which left Columbia, Missouri, with "Take It Easy" playing in the background.   I rolled into the shelter in the dark, climbed into my sleeping bag and slept fitfully. Mostly thanks to the caffeine.

My pals never even stirred.

A million people have likely stayed at Icewater Spring shelter in Great Smoky Mountains National Park; and if it wasn't a million, it was enough to leave the place worn and tired and the land around it scarred. In 1987, the building was solid as a rock and overrun with mice and other critters. It was nearly impossible to find an unused spot to dig a cathole without walking halfway down the mountain. Most had walked a few feet into the woods, scratched a shallow trench in the rock-hard surface, done their business and half-heartedly covered it. Leave no trace? Hardly. Plenty of people had left lots and lots of traces around Icewater Springs shelter. It was kind of disgusting. Finding a place to poop required picking a delicate path through a treacherous minefield. Despite being set amidst the most beautiful of surroundings, it was, I believe, the least appealing spot along the entire two-thousand miles to "take a break."

Hugh and I cruised in after a leisurely twenty miles from Cosby Knob. In the two days before, we'd logged forty from Hot Springs, NC, where we'd lingered at the Jesuit hostel to read by the fire and eat in a local cafe. At a local's urging in hot springs, we'd climbed a fence, squeezed between some loose boards around a window and found our way into the ruins of the old bathhouse. The walls were lined with tiled stalls, half-filled with silt and old boards except for one. That one had been painstakingly cleaned, perhaps even restored, and was near immaculate. There was not a bit of sediment in the pool or litter anywhere. Half-burned candles lined the walls here and there. Clearly, this was someone's favorite spot, and they cared for it. We lit the candles, stripped down to our skivvies and sat in the warm springs for quite some time. We laughed and joked as we did more often than not. Laughter is part of what makes thru-hikes genuinely amazing.

Icewater Spring shelter was like a fortress built with rocks from the surrounding landscape by some of the three million unmarried men, seventeen to twenty-five, who served the in Civilian Conservation Corps, between 1933 and 1942. A good part of the backbone of the AT still trails over bridges and paths built originally by the CCC.

As we hunkered down in the shelter sipping instant international coffee and sharing Jello cheesecake, a rather bold skunk emerged from under the wire bunks to check things out. At the same time, a mouse slid from the rafters down a piece of piano wire to the food bag at the end. Unfortunately for the mouse, his robbery attempt ended in the snap of a trap balanced atop the pack and baited with a spot of peanut butter. Fortunate for the old guy who owned the trap and for us, the sharp snap didn't startle the skunk who was quite unperturbed by our presence.

My favorite thru-hiker tale, its truth likely twisted some by the time I heard it, took place in Icewater Springs Shelter and probably featured that very skunk. It featured two hikers from overseas known together as the "The Brits." I'd met them north of there, in New York, maybe, and heard part of the story straight from them. Through their Cockney accents, I managed to understand bits and pieces. While overnighting in Icewater Springs, one had awakened to a black and white "kitty" standing at his feet. Reaching to pet the "kitty" was apparently not so well-received, and it exploded in a cloud of noxious gas. Skunks, apparently, are not so commonplace in Great Britain. Or at least not in London.

Did that really happen? Likely not just that way. Tales along the AT have a way of "maturing."

The CCC built Icewater Springs Shelter plus a whole lot more. Modern AT hikers owe at least a tip of the cap to the Civilian Conservation Corps, a work relief program that focused on environmental projects during the Great Depression. The CCC built the foundation of a nation wealthy beyond measure in well-managed parks and public lands. They planted three-and-a-half billion trees, constructed trails and shelters in more than eight-hundred parks nationwide between 1933 and 1942. The CCC shaped the national and state park systems and built the backbone of the AT as it's enjoyed today.

The CCC was part of FDR's New Deal. Within months of the legislation that established it, 1,433 work camps had been built, and 300,000 men were at work fighting forest fires, planting trees, clearing and maintaining access roads, re-seeding grazing lands and putting soil-erosion controls in place. They built wildlife refuges, fish-rearing facilities, water storage basins, and constructed bridges, campground facilities, and park infrastructures to encourage Americans to enjoy their natural resources. It was the most rapid peacetime mobilization in American history.

The CCC enrolled mostly young, unmarried, unskilled and unemployed men from families on government assistance. Each received thirty dollars per month plus food and shelter at a work camp. They were required to send twenty-five dollars home to support their families each month. 57,000 men, as an added benefit, learned to read and write in CCC camps.

Eighty years later, without the success of the CCC and the manual labor of three-million men, we'd live in a very different, much less healthy nation with fewer connections to the natural world. Every mile on the AT deserves a nod to those men who broke their backs to lay the infrastructure for the places we love, learn in, and derive life from.

By the time we reached Double Springs Gap, the wind had turned cold, and the sky was spitting little pebbles of ice. In Maine, I'd have cursed such weather. In North Carolina, though, it was just another day. Taking hardships in stride came naturally now.

We rolled in refreshed, Hugh and I, after a good day in Gatlinburg. We'd hitchhiked from Newfound Gap, spent most of the morning grazing at a Shoney's breakfast bar where the manager watched with some consternation as we each ate what four others might consume. Then we wandered the crowded sidewalks. Every step required great care not to bang into tourists or knock things off shelves. To tourists and sightseers who walked Gatlinburg, mostly older folks and visitors from other countries, we must have seemed like monsters milling through the streets.

Thru-hikers don't look like everybody else.

We slept off the 10,000 calories from Shoney's for a good long while in a field outside of town, read some in the sunshine, and caught a ride back to Newfound Gap in the back of a pick-up. By the end of the day, and before dark, we'd still made 14 miles without effort. In the higher country, the winds picked up and the rain started to freeze.

When the challenges of a hard day were well-met, the next day was easy. That was one of the most important lessons of my Appalachian Trail. Work hard one day or several days in a row, then take a well-deserved break the next. Even if it was just ten or twenty miles of two-thousand, any day when I could look at a map and see evidence of progress, I knew I'd sleep well that night and dream the kind of dreams worth remembering.

A good day always contributed to a sense that I was going somewhere, and that felt right. That's how life works, I guess. If we're moving towards something that matters, everything else seems okay. If you're spinning your wheels, though, then it feels like you're stuck going nowhere and then nothing feels right.

What makes the difference between feeling like you're going somewhere and feeling stuck? Intent. Hard work. Focus. How do you eat an elephant? One bite at a time. How do you hike the A.T.? One step at a time. And with a smile in your heart. If you can't smile at the tough stuff, going home might be a better choice. How do you accomplish just about anything? Accomplish a little each day for a whole lot of days in a row.

By the Smoky Mountains, that's something that was ingrained in my head.

From a hundred yards out, Double Springs Gap shelter looked empty. At least it wasn't overrun by refuge-seekers. Ice was starting to spit from the sky, and the wind blew harder and colder. It was a proper shelter. Solid. Stone. Built by the CCC. It had a dirt floor and log bunks along the back wall; there was a chain-link fence across the front to keep bears at bay. It was almost luxurious, especially in the face of the weather blowing up outside.

There was room for caution when one entered a trail shelter lest he might hazard upon someone or something undesirable. Or perhaps even downright dangerous. But there had not been anyone unpleasant or scary since New York, and tales of fearful encounters from Northbounders were few at best and very occasional. The trail proved to be a safe place and abandoning the idea that evil lurked in the shadows was freeing. Embracing the belief that good and wholesome types outweighed less-desirables brought out the best in others. In the months since we'd started, we'd weathered enough nights with friendly sorts that any notions that bad people hung out in shelters just waiting to pounce had long before been dispelled. When you expect the best, I believe, you tend to find it. And when you can let go of fears, you sleep far better at night.

Not since the initial minutes of my encounter with the massive snake back in Arkansas had I ever wished I was carrying a pistol.

It was getting cold and dark, and we were hungry. We quickened our steps and rolled into Double Gap without a care, not the least bit concerned about highwaymen or vagabonds as we once might have been.

We were just ten days from Springer. Two more food drops to go and then on to the rest of our lives. Being part of the Appalachian Trail was no longer stressful in the least. It was home and perhaps we'd even grown a little careless.

It was nearly dark outside and all the way dark inside when we burst into Double Gap Shelter as if we owned it. We were considerably self-absorbed as we tossed packs on bunks and missed the middle-aged men huddled in the dark behind ponchos slung on the fence to block the wind. We went about our work loudly, making tea and instant soup and sealing the shelter from the chill winds with tarps. Had the men in the corner been bears they'd have mauled one or the other of us and ransacked our packs. Then suddenly we saw them hunched and cold in a corner, staring and not doing much more. They were pale and a bit startled. They shared a meager freeze-dried meal between them without speaking. Or blinking.

One or the other of us noticed them rather all-of-a-sudden. No one spoke. All of us stared. And in the minutes of awkward inaction, opportunities for convivial greetings just sort of passed us by.

We'd scared the piss out of them, I'm sure. The shorter of the men sat on the bunk, one hand deep in his pack as if maybe reaching for something concealed there, something perhaps that consoled him some. Had their thoughts turned to pistols tucked in their packs? They were law-abiders, for sure, and careful. Did they now worry how they might unpack their pieces from deep in their bags, load them, and level them at our heads before we could set upon them? In the minutes before either Hugh or I noticed them, impressions had been formed, I'm sure, and not likely favorable ones.

The next minutes were awkward, even a bit tense. No one spoke. The men, I'm sure, wondered if, in the next seconds, we might bash them in the heads, tie them up, and abscond with their valuables. We just went about fixing dinner and getting warm.

We watched, and they waited. They watched, and we waited. Each of tried hard to watch the other without looking like we watched the other. I could feel their eyes on my back. I'm sure they could feel mine on theirs, too.

Hugh wasn't bothered by any of it He was an Englishman to the core. At this point in any day, nothing was more important than tea. It was his daily ritual when he rolled into camp to boil water before anything else. Our way was for him to make the tea and me to prep instant soup. Neither of us spoke much just then, there seemed to be a rather large elephant in the room, and perhaps that "elephant" clutched a pistol, loaded or otherwise.

The men watched as if they expected us to spring at any moment and stcal their brand-new packs, likely purchased recently from a discount store like K-mart. To them, we were naught but drifters. And likely dangerous, desperate ones. They were quick to judge, we figured, and went about our business with some disappointment. And watched them almost as closely as they watched us.

We were unlike them, especially in appearance. Neither Hugh nor I had shaved nor groomed ourselves recently. Our equipment and everything else about us showed the stresses of two-thousand miles. And our boots? Hell, they'd endured a few million steps. How could the men recognize they were among the very best. Even a few days into their hike, the two were clean-scrubbed. Like their stuff, they were new and shiny. We, obviously, were not.

They likely remembered their last shower. We did not. The backpacks, sleeping bags, and rain gear they carried resembled something one might pluck from the shelves at a big-box store. No stains, nor tears, no scars from sitting too close to a campfire. Their boots were unblemished and stiff. Ours looked like ten days might be too much more to ask from them.

It was perhaps the first time I'd ever seen a blaze-orange pack. That color in outdoor gear among serious hikers who don't hunt tends to blast messages like, "I've never done this before," "I bought my pack at ACE Hardware," and "Help, I'm in over my head."

While we sipped tea and soup in a quite civilized manner and rice and noodles simmered with canned chicken and bacon on stoves, they tried not to look like they were staring. We hung tarps neatly on the fence to block the wind, lit candle lanterns to flood the shelter with warm light, and settled into a warm and hearty meal. Just 20 minutes had passed between our arrival and the moment dinner was served.

We each prayed silently before we ate.

It was Art who broke the ice. He was an accountant from Illinois, I think. Or Pennsylvania. He had kids in college. He looked pretty much like you'd expect an accountant from Pennsylvania to look. He was well-groomed and soft around the middle with thick glasses and less hair than he'd likely had in previous years.

He'd long before taken his hand out of his pack; he walked our way slowly, as if not wanting to startle us. "You guys have obviously done this before," he said. "That was impressive to watch."

"Yes, sir."

"We're new at this," he said. I didn't say anything. His was just a statement of the obvious.

"You don't say?" I grinned at him.

"Where are you heading?" Art asked.

"Georgia." No one was ever impressed by where we were going.

"Where'd you come from?"

"Maine." And that's when the tone of everything changed as it always did with trailside conversations. People cared more about where we'd been than where we were heading. Miles hiked, like in other areas of life, gave credence to whatever you had to say.

"Thru-hikers?"

"Almost. 180 miles to go. Then we will be." Aby tension in the shelter was now gone. Instantly.

Having purpose gave us legitimacy. We were no longer bums. Or wanderers. In their eyes, our dishevelment was understandable. Even admirable. We were on our way somewhere. They recognized our appearance as the price paid for our expertise and from that point, they embraced us as experts.

From Maine to Georgia, people were quick to distrust when they didn't understand. Or when you didn't look like them. Or act like them. Once they understood your purpose, though, and recognized you were working towards something higher -- and didn't want to eat them or take their stuff, most wanted to know more. Some were even impressed. People admire expertise and commitment and like to share in other people's success. Give them a reason to be drawn to you, and they will be. Ignore them, and they're likely to ignore you. And distrust you. Want people to care about what you have to say and to give you a chance? Then you need to give them a reason to believe in you as an expert and show them that you care about them. And be sure your story is of consequence to them, too.

"I wish I had the time to do that."

"Nobody has the time," I said. "You've gotta make the time. It's about choices."

"Yeah, your right," Art nodded.

Everybody introduced themselves. Hugh, David, Art, Joe.

"Can I pick your brain about gear and food and stuff?" Art looked tired and relieved we weren't after his stuff.

"Sure." And thus unfolded one of the most pleasant encounters along the entire AT And one of the more meaningful.

"You guys aren't carrying dehydrated meals. Why not?"

"Too expensive. Not necessary. Not enough fat. Not enough food." My responses came between big, sloppy bites of buttery noodles and chicken and bacon I shoveled into my mouth.

"The guy at the store told us we needed dehydrated stuff. The packages said 'two servings,' so we got one to share for every meal. Turns out they barely feed one. Art shook his head and laughed, "We learned the hard way."

"The guy at the sports store is a dope," I said. "Likely he's not even tasted the stuff. Pretty bland, I'm guessing." In the light, it was obvious they were ready fora hotel. And Shoney's. "You need more than dehydrated meals to stay warm and keep going."

They'd been hiking several days, it turned out. They'd been living off half-rations and barely eating enough to stay warm. Not only were their portions small, but there was no fat in their diet either. There was nothing to burn to keep them warm. They reminded me of Mack and the Boys when we were four-strong in Maine and only slightly smarter than rocks.

"We have a name for guys like you," I smiled at them; they waited expectantly. "Goofers."

"Goofers?"

"Yeah, guys who don't have a clue, but think they do and who get by accidentally more than anything they do. 'Goofers' rough their way through life on the trail and get where they're going by accident. Thru-hikers, though, well, eventually they figure out lasting two-thousand miles takes building a sustainable lifestyle."

They laughed about being 'goofers,' and we fed them well -- coffee, cheesecake, Snickers bars, and crispy fried bacon. And we made a gift of extras we could spare -- mac and cheese, canned tuna, and oatmeal. We talked about life throughout the evening often in terms of the difference between those who lived as goofers and those who lived as thru-hikers might.

More than anything, Joe and Art were decent men. That's what I remember. Joe and Art were anything but goofers when it came to living satisfying lives. Both had raised families. Art was an accountant; Joe was a mailman and a Vietnam veteran who struggled with the effects of Agent Orange exposure.

If you don't know what Agent Orange is and the devastating effect exposure had on the lives of four million people during and after the Vietnam War, you should. Agent Orange was a chemical defoliant that cleared jungles. It also resulted in destructive health impacts on those exposed to it. It's a consequence of war not addressed often enough or with full honesty.

There are 58,272 names on the Vietnam War Memorial. To honor the four-million impacted by Agent Orange with their own monument would require another wall almost eighty times longer.

Along the Appalachian Trail, I felt alive and free to learn and grow. Most of the time, I felt safe. Wrapping one's head around the horrors men and families impacted by war struggle with was often far from my mind. Joe brought it home, though. He was a good-natured sort and struck me as one who lived simply and thankfully. I admired him deeply.

Art watched over him like they were brothers. He'd done so since they were kids. Their relationship reminded me of Doc and Mack from Steinbeck's novel, Cannery Row -- the same Mack that inspired my trail name, only I don't think Art's commitment was motivated at all by guilt like Doc's was in the novel. Art laughed at Joe's failing memory which was apparently not quite what it had been in their earlier days. They loved each other as friends, and Art watched over his friend as brothers-in-arms. It was the kind of friendship, I thought, that every man should have, the type that might change the world if more of us had such connections. Altogether, they were fortunate men. They were blessed with something valuable and exceedingly rare.

Both men spoke of wives and careers; each talked of children and futures. They'd been friends all their lives and would be for the rest of their days, too. On the A.T., they were goofers who lacked a clue. In their

176

lives, though, they were anything but goofers -- at least that was my impression from our brief time together. After completing the Trail, Joe and Art came to represent for me a valuable lesson about living and friendship, a lesson one I wish I'd embraced earlier and with more gusto.

Two-thousand miles into the A.T., I was no longer a goofer in the context of hiking the Appalachian Trail. Not even close. There was little I couldn't manage out there, and I could claim to be an expert. I'd achieved not just competence but extreme competence in my small world. Being an expert for that short time and in that specific world was amazing. Unlike any other point in my life, I was better prepared than almost any other person I knew or encountered. It was a valuable lesson and one that left me with great respect for those with the ambition and resilience to become the best. That's an impressive way to live.

Expertise gleaned along the Appalachian Trail was limited mostly to the realm of the Appalachian Trail, though. What I would be after Springer Mountain remained to be seen. How much of my competence on the trail – my extreme fitness to thrive in that environment – would translate back to living life well when I was off of the trail? Not as much, it turned out as I guessed.

I've hiked to the top of many mountains and enjoyed some spectacular views. One thing's always the same at the peak of each of overlooks, though. I could never stay there for long – certainly not forever. At some point, no matter how beautiful the view or how hard you worked to get there, you had to hike back down the mountain and get on with living. The same is true for the AT. And for life. One can thru-hike the trail, even bounce back north or south and hike it again, but at some point, thru-hikers need to go home and move on with the rest of their lives. What makes the difference is not that you hiked the A.T., but whether you can approach life in a manner similar to how you thru-hiked.

Two-thousand miles into the experience, thru-hikers are perfectly adapted to trail life and capable of things few others can do easily. It is a fantastic feeling. In a single day, an average thru-hiker can walk 30-miles with a full pack, weather an unexpected storm, take a two-hour nap in the sunshine atop some scenic point, yogi a meal or a shower, write a heartfelt letter home, track down a payphone from which to make a collect call, and still set up camp in a shelter by nightfall. Not yet finished with their day, he or she can prep a satisfying meal over a camp stove as if machined to do so, write in a journal by candlelight, and turn in early enough to get a full and refreshing night's sleep with a clear plan for what needs to happen the following day.

Thru-hikers are amazing beings -- At least they are when they are on the trail. But what happens when they are transplanted to the "real" world? I wasn't far from finding out.

It would be awesome if once we climbed to the summit, we could stay there. Most of us can't. The skills that matter a whole lot along the trail don't matter near as much when you get home. What happens on the AT, as beneficial as it is, isn't perfect preparation for what comes after Springer or Katahdin.

I doubt there has ever been a thru-hiker who was still a goofer when he or she reached either terminus, north or south. Plenty of us, though, go home to discover that we are goofers at home. The challenging task facing hikers is not finishing their hike, it's taking what they learned from their trail experience home and incorporating lessons learned about simplicity, hard work, consistency, and focus to life in general and ensuring you don't wind up a goofer for the rest of your days.

I knew Joe and Art for a day, but the impressions they left are alive and well 10,000 days later. And they still have meaning. That should be an objective for each of us – to still be relevant even in the lives of those we connect with for short periods of time for 10,000 days or so. That's the kind of thing likely to forge a better world if a significant number of us strived to do it.

NORTH CAROLINA

October 19, 1987

From my Journal:

"It's impossible to write with mittens on. Nightly temperatures range from low thirties to upper 20s making writing difficult at best. The most efficient system seems to be writing a few sentences then warming my fingers over a candle or under my armpit until I can write a little bit more."

"I can smell the home fires burning. 400 miles to go. I've spent a great deal of time by myself thinking and figuring. I'll come home with a supply of confidence and direction that wasn't there before. And I'll bring a greater understanding of limitations than I've ever had before. I am excited to take these lessons home, though there is so much I will miss."

"I woke up to a wonderful site this morning. The sky was clear as crystal and bluer than any blue I'd ever seen before. The air was cool, but the sun warm. I was standing on Iron Mountain looking down on what should have been Watauga Lake. Instead, there were only clouds -- a valley full of them -- far below. It was an ocean of swirling white; the peaks of the opposing ridge rose above the clouds like Islands. There was not a cloud above me, but a thousand feet below was a blanket so thick as to completely obscure the valley floor. Today I understand the meaning of "breathtaking" beauty even more."

"I still learn a little each day even though I've traveled seventeen hundred miles. There's no reason not to stop."

One crosses from Virginia into Tennessee then into North Carolina. Through the Smoky Mountains, Tennessee, North Carolina, and the AT share a seventy-mile long border until the trail crosses wholly into North Carolina just south of the Smoky Mountains for a while. Eventually, it passes almost unceremoniously into Georgia.

In Hot Springs, I stepped into a diner; l more appropriately, I stepped 'back' into a diner. It was a snapshot of a time long before. The accents were heavily southern; the people were fresh from whatever fields they'd come from. Most likely made their livings with their hands or spent good parts of their day plowing up the earth, hunting, fishing, or tending stock. Most of them had likely been up for a long while, and it was still early morning. They were hard working sorts. Little more than long dresses on the women and worn grey coats and battered kepi caps on the men would have transformed the place to the 1880s, except that the Andy Griffith Show played on a TV perched on a shelf above the counter. The place was alive like a Norman Rockwell painting, filled with older men mostly, and a few younger ones who'd probably hunted that morning or tended livestock and fields. A few sat with wives, not many, though. There were just a handful of people breakfasting and sipping coffee in the place. Among them, though, one could feel the buzz of a million stories waiting to be told.

No one acknowledged me as I stepped through the door except the waitress who stood with her back to me, eyes fixed like everyone else on the television above the counter. It was now on The People's Court, the first of the on-air courtroom reality dramas starring silver-haired Judge Wapner. The waitress never looked at me, just said, "Sit anywhere." I sat at the counter next to an older man in dirt-stained clothing and tobacco-stained hands. He looked at me and smiled. It was a nice smile. And nodded. Still not looking away from the TV, the waitress asked, "Coffee?" and set a steaming cup in front of me before I'd even responded.

I'd left my pack at the Catholic hostel down the road but still toted the unmistakable markings of a long-distance hiker -- gaunt face, burned skin, disheveled hair, and an insatiable hunger for food. Any food.

I fit in with the patrons. No one was the slightest bit concerned or passed the most minor judgment.

"You one of those Appalachian hikers?" The man asked.

"Yes, sir."

"Why are you doing that?"

"I want to see the country."

"You like what you've seen?"

"Yes, sir. Seems people are inclined to help when they can. Most are working hard just to get by. Aren't many nasty ones out there, at least not in the places I've been. And the unpleasant ones, well, they're dealing with tough stuff or they never learned basic things about being decent. They're okay, though."

"This country ain't perfect," he said. "But it's what we've got, and people are good most everywhere you go. You know Ernest Tubbs?"

"Musician? Had his heyday in the forties and fifties?"

"Yep. Philosopher of sorts, old Ernest. Wrote many a good song. They're the soundtrack of my life. He said, 'If you want better neighbors, you gotta be better to your neighbors.' I buy that. It's the secret, I think. Simple. Just another way of saying, 'Do unto others' and 'Love one another' as the Bible says. If we all did that, this world would be a helluva place to live."

I smiled and ordered breakfast.

"God made it pretty clear what he wants, didn't he? Said, 'Make me first. Live unselfish-like. Love one another'. What's hard to figure about that?"

He took a long pull from his coffee mug. The waitress threw down a plate of eggs, ham, grits, toast, tomatoes, pancakes, a waffle, butter, and syrup in front of me.

"Anything else?"

"Give him a piece of pie, Rosy, if he finishes all that. On me." He smiled. "Apple's the best."

"Where are your shoes?" I asked him. He sat at the counter in his socks.

"My wife, bless her soul – and her soles -- said 'no shoes in the house, Mr. Tom Joseph – ever.' Now, I take most of my meals in this place, so I figure it's kinda like my house. I never wear shoes here. Left mine outside the door. It's a respect thing fer my wife, I guess. I lost her year before last."

"I'm sorry."

"No need. God's with me. And she's with God. It's not the way I would've written my life, but I'm sure there's a plan behind it. I'll bide my time patiently and do the right things so's I get to see her again. We're all living on God's time and His time ain't never the same as what we want. That I'm sure of."

I could only nod and keep shoveling food in as fast as I could. I was intent on earning my free pie slice. Tom Joseph had thrown down the gauntlet. I was intent on showing him that the appetite of a thru-hiker was nothing to be trifled with.

Tears sparkled in his eyes. I could tell he missed her more than anything.

He talked about his days soldiering in France, Germany, and Italy during World War Two. He told about things he'd seen, talked about how men are capable of the highest good and the most terrible of deeds, and shared stories about the Battle of the Bulge. He told about men laying down their lives for others, giving all they had so others might live. "Yep," he said, "Most men are capable of more than we give them credit." He named some of them and shared specific deeds he'd witnessed. Then he leaned in and said, "I've never told anyone that before." He told me about two boys he'd known while the Battle of the Bulge raged and how a grenade had landed among them at breakfast. In their haste to be the right kind of men, both jumped to throw themselves on the grenade to save the other and those around them. Only in their enthusiasm to do the right thing, they'd collided with one another and fell to the ground next to – not on – the grenade. "Dummies," he said. "Both them boys were killed and a few others. It's how I lost hearing in my left ear." He stared far off into the distance. I guessed he was for the moment back to France forty years before. For the time, he forgot Judge Wapner, "Boys like that would have gone on to do great things as men. War is such a waste."

I was humbled in the man's presence, wrapped in his wisdom, and thinking maybe, just maybe I should stay a few more days just to listen to his stories. And maybe write them down. He seemed so filled with understanding about men and greatness and living well that he could, with his message, perhaps, change the world, I thought. "So much to learn," I told myself. "This man might teach you something that matters."

The waitress refilled my coffee mug for the tenth time. He stopped her from filling his with a hand over the cup. Another episode of The People's Court came on. It commanded everyone's attention such that if I'd been so inclined, I could have slid over a couple of stools, picked the cash register clean, and gotten away without anyone being the slightest bit wiser.

"I seen this episode," old Tom Joseph blurted out to everyone in the place. I braced myself for more wisdom from this modern day philosopher as he addressed everyone in the place. They froze like me, it seemed, hung on the words about to come from the man. And there I sat ill-prepared -- without pen and paper -- to record his wisdom. I waited, fully expectant that whatever might come forth could be life-changing. I trembled. I zeroed in on the sound of his voice; focused like a laser on whatever it was he was about to say. For the instant, time stopped and waited. Then, he spoke. I wasn't at all prepared for what he said, though. He gesticulated towards the television, captured their attention, and announced to everyone in the place, "That nigger woman says that white fella cheated her out of rent money or something. I believe she's telling the truth. That other fella with the nose like a hook -- He's a Jew, I suspect, and you can't trust them when it comes to money."

I choked on the chunk of apple pie I'd just shoveled into my mouth. Tom Joseph picked up the tab. It was a beautiful thing. More art than food, warm and topped with vanilla ice cream. Old Tom Joseph got sucked into the TV. I was inclined to educate him then and there about the injustice of his hatred-fused words. "Yeah," I thought with self-righteous indignation, "Sometimes it's not okay to let others hike their own hike. " I started to indict him for his horrible, hateful language. Fortunately, in that instant, I couldn't have spoken without spewing pie over the counter. So instead of spitting my own brand of indignation, I said nothing and thought some instead. It's lucky that I did.

In the natural pause that ensued, it occurred to me his words were not loaded with venom as I'd concluded. Nor were they a conscious choice to denigrate anyone or any group. Instead, his words were just those available to him. They were holdovers from a different era. Perhaps they were laced with ignorance, but not with hate. Were they okay? No. Were they reason to indict him as a monster? No. Was it my place to pass judgment? No.

Tom Joseph had been born when there were fewer than a thousand miles of paved roads in this country. It was an era when memories of civil war and slavery -- not things he'd chosen -- were as recent for older people as memories now are of things like the hula hoop, the Vietnam war, the Beatles wearing jackets and ties on the Ed Sullivan Show, Kennedy's assassination, and the 1965 Ford Mustang. His words were a snapshot of history not a glimpse into his soul. I almost lashed out wrongly and judged him as terribly evil and branded him and others like him as the reason for so many wrongs in the world when in fact he and his kind were the reason for so many good things in the world. I could have challenged him about God and his beliefs. I could have become Tom Joseph's self-appointed judge, jury, and hangman that morning, but to assume those roles would have been a greater injustice than his misuse of language. Old Tom Joseph was a good man, more perfect than me. He was steeped in the language of another era, sure, but he was still just and fair and good in so many ways. Almost to a fault.

He got up and shuffled towards the door in his stockinged feet. He lightly patted my shoulder as he passed. "Good luck, young man," he said. "You're doing the right thing." I sensed he was going home to his small and lonely house where he would talk to himself and miss his dead wife terribly. My heart hurt for him.

He wasn't perfect, but he was special, I thought. And he'd paid his dues.

I finished my meal, satisfied that the man's goodness wasn't tainted by his ignorance. I walked to the cash register to pay. "No need," the waitress whispered. "Mr. Tom Joseph paid your tab and gave me a nicer than normal tip. He's a good man, isn't he?"

She seemed to understand that his language had been inappropriate. "He's from a different time," she said. "White or black, if you were broke down on the road, he'd be the first to stop and help. Most of the people here are like that. They just care about living good and getting by."

I nodded politely and walked into the sunshine. Tom Joseph's words swirled like a storm through my head, "God made it pretty clear what he wants, didn't he? Make me first. Live unselfish-like. Love one another. What's hard about that?"

I've thought about his words often. Apparently, those things are pretty hard.

A mile or so down the road, a passage from the gospel of Matthew came to mind. I realized that it was a perfect complement to the idea that one should hike their own hike and let others hike theirs. It doesn't matter whether you're a believer or not, there's wisdom in the quote:

"Why do you look at the speck of sawdust in your brother's eye and pay no attention to the plank in your own eye? How can you say to your brother, 'Let me take the speck out of your eye,' when all the time there is a plank in your own eye? You hypocrite, first take the plank out of your own eye, and then you will see clearly to remove the speck from your brother's eye." -- Matthew 7:3-5.

Aren't Matthew's words as appropriate for clean living as something like, Hike your hike, and let others hike theirs?" I'm glad I listened to old Tom Joseph without kicking him to the curb in some misguided kneejerk reaction.

South of the Smoky Mountains, it was as if North Carolina were on fire. The fall colors were beyond comprehension. Near Grandfather Mountain, they mixed and swirled with the fall sunset to create a confusing illusion of the woods being on fire. Everything was pink and orange and red and alive and moving. I tried to take a picture, but you just don't capture such beauty with old-style point-and-shoot cameras. I leaned against a tree, dizzied by the overwhelming display, and soaked it all in. Gorgeous. Even now, when I need to be swept away by things spiritual and mystic, I drift back to those amazing colors.

I spent that night in a bunkhouse at Nantahala Outdoor Center, ate the "River Runner's Special" in the restaurant there, then did it again a few hours later. Before I set off on the trail, I ate the same thing again. I thought about flirting with the pretty waitress, but I'd caught sight of myself in the shower-house mirror earlier. I was lean and brown, and nearly emaciated. I looked like one who'd stepped recently from the wilds – which I had. I wasn't so pretty as I once was. My face, arms, and thighs were brown as raw earth; my chest and legs below the knees were white as snow where gaiters and a shirt had shielded them from the slightest sun for months. The haircut Scotty gave me in Harpers Ferry West Virginia had not grown out well. Somewhere along the way, I'd stopped combing my hair, choosing instead to tame it most mornings with a wet bandana. My beard was unruly and wild, and the chest and shoulder muscles I'd worked so hard to build up pumping weights before setting out were stripped down to nothing. I was barely recognizable as the bulked-up version of me who climbed Katahdin. Any muscle not needed for hiking in the mountains was long gone, but those required there were like rocks. I felt as much animal as I did man.

No, I thought, no flirting that day, just stories about where I'd been and what I'd seen. I was an outsider in most places now where I used to be just like any other. With one-hundred-fifty miles to go and two-thousand behind, I was from a different world than the waitress and almost any others. Trail life was something I understood, though few others could grasp. Hugh, Brett, and Ken were from the same universe. Hanging with them was simple. I loved the identity and simplicity of being a thru-hiker. At the same time that I sensed a balance within my personal cosmos, I wondered how much of that balance could be preserved when I went home.

That's when I started worrying about what was next. Just a few more days remained. Worrying about what it would be like to go home occupied much of my daydreaming. Soon I'd have to face my father and Rusty -- who I hadn't kept touch with since he left New Hampshire. And I'd have to thank all those who supported me. How does one do that? So many had faithfully written letters and accepted expensive collect phone calls from out of the blue. What did I owe them? Most of all, I'd have to come to terms with who I'd become. I was hardly the same man. My head was screwed on better than before, at least it seemed so, but was it? Out there it absolutely was, but what about when I was back?

And Lori. She wasn't from the same world. What would happen when I saw her in a few weeks? Picking up where we left off wasn't an option. Did she know that? I wasn't the same; she likely wasn't either. I'd have to choose; and she would, too. Maybe that would be painful, maybe it wouldn't.

The often spouted wisdom, "Failing to plan is the same as planning to fail," echoed in my brain as I approached Springer Mountain.

I didn't have a plan for what would come immediately after the AT "Paddle the length of the Missouri River" or "Hike the Pacific Crest" seemed to be valid options. More likely, they were just the easiest. I hadn't planned for what was to come after the AT beyond taking two or three weeks to get my head straight, going to see Lori, and then figuring out what to do next. That was a mistake. I should have planned better.

I don't remember much about my stay at NOC – the Nantahala Outdoor Center in Wesser, NC. I remember flipping on a light switch in the bunkhouse and thinking it an odd sensation. I remember flipping that same switch on and off a few times and considering how many habits I'd soon have to unlearn and relearn. Changing underwear every day hadn't been necessary for a few months. I'd have to resort to using a fork, too. I'd rarely used anything but a spoon for the last five months. And I'd lick that clean rather than wash it with soap! Things like that, I knew, wouldn't be acceptable at home. Combing my hair and not just taming the tangled mess with a wet bandana would become important again. And shaving. And hardest of all, perhaps, I'd have to re-learn to live by a schedule that ignored sunrise and sunset. In less than two weeks and 140 miles, I'd be back in Missouri, something I wasn't sure I was ready for.

We headed south out of Nantahala, as individuals as we always did, each traveling at our own pace, lost in very personal thoughts of what was one the horizon. I headed up the steep climb out of Wesser to the sharp ridges of the Stecoah Mountains. I hadn't gone but a few miles when an unfamiliar sound drifted in from a distance. I didn't recognize it precisely, but it sounded like dogs. Lots of dogs.

I neared the top of the mountain along a trail that followed a knife-edged ridge. There were spectacular views to the east and west and thin lines of trees along either side separating me from a precipitous drop into the valley way below. The unfamiliar noise rose to a fevered pitch almost suddenly. Still, there was nothing to see. Whatever was making the sound was closing faster than expected. I looked for an escape, but there was nowhere to run, and now I was sure they were dogs barking and howling with great urgency. And then they were upon me. They were in front, behind, to the left, and to the right, too. There must have been ten or maybe fifty of them, all moving like lightning straight at me and raising a hell of a racket. I was sure I was about to be torn limb from limb, but then the pack parted to my left and right and whisked past without so much as an acknowledgment or even one of them brushing against me. Then, they were gone. Only the sound of their barking was left, trailing up from behind and below where I stood on the ridge. I stood sweating and panting, wondering what the hell had just happened.

It was ten minutes or so before the four men cradling rifles and radios trudged up the trail from the direction from which the dog's had come. They stopped to catch their breath when they saw me and to check-in with unseen others on their radios.

"Hunting bear," one said in an almost-impossible to decipher dialect. I must have looked puzzled. "Dogs are closing in. They'll tree him soon. We been on him all night. Yep, he's a smart one, that old bear. Don't you worry, though; we'll get that son-of-a-gun soon enough."

At that moment, I wasn't worried about anything but the bear.

The men were considerably more weathered than me. It was as if they'd been thru-hiking for a lifetime. Collectively, I guessed the men had fewer teeth than me. It was a cordial exchange, but what they were doing didn't make sense to me, especially as a thru-hiker. I'd seen three bears in two-thousand miles; both sightings were in Virginia. There were the twin cubs high in a tree just beyond Shenandoah National Park, and another somewhere in middle Virginia. I'd only caught a glimpse of that bear's backside as he hightailed in the opposite direction from me. Clearly, he had no intention of being social with me. I was overjoyed to see those bears and remember offering up a prayer of thanks both times for the privilege of sharing in the beauty and majesty of creation each time.

Now, I'm not opposed to hunting, especially when it feeds those who might otherwise go hungry or when it's practiced more as art rather than sport. A pack of dogs, eight men, radios, and rifles against a frightened bear just didn't seem fair.

An hour or so later, as I sat on the mountain reflecting on the beauty of the Blue Ridge stretching before me, two gunshots echoed up from the valley.

I guessed that meant the hunt was over. More than likely, the men and dogs and few others -- least among them the bear -- would be celebrating the conclusion of the hunt.

GEORGIA

November 7, 1987

From my Pre-Trip Journal:

   "Nature meets many of man's needs. Among other things he finds beauty for his soul, healing for his body, knowledge for his inquiring mind, communion with his creator, and peace for his troubled heart."

– Esther Baldwin York

   There's a much-photographed tree at the Georgia-North Carolina border. It's gnarled and distinctive, and it has drastically different meanings depending on a thru-hikers direction of travel. For Northbounders, it marks the end of the first state. Most hikers probably think, "One down, 13 to go," as they pass the tree -- if they even see it at all. For Southbounders, though, it's the last boundary between two states. It signals 80 miles left of a 2,100-mile journey. That's a week of hiking at best and as few as four days for some. It's the point where Southbounders are reminded that the future's coming fast – probably even quicker than most they want it to.

   I sat in the tree drinking warm water from a Lexan bottle, eating handfuls of granola, and basked in the sun. It was situated almost exactly on the North Carolina - Georgia border. It was a place I hardly dreamed I'd ever reach. It was among the most grounded moments of my entire experience. Maybe my whole life. Less than a week to Springer.

   Why anyone would give up this lifestyle for something much more complicated? I wrestled with that notion most moments over the next four days which were more picnic-like than any others. Ever. The trails were easy, my spirits and those of my companions were high, the weather was mild, and stress was nearly non-existent – except when I thought about what was next.

   We breezed into Neels Gap to find the owners of the inn there, Jeff and Dorothy Hansen, recent thru-hikers themselves, waiting to welcome the first Southbounders with a little trail magic.

They'd recently purchased the building and business now known as "Mountain Crossings" by recent generations of thru-hikers. They had planned a grand and elegant feast – quail, venison, bread, fruit, vegetables, and pastries -- for the first Southbounders to pass. It was to be their way of giving back some of the kindness they'd encountered as thru-hikers. Unfortunately, there was a power failure that day, and the more exceptional delicacies couldn't be prepared, but they brought each of us a tray neatly arranged with a loaf of bread, a block of cheese, a stick of butter, apples, grapes, and chocolate. They understood a thru-hiker's appetite. We sat in the dark, ate like kings, and shared stories.

I doubt Jeff and Dorothy would remember that day. They were thru-hikers who'd returned to the "real world" with a vision. They hit the ground running and parlayed their experiences into a thriving enterprise. I remember walking away from there infused with confidence and shaken by the enormity of what was about to happen. In less than a week, the most essential thing in my life would be updating my resume.

I completed the Appalachian Trail with few regrets. That has been a great thing and something that should be the target of every hiker. As mentioned previously in this book, my few regrets have to do with having a less-than-concrete plan for my next steps once I got home. Completing a thru-hike defined my capacities in many ways. I wonder, though, if I had returned from Springer with a plan that had allowed me to hit the ground running, if I might have benefitted even more from strength garnered from my thru-hike. Maybe I might have written this book decades ago instead.

It was early November 1987, cold and overcast. I woke up in Gooch Gap shelter and stuffed my sleeping bag into my pack one last time. I was aware it was the end of the road – or at least close to it. My stomach was a mix of butterflies and anticipation. I ate only because I had to, not because I wanted to. The instant oatmeal and pop tarts tasted more like cardboard. They were hardly satisfying for the first time in months.

I flew more than walked those last sixteen miles. My brain covered ten times the miles that my feet did. My thoughts bounced around at light speed. There was so much to think about.

People have often asked me at what point I knew I was going to finish the entire trail. It was on that last day that I knew I was going to finish. Before that day, though, I sensed unknown things might pull or push me home. On that day, though, nothing could have stopped me from reaching that final last white blaze. Interesting, I've always thought, that the first time I was absolutely sure I would complete the Appalachian Trail was on that last day of hiking.

The final sixteen miles were nearly effortless but not pain-free. To my surprise, uphills still strained the heart, and downhills assaulted the knees as much as ever. Early on, I had the unrealistic expectation that I'd reach a point where nothing hurt anymore and where I'd enjoy a certain superhuman-ness. That never happened. Things never stopped hurting.

Hiking up mountains is generally a satisfying thing. Seldom, though, does it come without pain. Or work. Expecting to get somewhere worthwhile -- like the top of a mountain -- without doing the work is a goofy notion. Plain and simple. Embracing discomfort as part of the experience was essential to enduring. And succeeding. And not quitting.

Some truths like that one never stopped being truths no matter how much I wanted them to be different. On the trail or off. And accepting them kept me from going crazy. The further you hiked, for example, the more things hurt. The heavier your pack, the more tired you were at the end of the day. The more tired you were, the more corners you cut, and the more corners you cut, the more likely you were to screw up or find yourself in a tight spot. And of course, the longer you were away from home, the more you missed it.

I moved up the last mile of trail like a machine. I tried to make it last, tried to slow my pace, but 2,100 miles of training in the previous months made that impossible. My body worked at one speed, and that speed was not slow.

The last sixteen miles felt like nothing.

I stifled a sob when I saw it, the brass plaque marking the southern terminus and the last white blaze on the rock next to it. I'd passed perhaps fifteen thousand similar blazes since Katahdin, but none evoked the slightest emotion compared to this one. I'd seen pictures and knew exactly what I was looking for.

I'd daydreamed about it, even awakened some mornings thinking about it. Nothing could have prepared me for the realities of that moment, though. It took a supreme effort not to explode. The emotion permeated absolutely everything.

I made the last few feet without physical effort, probably floated above the trail even, but the emotional energy required was almost too much. It was the step I'd dreamed of for months, the five millionth one, and now that I was there, I didn't know what to do or how to feel or if I really wanted to take it.

What would it mean to finish a thru-hike? It's not something I'd really considered enough to that point even though I'd lived the moment in my dreams a thousand times before.

Springer Mountain wasn't what I expected in some ways and much more than I bargained for in others. I've hiked in some spectacular places since then -- Scotland, Croatia, the Western U.S., China.   Springer's not exactly in league with such world-class beauty, but for an area steeped in meaning and significance, I've never been anywhere that compared, except maybe the top of Mount Katahdin.

I tagged the brass plaque like I was touching home plate, and dropped my pack for the first time in five months without caring where it wound up. The five millionth step brought me to my knees.   I prayed a little, said thanks, let tears stream freely down my cheeks. I didn't bother wiping them from my cheeks, burned and brown as they'd ever been. I wasn't embarrassed to let people see me pray. God had been a constant companion every one of those five-million steps.

I didn't recognize the girl who handed me the bottle, but I turned it on end and guzzled deeply. The champagne was cheap and three-quarters empty when I came up for air. I let out a belch, a good belch. I didn't care, she didn't care, and nobody near me did either. They politely gave me space. It was a celebration after all and one they couldn't fully understand. I'm sure I didn't smell that great besides.

In that instant, I'd become one of an exclusive band, something more than I'd ever been. From that day on, I was a thru-hiker who'd walked every step between Katahdin and Springer.   I was an end-to-ender and a south-bounder. And no one could take that portion of my identity from me. Ever. I'd earned it.

At that moment, though, I didn't fully understand what any of that meant. It was too new.

The shock of that last step was like a hammer to the head and a knife to the heart.   I stood there in shock, finished finally and free to go home with my accomplishment, whatever that meant.

The drink got to me, maybe, or perhaps I was just afraid to leave the path and the life that had grown so familiar. I took another long pull from the bottle. It was near empty then, and I was giddy, goofy, and kind of drunk. I shook off the solemnness of the moment and joined my brothers in celebrating. Since Harpers Ferry, they'd become family -- the White

Rabbit, the Fireman, and Kenny Bob. Though we weren't destined to share future adventures, the ties forged those couple of months would last another ten-thousand days, if only as memories.

I've experienced pure joy on several occasions – the day I first kissed my wife, the day I married her, the births of each of my three children, and the day I completed the Appalachian Trail.

The southern terminus was just a brass plaque embedded in rock. Springer was so less grand than where I took my first steps in Maine. That brass plaque, though, and the final 2"x 4" white blaze brought me to my knees. On top of Katahdin, I remember thinking Springer might well have been the moon. It was impossible to reach and months and months away even with luck and hard work. And then, one-hundred sixty days later, I stood on Springer, dumbfounded, almost-satisfied, but seriously considering turning and heading back north.

What would my father say about that?

Five months had taken their toll on my manners. I was suddenly aware of that. I was unkempt and oblivious to so much about my appearance and presence. It seemed forever since I'd eaten consecutive meals at a table. Or shaved. My beard was bushy and ragged. I hadn't showered since Nantahala, a week before. I was aware that I was not the person who'd started this journey the previous May. Or perhaps the July before that.

I'd dropped 30 pounds and grown philosophical. I was long past caring about little things that had no bearing on trail life. And I listened more. And considered things more. A whole different set of details and boundaries and parameters mattered. I sensed I was wiser about lots of things then. Or maybe I just understood how many things I didn't know that much about. A significant part of being wise, it turns out, isn't knowing things. It's instead knowing what you don't know and being alright with that.

I stood there on Springer Mountain not sure I was ready for whatever was to come next. I stood both empowered and terrified that I might not fit in once I got home. Heading back north seemed a better decision all the time. What would my companions say when I told them. I'm going back to Katahdin.

For the first time in a long, long time, I was aware that I smelled.

My metabolism was stuck at light speed, and the effects of the champagne were short-lived. The goofiness and giddiness were soon gone and replaced with somberness. The future was ahead, and I didn't really know what that meant.

I'd been off the trail all of ten minutes and the idea of heading back from where I came was looking better all the time.

Brett's family was there to greet him. We piled into their cars and went to dinner at the all-you-can-eat Smith House in Dahlonega, GA. The Smiths lost money that night. Four thru-hikers can eat absurd quantities. As high as my metabolism was then and as my lifestyle was as a hiker, If I didn't eat six-thousand calories per day I'd waste away to nothing. Six-thousand calories were barely enough to keep me at my present weight which was 30 pounds or so below my reasonably trim weight upon departure.

At the Smith House, I made it a point to eat a chicken. Two breasts, two thighs, two legs, and two wings. It wasn't enough, so I ate another chicken and a little of everything else. Or a lot of everything else. I knew I wouldn't be able to do that again. Ever. As high as I was on life and champagne, there was an overriding sense that things would change rapidly from that moment on.

On November 7th, 1987, I balanced uncertainly at a pinnacle. I was perfectly adapted for walking in the mountains. Everything was near perfect, except that I couldn't stay where I was forever. I could go back the way I came or continue onward. I just couldn't stay where I was -- at the southern terminus of the Appalachian Trail.

That night, I lay in an unfamiliar bed thinking. I'd only been off the trail for ten hours, but I could feel things changing. Hell, the whole world was becoming something different, and I wasn't ready.

It was November and daylight was short, but I could hike thirty miles with the weight of half-a-man strapped on my back. Even if I napped atop some mountain bald for an hour or two and dawdled at overlooks here and there, I could make it to where I intended to spend the night before dark.

I could hike forty miles in a day with a headlamp if needed, but I'm not sure why I'd ever need to. I could wash ten sandwiches down with a quart of milk for lunch, follow that with a half-gallon of ice cream, and eat double that for dinner. As an Appalachian Trail hiker, I was spectacular. As a man, I was just like anybody else.

I appreciated the slowness and freedom life offered. I become well-acquainted with the natural rhythms of day and night. For six months, I had been early to bed and early to rise. Rarely had I been awake at midnight or asleep after seven. Nothing was rushed, and insomnia, well, there was no such thing as far as I was concerned. There were plenty of reasons to laugh.

For the last few months, stress had been measured in terms of things like rainclouds and dry springs, a hole in your sock or a loose sole on a boot or maybe in a trailside grocery closing before you got there. Altogether it was a beautiful life, thru-hiking, and I wondered why anyone would give up such simplicity. Was I stupid to even think about going home?

Heading back to Katahdin was just five million steps more, and all I needed was a reason to turn around and head back north. And not even a very good one.

More and more I found myself almost convinced that heading back to Katahdin might be best for my soul. , but I hadn't seen anybody I knew well for five months plus a half or felt the warm embrace of family and friends. As scared as I was to give up the balance of trail life, it was time to go home, I knew deep down. It was time to start building something of substance, though I wasn't altogether sure what that might be.

Barely thirty-six hours later, I was on a plane heading back to Missouri. I said goodbye to Ken, Hugh, and Brett. I didn't consider it would be the last time I'd see any of them for at least thirty years. Perhaps forever.

Getting on that plane might have been the hardest step of five-million.

MISSOURI

November 9, 1987

From my Pre-trip Journal:

"You cannot stay on the summit forever; you have to come down again … So why bother in the first place?   Just this: what is above knows what is below, but what is below does not know what is above. One climbs, one sees. One descends, one sees no longer, but one has seen. There is an art of conducting oneself in the lower region by the memory of what one saw higher up. When one can no longer see, one can at least know."

– Rene Daumal

"You coming or going?" The man next to me asked. He was pale and overweight. His shoes weren't the least bit sensible -- shiny and slick-soled. They were the kind that would get you killed on a rugged mountainside. Or cost you an ankle.

"What?" My thoughts were jumbled and all over the place. I was somewhere back in Maine in my dreams. Or maybe even on the banks of Sunfish Pond in New Jersey. It took a moment for me to collect my thoughts and focus on the man who'd spoken to me.

I was nowhere near what had become my element. I was on a plane, in the air, moving at 600 miles per hour, and uncertain of what lay ahead. I didn't have a map nor was in control of where I was going or how fast I was traveling. There was no job in my immediate future, no discernible direction, not even any appointments or commitments beyond getting off the plane in St. Louis. Lori told me not to expect a hero's welcome. I didn't.

Five months before, my father had called hiking the Appalachian Trail the stupidest thing ever. For a good while, I was convinced he was absolutely wrong. Now, as I headed home to uncertainty, I wasn't starting to think he had been right and the last few months, while satisfying had been little more than a diversion.

I wrestled with the fear that no one would be at the airport to pick me up and that I'd find myself wandering the terminal in search of them. What if they'd forgotten? Or more important things had come up?

I figured the man next to me didn't really care if I was coming or going. He just wanted to know why I didn't look like him and the other passengers. He really wanted to ask why I hadn't shaved for a while or why my skin was so browned or why my hair was a mess.

I'd knelt and cried on Springer Mountain just two days before. For five months before that, I'd been caressed by and beaten by sun and wind and elements except when my face was buried in my sleeping bag. A clean shirt and a shower couldn't hide that. "Why don't I look like you? Because I'm not like you," I wanted to tell him.

I guess I waited too long to respond. The man repeated himself. "You heading home or leaving home?"

That was a hard question. The AT had been my home for 5 months. Before that, it had filled my thoughts and imagination for nearly a year. I answered honestly. "I don't know." That took the man by surprise. If he could have moved to another seat, I'm sure he would have. We sat in awkward silence after that, he likely convinced I'd lost my mind and thinking maybe I was crazy. Or a drug addict. Or a recent parolee. It didn't matter much to me what he thought, but I felt obligated to smooth the confusion. "I've been gone six months," I told him. "Hiked the Appalachian Trail from Maine to Georgia. 2100 miles. It feels strange to be heading home."

"That's a lot of walking," the man said, far less impressed than anyone I'd ever met along the trail who'd asked where I'd come from. "My wife and I love walking," he announced. "We have a place on the beach down in Florida. We walk every morning when we're there. Along the ocean mostly. We must hike thirty miles or more by noon. We just love it. It's so relaxing."

He seemed to be waiting for me to be impressed. Thirty miles in a day? I'd done that once. I'd hoofed it from Hot Springs to Hogback Ridge. I'd stopped for a couple-hour nap on a bald patch along the way, too. And had a substantial breakfast at the diner in Hot Springs. I could have still done the same that very day, but I was on a plane. Hell, a day after finishing the trail, I could have hiked forty without a pack. Maybe more.

In a week or so, I knew, I wouldn't be able to do near superhuman like things anymore. At least not without a growing effort.

That day on the plane, I was at a peak, and I knew it. From there, I would start my slow, steady descent to being just like everyone else.

I looked at the man next to me. I knew he had never walked thirty miles -- at least not for a long time. Nor was he likely to ever do it. He was pear-shaped and breathed like someone was standing on his chest. He was wrong and blind and stupid. Thirty miles before lunch was extraordinary. I knew that; he didn't. He had stolen my thunder on purpose, I sensed, to exert his superiority over someone who looked like more of a misfit than him.

Was that the world I was going back to? Maybe I should have turned around at Springer and headed back north. It had been just two days since Springer, and I was beginning to regret my decision not to keep going.

"How far did you walk each day?" He asked.

"Averaged around fourteen."

The fat man was unimpressed. He yawned, and our conversation trailed off to nothing. It ended not because I stopped talking but because he seemed satisfied that he'd one-upped the shaggy, sunburnt man next to him who he assumed was his inferior. The man was likely convinced that he and his probably equally unfit wife did indeed regularly walk thirty miles before lunch and that he was better and more valuable than me because of it.

I figured the most significant difference between us was that I had tasted adventure and knew it. And he had not. Or if he did, he didn't know it or he'd lost touch with it.

It was a short flight, thankfully but it seemed forever. I wanted to poke the man in the eye. Or maybe remove my boots and thrust them in his face. When they were wet, and it had been a while since a town with a laundromat, they smelled worse than any months-old thing I'd ever discovered in my refrigerator. Oh, how I wanted to teach him a lesson.

I missed the humility and honesty of thru-hikers. And the Appalachian Trail. I was glad to be an honest man in that conversation. Even more, I was happy to understand how fortunate I was to know that I was the honest man in the conversation – and not the man who erroneously believed he was the honest man and perhaps based much of his life and identity on falsehoods.

I thought of the well-dressed young man in the apothecary in North Adams, Massachusetts, who'd bought Joe and me an ice cream soda the previous August. He was batshit crazy. I remember how he so politely and elegantly prattled on about all matters of insanity if his ramblings and he were both right as rain. He'd talked about civilizations on Pluto and how their survival tied to him. He shared that he could hear dogs think and that Elvis still lived happily in some corner of the solar system. I remember how Joe and I had looked uncomfortably at each other when the boy in North Adams shared that he'd been released from a mental institution the previous week. I thought about borrowing his persona just long enough to scare the piss out of the bastard next to me. While convinced that I could literally scare the pee out the jackass, I figured it wasn't quite right to do it.

Socrates said, "An unexamined life is not worth living." I'd done a lot of examining my life for the last five months, I knew things then that I had not understood before. Thinking is a powerful methodology that leads to understanding. Five months of thinking about my experiences had built a firm foundation on knowing because I'd been tested.

I looked at the man next to me long enough to make him uncomfortable. I didn't like him. What happened to the "You hike yours, let others hike theirs" business? Was I heading home a self-righteous ass or was I genuinely doing the world a favor by making him squirm?

How hard it must be to go through life spouting off things that you think are true but which in reality are just stupid and flat out wrong. That's when I wondered if I was violating my own principle – Hike your hike, let others hike theirs. If this man wanted to live in the dark, then perhaps it was his privilege.

I decided working a crossword puzzle was probably more appropriate than harassing the man. Twenty minutes to touchdown in St. Louis. Oh, how wrong I was to think that my adventure would end there.

Unfortunately, the man with the ridiculously impractical shoes had planted seeds of doubt in my brain. He'd left me wondering if my accomplishment mattered at all. What would happen when I landed in St. Louis? Would anyone be there? Would anybody care that I could hike thirty miles before lunch without a pack? I squirmed in my seat and tried to prepare for the moment when I would get off the plane and head up the jetway? Would anybody be there? I was trying to come to terms with the reality that in the eyes of most everyone else, I might just be a guy returning from a long vacation.

The plane touched down, my heart pounded, people and people cleared out. I sat for a moment wishing now more than ever that I had turned north for another lap. The last hundred yards up the gangway to the terminal were some of the longest and scariest of the last 2,139.5 miles. What was about to happen, I wondered. What was I coming home to?

Those were the days before TSA checkpoints -- when visitors could walk right up to the gates to greet passengers. I moved up the gangway cautiously, aware that the next moments could be as life-changing as any other in the last months. What if Mom and Dad had forgotten? Or were late because they had errands to run or something good was on TV? Or what if their greeting would be as simple as a hug and a handshake and loaded questions like, "What are you doing tomorrow?" or " What's your plan for finding a job?" Soon, I figured, my dad would ask if I needed money for a haircut. Or if I needed to borrow his razor.

I saw my sister first. "Here he comes," she called back to unseen people behind her. I knew then I'd at least not been forgotten, but then I stepped into the terminal to something astounding and entirely unexpected. There were signs and banners, fifty family members and friends, probably more, cheers and whistles and hugs. And Rusty. It was overwhelming and in its own way, a moment as powerful as tagging the brass plaque on Springer Mountain.

The fifty of us moved as a group to baggage claim, attracting stares and occasional applause. And then all moved on to my parent's house. It was a celebration of personal achievement, sure, but I understood too that I'd written a chapter of family history. It was with their support that I'd finished my thru-hike. Without them, I'd have had no story to give to them to tell.

Later that night, my mother told me it had been my father who single-handedly set up the welcome home celebration at the airport. Apparently, he'd long past moved beyond thinking my AT journey was the stupidest thing ever.

I cried.

In the days following, I made my way back to Columbia to see Joe and Lori. I slipped into town like she'd warned me not to do, neither expecting nor receiving a hero's welcome. I wasn't a hero, I knew. I was just a guy who'd walked two-thousand miles who was now anxious to get on with the rest of his life.

"What now?" Lori and I stared at one another knowing it was the end. We'd never been soulmates, just friends, and our paths didn't go in the same direction. I had lots of figuring to do. She didn't.

"Hike your hike," I told her. "I'll hike mine." The words meant lots more to me than they did to her. In the end, she went the equivalent of North, and I turned metaphorically south without regrets. Mostly. I'm sure she's a multi-millionaire career woman now. And I'm better for having known her. Her friendship and her letters and her phone calls lightened my load some along the AT

Less than two years after I stood on Springer Mountain, cancer took my father. The line of mourners was long; he was respected and well-liked. I didn't know most of them, though he'd worked with many of them for most of my life. When their turns came to speak to me, they approached humbly, extended their hands, took mine respectfully in both of theirs, told me their names and said how sorry they were.

"Which son are you?" They'd ask.

"David."

"The school teacher who graduated from St. Louis U.? Who just got married? Who's expecting his first child? And who just bought a house?"

"No. That's my older brother."

"You must be the Wash U. grad who works with monkeys and apes? Didn't you just get engaged? And weren't you just interviewed on TV?"

"No, that's my younger brother."

As I started to get the idea that maybe Dad had bragged about my brothers more, their expressions would change. It would brighten just a little in that impossibly dark moment. "You're the hiker."

"Yes."

"Your father was so proud of you," they'd say. "He talked about you all the time. When you were out there, he kept us up-to-date on where you were the whole time. He was so impressed when you kept going after your partners quit. If you could deal with that, he'd say, then he guessed you could manage just about anything. He knew you would go on to great things. Yep, he sure was proud."

"Thank you for sharing that."

"We're going to miss him."

"Yeah, me, too.

I had the same conversation a hundred times that day.

When it was over -- the funeral and such -- I stood under the stars in front of our family home remembering the moment along the Orange Turnpike when I'd decided to quit my thru-hike. I remembered the trail angel in the beat-up Ford who salvaged my thru-hike with a little kindness and a six-pack of Coke. In reality, I realized, she salvaged much more than that. How different saying goodbye to my father might have been had he and I not shared the Appalachian Trail.

"Which one are you?" People might have asked. "The unmarried one? The one who dropped out of grad school to take some cockamamie hike or something? You must be the one who's still trying to figure things out. Your father hoped you'd get it together one day. Too bad it wasn't sooner. He worried about you. Good luck to you, son. Your dad was a good man. I hope you don't let him down."

What did I get from my thru-hike? Peace. My father's respect. A foundation for the rest of my life. Knowing I made him proud was alone worth five months and five million steps. It would have been worth it at ten times that much.

Two years later, I met my wife. The day we met, I was confident that we'd share a future. In my wildest dreams, I could never have guessed we'd marry and raise a family. A year after that, our entanglement became a romantic one, and I've never looked back since.

My good friend Jon – who wrote almost weekly letters to me as I hiked and who much regretted not throwing in with me when I invited him to in 1987-- cajoled me once, "She's out of your league." I shrugged and smiled. He never said another thing about it. I guess he saw something between us that convinced him otherwise.

The day we met, she and I became fast friends. Eventually, that friendship became a partnership, and that partnership went on to become the foundation of almost everything precious in my life.

My older brother has always maintained that I wore my wife down with my proposals until she finally consented to marry me. At our wedding, my younger brother toasted my perseverance. That may be true, though, in the end, it was she who asked me to marry her. The lessons learned thru-hiking blazed the path to a beautiful relationship, a fruitful marriage, three beautiful children, and much more.

Our three children, of whom I am immensely proud, are not perfect, but they are what I might call "adventure ready." They are prepared to seek their own paths and to drive their own learning about themselves and the world. That is in part a return on the two-thousand miles I invested back in 1987. The AT made me a better parent.

The specter of building relationships and families and satisfying lifestyles is not unlike the challenge thru-hikers face standing on Katahdin or Springer. Such things take time. And work. And luck. You can't wish them to be something that they aren't.

Often when we dream about really vital "stuff" we want out of life, achieving them is daunting. It's like they're a million miles away. The experience of wanting something that seems unattainable is not unlike the feeling one has standing on Katahdin at the start of a southbound thru-hike. Or on Springer at the beginning of a northbound one. At the start of a thru-hike, no matter how excited people are about the adventure before them, their dreams turn to the opposite terminus. They wonder what it will be like to stand there. They are keenly aware that their destination is impossibly far away, though, and are burdened with knowing that no matter how impatient they are to get there, one can't get there without putting in significant work over significant time. That knowledge is almost overwhelming.

That's one of the universal lessons thru-hikers are most likely to connect with for the rest of their lives. If you want to accomplish something big, you have to do the work. One step at a time. They know you can't wish yourself to the end. There are no free rides. No escalators. No magic. And doing the work is neither comfortable nor pain-free. It is satisfying, though, and worth doing. A little bit every day eventually gets you where you want to go. That's one of the most applicable lessons of a thru-hike.

People who live like thru-hikers live better, I think.

So many of the lessons learned along the trail apply directly to things like life and love and building things that matter. That's true for most lessons learned from an epic adventure. Such lessons apply to every aspect of living and continue to impact the adventurer long after. Maybe even forever.

I don't know that there was anything I could have said to my father on the day he called my plan to set off on a six-month hiking adventure, the stupidest thing he'd ever heard. Here's something I know 10,000 days later: every day since completing my thru-hike has been just a little better than it might otherwise have been. I would not be the person I am if I had not taken the risk and embraced the challenge. I believe the same is true for any adventure as long as it is epic enough, doesn't guarantee success, and pushes the adventurer beyond what he or she knows they are capable of doing.

What I Would Have Done Differently

Thirty years later, I have very few regrets about thru-hiking the Appalachian Trail. None are significant and none too painful to think about. Altogether, I'm pleased with the million memories associated with those many, many steps, and I'm richer because of them. Being at peace with the experience has been an essential positive of the last thirty years.

There are, of course, things I wish I'd done differently, but not many. Being able to claim "no regrets" years and years later should be the goal of every thru-hiker.   Honestly, it should be the goal of every human being, hiker or not, to be able to claim "no regrets" as they make their way through everyday life.

In retrospect, there are things I wish I would have done differently. I've included fourteen of them here, one for each state. Some part of each reflection applies not just to hiking but to a living a good and satisfying life beyond the AT.

I wish I had worn a tin pot on my head like Johnny Appleseed. I took myself too seriously, I think. Though I laughed lots along the way, I should have made it a point to laugh even more. Each of us should make laughing a more significant part of everyday living -- on or off the trail -- and as long as its wholesome laughter and not mean-spirited. We'd all be a lot healthier as a result.

I am glad that I didn't "moon" the Cob Railway as it chugged up Mount Washington. While it may be a grimy, environmentally unfriendly, undesirable, smoke and coal-spewing relic that hauls tourists to the summit and has done so for the last hundred years, it's a favorite of families and folks unable to walk to the top. And people like the 10th Mountain Division veteran I encountered atop Mt. Washington. Flashing one's bare butt at such folks just isn't funny. I learned that as a parent trying to explain such things to my kindergarten-aged children.

I wish I'd carried a ukulele and learned to play along the way or carried an umbrella or let my beard grow even longer. It was the unique personalities that added interest to the experience rather than those who came and went without leaving much of an impression. I should have tried harder to add interest to the experience of others by being a little weird or just a little different. And I should have taken more time to ask questions and get to know the people I met. I am glad I kept my clothes on, though, unlike the naked backpacker outside of Unionville, NY. I've often wondered if he knew we were standing in an overgrown field of poison Ivy. He didn't add much to my experience, and his chattiness probably didn't add to his comfort a few days later when the rash spread over most of his body.   I am a firm believer in the wisdom, "Hike your hike, let others hike theirs," but I only believe that if you're going to do your darndest not to do stupid or unjust things.

  I wish I had written more down. Thirty years later, I'm startled by how much I've forgotten. I'm left wishing I'd taken more photographs of the people who made the trip special. Unfortunately, I remember most of them as faceless blobs who played bit roles in my experience. I snapped plenty of photos, most were vistas and lovely views but few were candid shots of people. And I did a poor job of labeling those. I assumed remembering just happened and that details never got jumbled. That's not the way brains work, though. Thirty years later, I've forgotten as much as I can recall. I did chronicle my experience in a hundred letters written home which my mother compiled in a binder and saved for me. Without those, so much of my experience would have been lost.

  I wish I'd taken more pictures – mostly of people. Memories fade with time and are near-impossible to recover once they do. I've stood in beautiful places all over the world and snapped photos. Years and years later, looking at those photos does nothing to recreate the experience of being there. When I pull out pictures of people, though, I usually smile and even laugh. They are so much more potent than generic scenery shots.

  The internet's a powerful thing.   I can find photos of most shelters where I once stayed; I can find pictures of most of the overlooks that left me breathless along the way. But even the internet can't help me re-see the faces of people I met so long ago or recover the stories that unfolded along the way. I would not today recognize a single person I met then even if we passed on the trail again. I should have written things down and not trusted the power of memory to preserve little things. Big ones, too.

  I wish I had written back to Mountain Laurel. She was heading north. I met her in Pennsylvania or maybe Vermont. We talked at a crossroads for a while, not long, just a few minutes. She sent encouraging letters after that -- lots of them -- but I can't remember ever responding. I don't think I ever said 'thank you' to her for her support. I wish I would have thanked all who sent cards and letters and care packages. I wish I'd held onto memories of those who made the experience worthwhile, and not just those I met along the trail, but those who supported me, and those who I've met since. I wish I'd been committed to never letting someone out of my life without telling them how they'd contributed to my experience. I wish I would have at least sent Christmas cards or "Happy Anniversary of Completing the A.T." cards to Ken, Hugh, and Brett each year for the last thirty.

I wish I had rafted the Kennebec. An outfitter offered to take Rusty, Joe, and I down the river. It was pre-season, and his crews needed practice. We'd have been guinea pigs for his brand new guides, but it wouldn't have cost a dime. Back then, though, it seemed like a distraction from the business of hiking, so we declined the invitation. Looking back, it would not have been a distraction. It was an opportunity to add depth to our experience and my story. Opportunities like that enrich AT experiences. Heck, they add value to life, in general. I should have embraced every one of those opportunities with gusto, and not worried about a schedule. They weren't, after all, distractions or shortcuts, they were detours. At the very least, they'd have added texture to my stories years later -- and all it would have cost was a day or so.

Would my life have been so different if the AT had taken 164 days or 175 days or even 200 days instead of 160? Would my life have been so different if I'd come home with 25 more stories or having met another 50 people? Thirty years later, I wish I could remember rafting the Kennebec, but I can't because I was in a hurry that day. I guess that's what happens when you make life too much about a destination instead of the journey.

Life is better lived when we embrace opportunities and experiences that build our story. I should have rafted the Nantahala and the French Broad, too. And I should have taken detours to the beach in Delaware, spent a day wandering the fields at Gettysburg and found my way to some seaside spot in Maine where I could have enjoyed lobster and beers in an off-the-beaten-path tavern. Those are the sorts of memories that add value to life ten-thousand days later, and I missed some of those opportunities because I was in a hurry to reach nowhere fast.

I wish I'd lingered at more scenic overlooks and for longer. I wish I'd napped longer on top of Max Patch and McAfee's Knob, and the field outside of Gatlinburg where I slept off a few hours at a Shoney's breakfast bar. There were a hundred places just as beautiful that I strolled right past. Without noticing. I wish I'd thought more about life or written about beauty and people and life while immersed in it. Don't get me wrong -- I caught some pretty satisfying naps in some pretty awesome spots, and I penned a few letters in some beautiful spaces, but what harm would a few more minutes have done? Would I look any older or have any less money in the bank if I had? Probably not.

I wish I'd been more gracious to more people and thought more about what I could give instead of what I could get. "Yogi-ing" is an Appalachian Trail tradition, mostly fun and innocent. I was pretty good at it, but I wish I could say I gave at least as much as I got. I didn't.

I wish I had turned and headed back north the day after I reached Springer Mountain. At least for a little while. It would have made an even better story. And who knows what else I might have learned that could be applied to building a better life. There's a certain ring to monikers "Yo-Yo", "Bounce-back", or "Re-bound."

By the time I reached Springer, I'm not sure I'd fully reaped the benefits of my thru-hike. Another half-lap or so might have done me good. I didn't want to leave; I wasn't ready to leave, but I left anyway. I thought I was done, I'm not sure I was. And, hell, whoever said hiking the Appalachian Trail has an end? It doesn't. The trail has two terminuses, sure, but the benefits of living like a thru-hiker continue if you let them. And you should keep living like a thru-hiker to get the most from your experience.

Unless one thinks about the experience deeply as it unfolds and embraces a clear understanding of what they need from a thru-hike, getting what you set out to get from it is just a crapshoot.   I wish I'd been more intentional.   The Appalachian Trail doesn't necessarily end at Springer or Katahdin. It ends when you get where you want to go. Unless you know where that is -- where you want to go -- how can you know when you're there and when you're ready to move on?

I wish from the start I had understood the AT as a stepping stone to greater things and would have lived the lessons even better than I have. I'm glad that I didn't make thru-hiking my life. It's neither real nor sustainable as one's life work. I do wish I'd never stopped living like I was thru-hiking -- At least not with the intensity I lived those values along the trail. In many ways, I haven't abandoned those lessons, but one just needs to look at the crap in my garage to see that I've moved beyond some of the more essential lessons like simplicity and how a lighter load makes for better living.

On the trail, I always knew my short-term and long-term goals. I could look at a map in the morning and know where I needed to go; at the end of the day, I could look at the map and see what I'd accomplished. That was satisfying. I wish I had done more of that in my life since.

I wish I had embraced the whole of the AT as a chapter and not as a whole book. I wish I had written the chapters of my life that came afterward more intentionally. Completing a thru-hike was not an end. It was part of a more significant and ongoing journey -- one that I'm still on. In the midst of my thru-hike, I understood success depended on concentrating on the journey rather than the destination. I wish I'd remembered that every day since. It's easy to get caught up in things that don't matter so much.

Don't bounce from finishing the AT to another starting point. Make sure all your steps extend as part of a continuous, well-planned journey. That's how you get further in life. It's important to connect all that you do as stepping stones leading to one great outcome. Before I started, I should have given substantial thought to what I was going to do when I got back. I should have defined the great thing I was ultimately going to do with my life. I left more of that to chance was wise. I'd have gone further and faster if I'd have had a post-adventure plan.

"Get a job and see what happens" wasn't enough of a plan to fully reap the benefits of a thru-hike. Picking a target and working towards it with the same passion a thru-hiker targets Springer or Katahdin might have taken me on a more direct and satisfying path.

I wish I had written this book much sooner. I wish I'd been able to call it "3,000 Better Days" or "The Day after Springer." I wish perhaps I could have included the tagline, "How I Plan to Continue Living Life in Line with the Lessons I Learned along the Appalachian Trail and Achieve the Very Most from Life as a Result."

I learned a lot from writing this book. More than anything, writing it put me back in touch with important things I've known for a long time. Reflecting on it even years and years later brought clarity to the lessons learned and refreshed the power of the experience. The sort of clarity that comes with critically thinking about something would have been helpful years ago, too. Don't worry, though. It's never too late to find meaning and direction in your experiences.

John Dewey, the remarkable educational philosopher and stellar librarian previously mentioned in this book, made the point that we don't learn from just doing things. Instead, we learn from thinking about the things we've done. When we think critically about our experiences, draw meaningful conclusions from them, and apply those lessons to directing our behavior and our lives in the direction we want to go, then, we are likely to wind up where we want to go and to reap the value of our experiences. To get the most from your thru-hike – or any experience – think about it critically. That's how we harness the power of adventures. Ask questions like, "Why?", "What for?", "What now?" and "What's different?" Draw some conclusions about yourself. When you've made sense of where you've been, then where you need to go and how to get there becomes a lot more clear. Don't leave learning from your adventures to chance.

I wish I'd prayed more. There was peace aplenty among the trees and hills. I experienced an abundance of it as I traveled, but there was more to be found, too, had I looked a little harder. Taking time to appreciate surroundings and experiences through prayer, deep thought, and meditation adds so much to adventures. For me, not praying while making my way north to south would have significantly diminished the experience.

I wish I'd acknowledged the role other people played in my success and found a way to involve them more. Thirty years later, I pulled out the letters received from friends and family. There are one-hundred-forty-seven of them. Each is marked conspicuously, "HOLD FOR A SOUTHBOUND AT HIKER."

I barely recognize the names of some of those who encouraged me from home and those I met along the way. As I read their letters, I wonder if I wrote back and if I adequately answered their questions. I sure wish I had.

One thing was apparent from their letters. When we thru-hike or adventure, in general, we live the dreams of many who will never, for whatever reason, hike the AT or do anything similar. It is our obligation to include them in our experiences. The lessons learned by thru-hikers apply to so much more than just hiking. They apply too to living a good and robust life.

Not once did I walk into a post office and not find a stack of letters waiting. There was always one from my older sister who beautifully chronicled six months of her very young son growing up while I was gone. My second sister kept me up to date on news from home as did my brothers. She came to see me in New York. My older brother asked meaningful questions in his letters and let me know he was proud and even envious. I remember a particular stout package from my younger brother picked up in Virginia. The box overflowed with pounds and pounds and pounds of canned oysters, roast beef, fancy soups, cookies, dried fruit and the like. All of it was impractical for packing along the trail, but every bit was wonderful. There was too much to eat in a setting, though I tried. Lord, I tried. I couldn't bring myself to sacrifice even an ounce of it. And so I set off up over "The Priest", a notoriously long and steep uphill on the northern side with eighty pounds on my back. Likely more. I cursed that mountain with every step that day. My load made one of the hardest climbs of the AT that much harder. That night, though, I ate like a king. And so did my pals.

A successful thru-hike relies on humility and not being in too much of a hurry. I'd have quit, I'm sure, if I'd hurried too much or if I'd been unable to rise beyond the thought that hiking the AT somehow made me better than others. That's not what a thru-hike is about for most people -- Proving something. Or one-upping anyone. At least that's not what it should be about. Success requires luck and the kindness of strangers and the support of family and friends. Yes, they were my feet pounding the trail step after step, but I would likely not have continued without the many others who kept me focused and confident and on the right track.

Most experiences that lent meaning to the journey had little to do with hiking. Or the equipment I carried. In the end, the most valuable parts of hiking the Appalachian Trail were rooted in people, solitude, an unhurried pace that afforded time and space to think. Being absorbed in nature was essential, too. I'm sure most long-distance hikers would say the same. People and boots and food and peace and laughter were as important as anything in giving the experience value.

In retrospect, I do have a single regret of substance. I hope you who would thru-hike or embrace some other great challenge will heed of this single bit of advice.

My sole regret is that I didn't continue to live the lessons of my thru-hike with the same intensity once I got home. I slacked off some as if I had finished something. Had I just taken that brass plaque atop Springer Mountain in stride as just another step on a much longer journey, I'd likely be even happier, healthier, and more prosperous thirty years later. And so might those around me. Don't let the last step of your physical journey become an end to the lifestyle.

I benefited plenty from my experience. I might have reaped even more benefits, though, had I followed the example of my good friend Miller J. Templeton who thru-hiked in 1982, and who, by his own admission, still lives much the same as he did then. He has made it a point to live simply, with few distractions, to stay sharply focused on what matters, has always been ready to laugh and always willing to lend a hand. Thirty-five years past Mount Katahdin and nearing eighty years old, he's without regrets and celebrates successes on so many fronts on most days.

My friend Miller traces much of his prosperity and well-being back to his deliberate decision to embrace the values of an AT hiker for the whole of his life.

Thirty years later, here's my advice for reaping the most from your adventure:

1. If you're going to commit to an adventure like the AT, make sure it's big enough and that success is neither guaranteed nor dependent on another person. Test yourself.
2. Immerse yourself entirely. Don't do it half-assed. Jump in with both feet. Don't hold back.
3. Be a purist. Hike every step and be certain to finish with no regrets.
4. Understand why you're there. "To hike" isn't good enough. "Neither is "to have an experience". Be sure your reason for being there is significant enough to keep you there when the going gets tough and the miles grow long.
5. Let go of things that don't matter or at least put them on hold while you're out adventuring.
6. Think about your experiences as they unfold and seek meaning in them. Experiences by themselves are just that – experiences. When we think about them, though, and seek deeper meaning in them, they become much more than just something we once did. Often they become the foundation for the next great chapters in our lives.

7. Write your story as it happens -- for yourself not for others. Thirty years will fly by. The more you write down, the more you'll have in later years, and the more you think about your experience, the more sense it will make and the rater it's value for the next ten-thousand days.

8. Have a plan for when you get back. Don't leave it to chance. Don't end your thru-hike at Katahdin or Springer. Bring the spirit of the whole experience home with you and live steeped in the spirit of adventure and challenge. Hold on to the lessons learned about living well and being part of a community like your life depends on it because in some ways it does. Hold tight to those values and make them part of the rest of your life.

9. Be open to the possibility that your thru-hike might not end where you planned for it to end. It could quite possibly finish before you expected or stretch long after. End you're thru-hike or your epic adventure when you're done. Not before or after.

10. Let each adventure be a stepping stone to the next big thing. When we slow down, we stagnate, and when that happens, life becomes far less than it was meant to be.

Times are different than they were in 1987. It's hard to deny our nation is mired in a mental health crisis. The impacts touch each of us directly and through loved ones. Mental health issues lead to higher crime and higher taxes; they spawn unspeakable tragedies -- suicide, abuse, murder. Many of the challenges facing our society result from people not taking opportunities to test themselves and to learn through clear metaphors for how best to live well. The need for the Appalachian Trail and adventure experiences like it is far more significant now than ever. Don't shy away from opportunities to test yourself because you don't have the time. A life well-lived is better served if you make the time.

You can't hike twenty-two hundred miles over five months without learning something of value about how the world works, about your place in it, and what it takes to accomplish something bigger than you are. You can't walk away without an appreciation for simplicity and hard work and an understanding that great things take considerable effort. And you can't walk away without a connection to nature -- which is essential for health and well-being.

Living in the moment is a great thing, but only as long as you're moving towards something meaningful. Otherwise, you're fooling yourself, and you'll wind up one day in the same place sometime later, with less energy, less opportunity, less time, and less strength. When you get home, be sure you're heading somewhere as if you're thru-hiking.

I close this book with advice applicable to all, advice that not only can change individual trajectories but could if embraced widely enough, change much more.

Want a better future? Find AN Appalachian Trail of your own and hike it end-to-end. It'll make all the difference, as long as you do it right.

Remember, yours doesn't need to be THE Appalachian Trail or even a hike at all. For best results, embrace a challenge that tests your limits and immerse yourself in it. It doesn't have to involve hiking; it just needs to be bigger than you. It could be serving in the Peace Corps or training for a marathon or committing to mission work for a year or studying abroad and traveling internationally on your own. Maybe it's paddling the length of the Missouri River. Or the Mississippi. Or the Amazon. Or traveling to every MLB ballpark in a single summer and writing a book about your experiences. Maybe it's building a tiny house and homesteading on a pretty piece of property. Or maybe signing on to crew a sailing ship that's making the journey around Cape Horn.

Whatever you do, don't do it half-assed or limit it to a few days or even a few weeks. Building a foundation takes time. Stay pure and intensely focused for the duration of your pursuit. And pay attention. This is about establishing a foundation for the rest of your life. It's not about raucous fun or drinking or meaningless hook-ups. Take it seriously. As Benjamin Franklin said, "Nothing ventured, nothing gained." You have to take risks to reap the benefits of adventures. "Play the game for more than you can afford to lose. Only then will you learn the game." That's what Winston Churchill would have said.

Simply put, we'd all be better off if more of us would commit to adventures bigger than ourselves. To any readers who seek something that might add definition and substance to your life: do something big. Learn well from that experience, whatever it is, and embrace the best of the lessons learned and live them for the rest of your life.

Never let your intensity or focus on those lessons wane. At least not for the next ten-thousand days.

Reducing what you need to live well to just that which can be carried on your back is a freeing experience. While not exactly realistic when you own a house and have a family and have a job to do, there's wisdom wrapped up in that memory. Value the little things. Forever. And keep life simple.

Except for that kid in Maine, I've never met a thru-hiker who lacked self-awareness, wisdom, work-ethic, grit, resilience, or at some level, humility. The same is true for many adventurers I've met, too. Make an effort to be one of those -- a successful thru-hiker – whether YOUR Appalachian Trail is the Appalachian Trail or some other grand adventure.

What will I say when my children come to me and say, "Dad, I'm going to hike the Appalachian Trail?"

"Fine by me," I'll say, but not without questions or worries. They are, after all, my children. "Just be sure it's the right trail," I'll tell them, "hiked in the right way and hiked for the right reasons. And be certain it's a stepping stone to something bigger and better for the rest of your life."

To you considering a life-sized adventure in the future, an Appalachian Trail thru-hike or something else, happy trails to you. Remember that the promise of an adventure done well and right is that the next 10,000 days might be better than they otherwise might have been.

Adventuring Right.

Several of those who proofed my original manuscript advised me to let readers make their own decisions about lessons and meaning in this book. "Let your stories work their magic," they advised. In response, I cut a good deal that might be perceived as "preachy." When I returned to those who'd offered the advice, most said of particular passages, "Oh, I didn't mean that one. That was good stuff." So, in response, I compiled these thoughts in a final section. These are the ideas that might have better prepared me to understand the experience and the opportunity I was about to embark on. Knowing these things might have prepared me to reap even more from my Appalachian Trail experience.

I don't believe thru-hiking is somehow magical nor is it a good idea for all – or even most. It can be powerful and positive beyond measure if done right and well, but so can any adventure. Hiking the Appalachian Trail is not about physical strength or equipment or logistics alone or even mostly. It's a profoundly personal experience, the meaning of which is greatly amplified by reflection and focus and having a purpose.

I believe every young person should hike AN Appalachian Trail; I don't think everyone should hike THE Appalachian Trail. Practically, there's not enough room. The AT grows more crowded by the year. Second, it's just not the right experience for everyone. Life-sized adventures come in all shapes and sizes and can happen anywhere in the world. They don't even have to take place in the great outdoors. But there is something magical about immersing oneself in pursuing something that matters, something well-defined, and then committing to a pursuit that doesn't guarantee success. Pursuing that goal through to the end promises better days.

Mark Twain wrote, "Travel is fatal to prejudice, bigotry, and narrow-mindedness, and many of our people need it sorely on these accounts. Broad, wholesome, charitable views of men and things cannot be acquired by vegetating in one little corner of the earth all one's lifetime."

Young adventurers, or even middle-aged ones, who prevail in the face of a challenging odds will find something irreplaceable years later when they look back and find themselves still able to say with complete honesty, "I did that." Owning such success changes one's perspective on who they are and what they are capable of doing. I'm pretty sure the world would be a better place if more of us challenged ourselves to achieve something remarkable and bigger than we imagined ourselves to be when we are young -- or when we are old, for that matter.

Among the older set, too many of us get into bad habits of believing we are no longer capable of such things. We prefer padded chairs and comfortable beds to sleeping on the ground and eating from the same pot we cooked in. Among those who are younger, there's a tendency to get distracted by things with little value – video games and the like -- or we follow pre-set and safe tracks that lead to the same place everyone else is heading. Such paths don't typically lead to better days.

Socrates, the great Greek philosopher, said, "An unexamined life is not worth living." Immersing oneself in an adventure – a life-sized adventure without guarantees for success -- naturally challenges one to think about themselves, about who they are, about who they are not, and about who they could possibly be. Done well, adventures lead us to understand the strengths that make up the foundation upon which we stand and on which we will stand for the rest of our days.

Every person – young or old -- benefits from setting distractions aside for a time, shouldering responsibility for something bigger than they are, living simply and focused on a goal, and making decisions that affect the outcome of their experience – for better or for worse. All of that is needed practice for building the competencies that guide one to greater happiness and satisfaction. Sitting on one's ass with a video game in hand or watching television until your eyes threaten to pop is not good practice for much of anything except doing more of the same. Neither is drinking or doing drugs or devoting one's life to trivial or selfish pursuits helpful in any meaningful way.

Those who are bound to excel in life are those who know themselves, who have a vision, and who have been tested. Those three things are all quite natural parts of a significant and life-sized adventure.

My purpose in writing this book was to share stories that still mattered to me 10,000 days later in the hope they might spur insights and realistic expectations that might better prepare others to get from their experiences what they want and need from them. Years later is when I really came to understand the value of thru-hiking the AT My life has been more than it might otherwise have been and quite possibly even a few years longer as a result. Adventures done well are good for you.

The only way to hit a target is to have a target. Without one, there are no guarantees that you are even close to heading in the right direction. If your best reasons for embarking on an epic adventure is "It sounds fun" or "I've got nothing better to do" or "I just always wanted to", then likely you have some thinking to do about who you are and who you hope one day to be because of your journey.

Hiking the Appalachian Trail is not a single adventure but hundreds of them, little and big, packed back-to-back in a relatively short period. The value results from thinking about each little adventure as it unfolds and understanding what each says about the nature of the individual hiker and the nature of the world in general.

When a thru-hiker – or any adventurer -- stops to consider what their experiences say about their capacities and limitations, they grow stronger. When they think about what their experiences say about bigger things like human nature and our nation, and about how to live a successful and satisfying life, then the world grows a little stronger. Adventurers who embrace their adventure with the right spirit emerge on the other side of o it filled with insights likely to fuel better days thereafter. The Appalachian Trail makes that promise, as does any life-sized adventure. If you commit fully to the experience, then the 10,000 days following are likely to be better than they otherwise might have been.

What will I say when one of my children announces to me as I did to my father, "I'm going to hike the Appalachian Trail"? I won't say, as my own father did, "That's the stupidest thing I've ever heard." I will urge them, though, to think carefully about why they want to thru-hike and how they want to be different as a result. I will encourage them to do it right and stress that to get the most from it, they'd be wise to take the experience seriously. "Hiking the A.T.," I'll tell them, "may well be the most important decision you'll ever make."

Through the years, a good number have approached me with their plans to thru-hike. They want to know about the equipment I carried and how far I walked each day and what advice I have about food and guns and safety. I surprise them when I tell them "stuff" isn't so important. I encourage them to get what they can afford. Earl Shafer and anybody who thru-hiked before 1980, likely did so with army surplus gear and packs that weighed 80 pounds at times.

Before there was Dri-fit, Lexan, Gortex, and breathable this-and-that, there was wood, metal, wool, and canvas. People succeeded with what hikers today wouldn't dream of carrying for whatever reason – too heavy, not pretty enough, bulky, or not state-of-the-art. Gear doesn't matter so much as character does. Don't get caught up in the technical aspects of your hike. Focus instead on a much more critical question, "What's going to keep you going when you learn that hiking isn't fun and games or easy?" Understanding why you want to thru-hike and what your long-term target is will prove as valuable as anything else in determining long-term success. That's far more important than what pack you carry, which boots you'll wear or whether you travel northbound or southbound, tote a gun, carry a satellite locator, eat freeze-dried meals, arrange mail drops or purchase food as you go.

The Appalachian Trail made me a better and more interesting person. I'm more resilient and self-reliant as a result. It became the foundation of 10,000 better days and plenty of opportunities. Without much stretch, I can tie about every significant part of my life back to my AT experience – my wife, children, home, career-success, overcoming health challenges, a better relationship with my father, and a strengthened spirituality. I suspect that's similar for most long-distance hikers. Was hiking the Appalachian Trail worth the effort? Absolutely. It wasn't finishing, though, that made a difference; it was not quitting when things got tough that mattered. What gave the experience meaning were lessons learned about who I am, about the greatness and generosity of people along the trail, and the reasonably hefty serving of humility I was force-fed along the way.

The experience remains significant years later because I paid attention to nuances and moments, thought about them, and put them into perspective. It's not the hiking part that mattered or even that I walked every step of the AT; it's that I regularly considered the deeper meaning in the hundreds of little things that occurred along the way – and learned from them. Enduring and overcoming things like powering up hills that nearly exploded my heart, pounding down slopes that tore my knees apart, and surviving situations that might have killed me like storms, streams, hitchhiking and plenty of other stupid decisions defined the experience and fueled the learning. Micro-experiences made for good stories, but as it turned out, the story-parts were just the keys to figuring out more profound insights about who I was and about life. The only way to unlock the meaning in such experiences is to think about them – sometimes critically.

I laughed more as a thru-hiker than I have ever laughed since, except maybe for the days when I had very young children. Don't take things too seriously. Laughter adds much to any experience.

There are lots of keys to a successful AT hike: keep your pack light, stay clean, eat well, laugh lots, invest in quality boots, get organized, know your stuff, stay connected with folks at home, and connect with a trail community – even if your plan is to go it alone. But you also need to know why you're going, how you're going to measure your success, and you need to take time to reflect often about what's happening in your head and in your heart.

So many trail philosophers have preached how the mental challenges of a thru-hike outweigh the physical ones, and they are all correct as can be. That's why it's essential to understand why you are committing so much to your thru-hike or to any adventure. If you don't know why you're there, it's easy to crumble when the going gets tough. Having a vision is an integral part of a successful thru-hike. It's also an essential part of lifelong success. A clear vision gives you the strength to keep going when you're at your limit physically, mentally and emotionally.

AT hikers should know something of John Dewey, who should not be confused with Melvin Dewey, creator of the Dewey Decimal System. Both were librarians, but John Dewey was also an American philosopher, psychologist, and educational reformer. He was influential enough to have a US postage stamp minted in his honor. Since so few of us have stamps named in our honor, I trust that establishes his credibility as a wise man. Dewey – John, not Melvin -- wrote about the link between learning and experience. He made it clear that we don't learn from experience, we learn instead from thinking about our experiences. That's a seldom-talked-about secret to getting the most from your thru-hike. You must think about experiences as they unfold and seek lessons in the tiny episodes that combine to define your thru-hike.

Going with the flow as if everything you want will magically happen because you took a long walk in the woods is pretty naive and a reasonably likely path to disappointment.

Hiking the Appalachian Trail is a string of little experiences strung together on a 2,100-mile cord. We don't learn much from the stuff we do, but we do learn incredible and enduring lessons when we think about what we've done and then do our best to make sense of it all. For me, learning from my Appalachian Trail experience has continued without interruption for 30 years – every time I think about it, I learn something new.

I finished the trail in a little over 5 months as a southbound hiker with a pack that rarely weighed less than sixty pounds. Completing a thru-hike doesn't mean much other than I was lucky enough not to get hurt; that I had resources to stick with it to the finish; that there were no urgencies back home that called me away; and that I found a satisfying place among other thru-hikers for the bulk of my time. Finishing a thru-hike doesn't mean I was stronger, better prepared, or better-adapted than anybody else. If anything mattered more than anything else, it was that my head was in the right place and that I immersed myself in the experience entirely. Letting go of distractions is part of a successful thru-hike. And the same holds true in life -- letting go of things that don't matter is a good thing. Finding meaning in each day beyond just logging a few more miles is an essential part of keeping your head in the right place.

There were lessons in it all. The most significant was that life, like a long journey, requires patience and work and living both in the moment and looking forward to what is to come. Those were obvious lessons – that success in life, like success as a thru-hiker, requires direction, maps, people and a sense of humor. It requires taking care of stuff like boots and feet, keeping matches dry and rain gear at hand, and being sure water bottles are filled with clean, fresh water. And it requires that you don't do anything really stupid – especially the kind of things that might get you killed. And if you do dumb things and survive them, continued success requires you to adjust your ways of doing things so you won't make the same mistakes again. Those are valuable lessons for both on and off the trail.

There's one lesson every adventurer can take to the bank – you can't wish yourself where you want to be. You've got to put in the work to get there, a little at a time. Keep your head and heart in the game, and eventually, you'll wind up closer to where you want and need to be. If you don't get to the place you thought you would wind up, well, at least you'll arrive wherever you do finish with a greater understanding of who you are and what's important. You'll also likely have a clearer understanding of better ways to proceed from there. It's understanding yourself, your strengths, your purpose, and your place in the world that matters. Epic adventures lead to such outcomes. Remember, it's not just that you walked from here to there that will lead you to 10,000 better days. It's that you used your time well to think about your adventure and how it defines you and your relationships with the rest of the world and with your future.

Life-sized adventures are worth your time – no matter what they entail and as long as they are not ill-conceived. If you invest in one, don't just walk or paddle or go through the motions required to get from one point to another. Instead, live the experience, and think about what's happening to you as you make your way. That's how you get the most from it.

Set your sights higher than Katahdin or Springer or whatever lies at the end of your adventure. Don't let the lessons or the learning grow stale when you find yourself back home. There should be no final destination -- Just a transition point.

The last step of an epic journey should be the first step of the next one, even if that next adventure is the seemingly mundane act of getting on with life. Living the values of a thru-hiker after you leave the mountains and streams keeps paying dividends long past when you can no longer endure the pace or stomach a diet of Snickers bars, ramen, and macaroni and cheese.

The benefits of a life-sized adventure done well will last for the next ten-thousand days at least, and that's a pretty good return on investment! Take your adventure seriously. It's a ticket to something bigger and better than you might otherwise find – even if what you find in this life is amazing! Whatever you do, don't squander the enduring benefit of stepping beyond what's comfortable and experiencing life and the world in the fullest way possible. Make sense of your experiences by thinking about every step. Remember they don't have to involve tents and boots or a long, green winding trail. They just need to be big enough. Here's to letting every future adventure be the beginning of a life lived even better.

Happy trails.

Made in the USA
Columbia, SC
20 September 2019